KV-647-978

THE ECONOMICS
OF UNIQUENESS

DRILL HALL LIBRARY
MEDWAY

The Urban Development Series discusses the challenge of urbanization and what it will mean for developing countries in the decades ahead. The series delves substantively into the core issues framed by the World Bank's 2009 Urban Strategy, *Systems of Cities: Harnessing Urbanization for Growth and Poverty Alleviation*. Across the five domains of the Urban Strategy, the series provides a focal point for publications that seek to foster a better understanding of the core elements of the city system, pro-poor policies, city economies, urban land and housing markets, urban environments, and other issues germane to the agenda of sustainable urban development.

Titles in the series include:

Cities and Climate Change: Responding to an Urgent Agenda

Climate Change, Disaster Risk, and the Urban Poor: Cities Building Resilience for a Changing World

The Economics of Uniqueness: Investing in Historic City Cores and Cultural Heritage Assets for Sustainable Development

Urban Risk Assessments: An Approach for Understanding Disaster and Climate Risk in Cities

4681989

THE ECONOMICS OF UNIQUENESS

Investing in Historic City Cores and Cultural Heritage Assets for Sustainable Development

Guido Licciardi, Rana Amirtahmasebi, Editors

THE WORLD BANK
Washington, D.C.

© 2012 International Bank for Reconstruction and Development / The World Bank
1818 H Street NW,
Washington DC 20433
Telephone: 202-473-1000;
Internet: www.worldbank.org

Some rights reserved

1 2 3 4 15 14 13 12

This work is a product of the staff of The World Bank with external contributions. Note that The World Bank does not necessarily own each component of the content included in the work. The World Bank therefore does not warrant that the use of the content contained in the work will not infringe on the rights of third parties. The risk of claims resulting from such infringement rests solely with you.

The findings, interpretations, and conclusions expressed in this work do not necessarily reflect the views of The World Bank, its Board of Executive Directors, or the governments they represent. The World Bank does not guarantee the accuracy of the data included in this work. The boundaries, colors, denominations, and other information shown on any map in this work do not imply any judgment on the part of The World Bank concerning the legal status of any territory or the endorsement or acceptance of such boundaries.

Nothing herein shall constitute or be considered to be a limitation upon or waiver of the privileges and immunities of The World Bank, all of which are specifically reserved.

Rights and Permissions

This work is available under the Creative Commons Attribution 3.0 Unported license (CC BY 3.0) http://creativecommons.org/licenses/by/3.0. Under the Creative Commons Attribution license, you are free to copy, distribute, transmit, and adapt this work, including for commercial purposes, under the following conditions:

Attribution—Please cite the work as follows: Licciardi, Guido, Rana Amirtahmasebi. 2012. The Economics of Uniqueness: Historic Cities and Cultural Heritage Assets as Public Goods. Washington DC: World Bank. DOI: 10.1596/978-0-8213-9650-6. License: Creative Commons Attribution CC BY 3.0

Translations—If you create a translation of this work, please add the following disclaimer along with the attribution: *This translation was not created by The World Bank and should not be considered an official World Bank translation. The World Bank shall not be liable for any content or error in this translation.*

All queries on rights and licenses should be addressed to the Office of the Publisher, The World Bank, 1818 H Street NW, Washington, DC 20433, USA; fax: 202-522-2625; e-mail: pubrights@worldbank.org.

ISBN (paper): 978-0-8213-9650-6
ISBN (electronic): 978-0-8213-9706-0
DOI: 10.1596/978-0-8213-9650-6

Cover photo: Bill Lyons. An ancient cistern in Hababa, Republic of Yemen.

Library of Congress Cataloging-in-Publication Data

Economics of uniqueness : investing in historic city cores and cultural heritage assets for sustainable development / Guido Licciardi and Rana Amirtahmasebi, editors.
  p. cm. — (The urban development series)
  Includes bibliographical references and index.
  ISBN 978-0-8213-9650-6 — ISBN 978-0-8213-9706-0 (electronic)
  1. Urban renewal. 2. Historic sites—Economic aspects. 3. Cultural property—Economic aspects. 4. City planning. 5. Urban economics. I. Licciardi, Guido. II. Amirtahmasebi, Rana. III. World Bank.
  HT170.E35 2012
  307.3'416—dc23   2012031079

Contents

Tables

Foreword

Can investment in historic city cores and cultural heritage help reduce poverty and promote economic growth? *The Economics of Uniqueness* tries to answer this question. In a world where more than half of the population now lives in cities and more than 90 percent of urban growth occurs in the developing world, cities try hard to modernize without losing their unique character, embodied in their historic cores and heritage assets. As cities expand rapidly, conservation and continued use of heritage can provide crucially needed continuity and stability. In other words, the past can become a foundation for the future.

The benefits of investing in heritage for livability, job creation, and local economic development have been increasingly studied and debated over the last few decades, with the economic theory underpinning investment becoming substantially more robust. Reusing built assets and regenerating underutilized land in central locations is very much linked with the World Bank Group's inclusive green growth agenda. A city's conserved historic core can also differentiate that city from competing locations—branding it nationally and internationally—thus helping the city attract investment and talented people. Cities that are the most successful at attracting investment and businesses to meet the aspirations of their citizens, while alleviating poverty and promoting inclusion, are those that harness all of their resources, including their heritage. In addition, heritage anchors people to their roots, builds self-esteem, and restores dignity. Identity matters to all vibrant cities and all people.

The World Bank Group has a robust practice in historic city cores and cultural heritage, with close linkages to natural heritage and sustainable tourism. Since we began our work in this area, we have financed numerous projects in both low and middle income countries.

This book is a collection of research papers authored by leading scholars and practitioners in heritage economics. It presents the most current knowledge on how these assets can serve as drivers of local economic development. It aims to inform, inspire, and encourage many more such efforts worldwide.

Rachel Kyte
Vice President, Sustainable Development Network
The World Bank

Acknowledgments

To the memory of Richard Clifford (+ April 26, 2012)

Exegi monumentum aere perennius
regalique situ pyramidum altius,
quod non imber edax, non Aquilo impotens
possit diruere, aut innumerabilis
annorum series et fuga temporum.
Non omnis moriar, multaque pars mei
vitabit Libitinam. Usque ego postera
crescam laude recens, dum Capitolium
scandet cum tacita virgine pontifex.
dicar, qua violens obstrepit Aufidus,
et qua pauper aquae Daunus agrestium
regnavit populorum, ex humili potens,
princeps, Aeolium carmen ad Italos
deduxisse modos. Sume superbiam
quaesitam meritis, et mihi Delphica
lauro cinge volens, Melpomene, comam.

I have raised a monument no king shall claim
nor bronze outlast nor pyramid exceed,
which neither puny North wind nor toothed rain
nor the innumerable years' stampede
nor flying time can tatter to the earth.
Not all of me will die. A part is strong
enough to flout Queen Death into rebirth
of people's praise long afterward. As long
as priest and virgin pace the Capitol,
I shall be spoken of where Aufidus spins
wroth waves against the land, where Daunus ruled
parched farmlands: I, a humble-blooded prince,
who brought Greek melody to Latin song.
O Muse! Take pride in what I am today.
My genius is yours, and we have won.
Grin down and crown me with the Delphic bay.

Quintus Horatius Flaccus, Carmina, III, 30.

The team would like to thank Erik Berg (Senior Advisor, Royal Norwegian Ministry of Foreign Affairs) and Carsten Paludan-Muller (Director, Norwegian Institute for Cultural Heritage Research) for the financial support for this book and the international conference "Harnessing the Hidden Potential of Cities," held in Oslo on April 11–12, 2012.

The project benefitted from the guidance and supervision of Zoubida Allaoua (Director, Finance, Economics, and Urban Development Department) and Abha Joshi-Ghani (Sector Manager, Urban Development and Local Government Unit). Martin Rama (Director, World Development Report 2013) advised and guided the team beyond the call of duty to shape the storyline.

The team dedicates this intellectual effort to the memory of Richard Clifford, who passed away unexpectedly just as the book was finalized.

Appreciation is due to the authors of the chapters: Rabah Arezki, Reda Cherif, and John Piotrowski (International Monetary Fund), John O'Brien (Ireland Industrial Development Agency), Peter Nijkamp (University of Amsterdam), Christian Ost (ICHEC Brussels Management School), Martin Rama (World Bank); Eduardo Rojas (University of Pennsylvania, formerly with the Inter-American Development Bank), Francesca Romana Medda, Simone Caschili, and Marta Modelewska (University College London), Donovan Rypkema (University of Pennsylvania), and David Throsby (Macquarie University). Several experts provided background papers to strengthen the concept note: Gianni Carbonaro (European Investment Bank, background papers on urban regeneration), Rudy D'Alessandro (US National Park Service, background papers on parks management), Christer Gustafsson (Heritage Halland, background paper on creative industries), Patrizia Lombardi (Turin Polytechnic University, background paper on tourism), Randall Mason (University of Pennsylvania, background paper on heritage conservation), Damia' Moragues and Jordi Pardo (Foundation Barcelona Media, background paper on tourism), and Pier Luigi Sacco (IUAV Venice University, background paper on cultural economics).

A World Bank steering committee guided the team and included: Stefania Abakerli, Anthony Bigio, Katrinka Ebbe, Christianna Johnnides, Stephen Karam, Chantal Reliquet, Victor Vergara, and Mark Woodward.

At various stages of the project, World Bank staff members served as internal peer reviewers: Janis Bernstein, Brian Blankespoor, Roberto Chavez, Ahmed Eiweida, Mila Freire, Nancy Lozano Gracia, Sarah Keener, Mihaly Kopanyi, Martin Henry Lenihan, Shaun Mann, Catherine Mathieu, Robert Maurer, Hannah Messerli, Pedro Ortiz, Nicolas Perrin, Monica Rivero, Taimur Samad, Roy Van der Weide, Hyoung Gun Wang, Shenhua Wang, and Belinda Yuen. Moreover, external peer reviewers ensured inclusiveness and further quality control: Nada al Hassan (UNESCO), Jyoti Hosagrahar (Columbia University), Fiora Luzzatto (formerly with Molise University), Fernanda Magalhaes (Inter-American Development Bank), Alfons Martinell (Girona University), Stefaan Poortman (Global Heritage Fund), Anna Trigona (Council of Europe), Jurien Van Der Taas (Aga Khan Trust for Culture), and Ron Van Oers (UNESCO). The Cultural Heritage and Sustainable Tourism Thematic Group, a community of practice of about 150 staff members, provided data and facts on World Bank-financed projects. Katrinka Ebbe (Senior Cultural Heritage Specialist) produced the boxes on these projects.

Francesco Bandarin (UNESCO Assistant Director General for Culture), Gustavo Araoz (President, International Council on Monuments and Sites, ICOMOS), and Luigi Fusco Girard (Chair, ICOMOS International Scientific Committee on the Economics of Conservation) offered guidance. Partner organizations shared material and data, notably the United Nations Educational, Scientific and

Cultural Organization (UNESCO), the European Investment Bank, the Aga Khan Trust for Culture, the European Commission, the Council of Europe, the US National Park Service, and the Global Heritage Fund.

We would also like to thank the Governments of Italy and India for supporting the cultural heritage agenda at the World Bank through a dedicated Multi Donor Trust Fund.

Guido Licciardi (Urban Specialist, Task Team Leader) and Rana Amirtahmasebi (Urban Specialist) led the project team. Ephim Shluger (former Senior Urban Development Specialist) and Kerri Rubman (Senior Researcher and Writer in Heritage Conservation) reviewed the drafts until the final version.

Fernando Armendaris, Adelaide Barra, Laura De Brular, Vivian Cherian, Santiago Diaz Gutierrez, Xiaofeng Li, and Berenice Sanchez offered organizational and administrative support. The translation of Horace's poem is by A. Z. Foreman. The Office of the Publisher provided final editorial and production services. Finally, we extend our gratitude to all our other colleagues who contributed to this project.

Overview

- *Balance conservation with an acceptable degree of change.* Stakeholders should weigh the different values and trade-offs between conservation and development, identifying the acceptable level of change and the extent of adaptive reuse.

- *Promote a blend of regulation and incentives.* Measures to conserve historic city cores and heritage assets are not limited to rules and regulation that restrict activities. Incentives are also essential for achieving "integrated conservation."

- *Ensure a dialogue between public and private sectors.* Heritage is a public good and the economic justification for public sector investment is well established. But, it is unreasonable to expect the public sector to be the sole investor, and the solution is to have a combination of public and private investment, with a balance between the two, varying depending on the project scheme and context.

What Are the Objectives of This Book?

To fill knowledge gaps in understanding:
(1) how investment in heritage assets[1] creates jobs and
(2) how the sense of place and uniqueness of a city can be maintained.

With rapid urbanization, cities featuring valuable historic cores and heritage assets struggle to modernize without completely losing their uniqueness. The level of economic activity these cities can sustain increases, sometimes substantially, but in the process these places risk losing their distinctive traits, becoming less vibrant and livable. This is not merely a concern for culture-loving intellectuals: all income groups of local communities may regret the loss of a sense of place, which makes them feel part of their society.

The good news is that there is an increasing trend toward financing projects aimed at conserving and incorporating heritage into development strategies. All countries, developed and developing, are indeed investing more into conserving their city cores and heritage, with projects focusing particularly on landmarks and other major assets. However, landmarks are surrounded by urbanscapes and landscapes of certain heritage value that contribute distinctively to the character and uniqueness of a place, and these areas are home to local communities looking for income opportunities and economic growth.

This book presents approaches to balance conservation and development. There are many interesting papers surrounding the topic, but policy and decision makers do not have any easy-to-digest compendium to guide them on how to decide when an element of conservation is warranted, and how much it is worth spending on it. This book presents approaches to combine investment on landmarks and on their surrounding areas, with investment to create jobs and prosperity for local communities, many of them poor, while also contributing to sustainable urbanization and inclusive growth. Chapters 1 and 2 analyze the optimal balance between conservation and development, providing a framework to leveraging heritage for job creation and incorporating a cultural dimension into urban development.

Who Is the Audience for This Book?

Public and private sector stakeholders who design
investment operations in historic city cores, heritage assets,
and underutilized land in central locations.

There are different approaches that projects can follow. One end of the spectrum is to look at historic city cores as any other neighborhoods of the city, as if all the housing and other assets in the area were indistinct or generic, and including only isolated investment on some heritage assets in the area as a component of the project. At the other end, there is the approach of investing in projects solely on landmarks of unquestionable significance, isolating them from their context and communities. In between these two extremes, there are innovative projects blending the two approaches, targeting simultaneously landmarks, historic city cores, housing, and land that would not qualify for protection individually but that taken collectively have enough character to be recognizable features that give to each city its uniqueness. Experts call this approach "integrated conservation."[2]

Projects applying the integrated conservation approach link heritage conservation and local economic development. The objective of these projects is to create livable downtowns—places where people like to go, meet, live, work, and invest, linking heritage conservation and local economic development. These projects typically include investment for conserving landmarks and infrastructure, but also investment to transfer resources to the local community, in the form of grants or loans for residents to improve their historic housing and to support job creation and retention. They may also include institutional mechanisms to facilitate the adaptive reuse of buildings and land with heritage value to meet the new needs emerging from rapid urbanization. Chapter 6 presents the cases of four World Heritage cities in developing countries and provides evidence of the positive impacts of integrated conservation, expanding on the governance and institutional mechanisms that allowed the transformation to create jobs and improve services while maintaining the sense of place.

What Is the Economic Rationale Underpinning Heritage Investment?

Several valuation methods show that heritage investment does have positive returns.

In economics, heritage can be seen as an asset, with the theoretical basis in capital theory. Economists conventionally distinguish between different types of capital, notably physical or manufactured capital, social capital, human capital, and natural capital. The concept of capital has then been extended into the field of culture and heritage, with the definition of cultural capital. This allows recognition of the distinctive features of certain cultural goods as capital assets, and captures the ways in which heritage investment contribute, in combination with other inputs, to the production of further cultural goods and services, job creation, and well being of local communities.

Interpreting heritage as cultural capital has a clear parallel with the definition of environment as natural capital. Like any other form of capital, both cultural and natural capital have been inherited from the past, might deteriorate or depreciate if not maintained, and impose on the present generation a duty of care so they can be handed down to future generations. The long-term management of both cultural and natural capital has been integrated in sustainable development and experts have developed practical tools to operationalize this new paradigm.

A central issue in heritage economics is the question of valuation of these assets. As is the case of environmental economics, it is customary to distinguish between use[3] and non-use values.[4] These are also referred to, respectively, as market and non-market values. A third category of value—the cultural value[5]—should be added to the equation in order to capture the full benefits of heritage investment. While the first two categories of value are easier to measure, cultural value, by contrast, is a multidimensional concept. Chapter 3 proposes that the various elements contributing to cultural value can be similarly assessed.

Economic valuation of heritage investment evolved from methods traditionally used in environmental economics. Five valuation methods are used to address different aspects of heritage valuation, and chapters 4 and 9 discuss their features. The first method is compensation, which seeks to evaluate the cost and benefits derived from changes in the availability or quality of a heritage asset. The second method is social cost-benefit analysis, which captures the benefits of an investment with large spill-over effects. The third method is stated preference, which is rooted in behavioral economics, and aims to uncover what individuals are willing to pay or accept when the availability of a public good changes. There are also revealed preference methods, which include travel cost (fourth method) and hedonic price (fifth method). Travel cost is based on calculating the financial sacrifice that a visitor makes to travel to a city or a site of cultural significance, but it has some limits, especially due to attribution and opportunity cost.

The hedonic price method, widely used in urban economics, is emerging as a better tool for evaluating heritage-related investments. This model can help gain a better understanding of the value of heritage assets by leveraging databases having detailed information on transactions in the real estate market. Such databases are especially useful if they comprise disaggregated data on the characteristics of the properties sold. In this context, Geographic Information System (GIS) techniques often offer the possibility to further enrich data with mapping of information about geographic neighborhood characteristics. It is, however, important that this method takes distributional implications into account. Chapter 9 explores the use of GIS in valuation and includes a relevant and feasible application in developing countries.

How Can Heritage Values Be Maintained?

Through a balanced blend of regulations and incentives, the public and private values of heritage can be enhanced and leveraged for job creation.

It is widely acknowledged that heritage has a value to the community in which it is located. While landmarks are often in public ownership, the vast majority of other assets identified as heritage are in private hands (e.g., housing, former industrial areas of significant cultural value in central locations). Most countries have some form of identification for heritage, called listing or designation.

The most appropriate way to protect this value is through a blend of regulations and incentives. Designation is usually accompanied by regulations that may limit what individual owners can do to their properties (e.g., specific uses, prohibition to demolish, specific materials to use, dedicated approval process for building permits). However, regulation alone might not be sufficient, because of the legitimate concern to limit property rights of individual owners, so it is often best coupled with incentives (e.g., tax reduction, grants). Through a balanced blend of regulation and incentives, the public and private values of heritage can be enhanced and leveraged for job creation and integrated conservation.

Are There City-Wide Benefits from Heritage-Related Projects?

They contribute to urban livability, attracting talent, and providing an enabling environment for job creation.

The cities that will be most successful at meeting the jobs and growth aspirations of their inhabitants, while alleviating poverty and working toward inclusion, will be those that leverage all of their resources to do so. Among the resources that these cities need to harness are their heritage assets, which are unique features that differentiate them from other cities. Investing in historic city cores and underutilized land in central locations can attract investment for job creation. As chapter 1 shows, heritage is a differentiator that attracts talent to cities. Furthermore, the linkage between a livable historic core and a city's ability to attract business is not confined to businesses that locate in or near the core: proximity to a livable historic core is also important for companies located on the periphery, especially for innovative, knowledge-intensive firms whose employees look for vibrant and unique places to live in.

Evidence shows that there is a correlation between projects aiming at regenerating historic city cores and underutilized land and a city's ability to attract talent and business investment. A number of cities in developed and developing countries have already successfully leveraged their historic cores and underutilized land creating powerful talent hubs, attracting world leaders in knowledge industries and foreign direct investment, while at the same time becoming hotspots for local business development. A number of successful stories about cities that leveraged their historic cores and underutilized land for job creation are presented throughout the book.

Does Heritage Investment Have Distributional Effects?

Yes, real estate values can increase significantly. With adequate policy measures, such investment can also distribute wealth.

Country-level data show that heritage designation, with its accompanying regulatory framework, creates a market-assigned value premium for heritage assets, in particular for housing and retails. Increase in real estate values in neighborhoods designated as heritage has positive impacts on local governments, allowing them to mobilize property-based tax revenues to deliver better services. However, increase in real estate values also has distributional impacts on lower-income households, who have limited capacity to pay increased rents, increased house prices, and higher property taxes, causing their displacement and leading to gentrification.

Attracting investment to historic city cores, heritage assets, and underutilized land in central locations raises the issue of how to distribute the capital gains between the local community (lower- and higher-income groups) and outside investors. Standard urban projects emphasize the importance of clear property rights, at the household level, as a prerequisite to attract investment. Because transactions are on a voluntary basis, clear property rights ensure that local residents are adequately compensated if they decide to transfer their properties. But if this process results in displacement, it can jeopardize the mix of higher and lower-income groups that made the historic city core livable, undermining its sense of place and uniqueness. These distributional issues should be taken into account at a very early stage of project preparation. Proper measures can minimize the negative effects of gentrification, including securing tenure and facilitating access to housing finance for lower-income residents. Other alternative property arrangements can be considered, including a shareholders approach in which long-term residents can have a collective stake in the project.

Chapters 2 and 5 expand on the impacts of heritage investment on real estate values, including distributional impacts, risks of gentrification, and ways of mitigating these risks through Poverty and Social Impact Assessments (PSIAs).

In development economics, it is well understood that investment projects and policy reforms can create winners and losers. It has therefore become common practice to supplement project preparation by analyses of the potential distributional impacts. Those analyses are known as PSIAs. When considering development policies or specific projects, PSIAs are often used to design complementary measures aimed at mitigating adverse impacts on the poor. From a political economy perspective, PSIAs identify measures to redistribute some of the gains from the winners to the losers. The discussion of distributional issues has so far emphasized the difference between those whose property is reclaimed for project implementation and those who can fully enjoy the windfalls created by the project. Chapter 2 tackles the debate on distributional implications.

What Is the Relation between Heritage Investment and Tourism?

Heritage investment develops tourism, a labor intensive industry that provides proportionally more income opportunities for the cities low-skilled laborers and the poor.

Tourism has emerged as one of the fastest-growing sectors of the world economy. The average growth of tourism arrivals, as the world economy recovers, is likely to continue to grow in the decades to come. This is especially due to growing interest in visiting and enjoying vibrant cities and heritage assets. Indeed, inspired by a number of success stories attributed to tourism specialization, more and more developing countries are contemplating such a strategy, supporting museums, conference centers, exhibition areas, parks, attractions in general, hotels, and infrastructure, as chapters 1 and 9 illustrate.

Tourism, by virtue of being a labor intensive activity, can allow the large pool of unemployed and underemployed individuals in developing countries to get jobs and in turn create the conditions for a sustained and broad-based growth. Indeed, there is a well recognized positive relationship between the extent of specialization in tourism and long-term GDP growth. Data show a positive correlation between tourism receipts (as a share of exports) and growth and that countries that have specialized in tourism have experienced better economic growth than countries that have not, all other factors being equal.

Tourism has spillover effects in other economic sectors: the foreign direct investment associated with it can in fact bring managerial skills and technology with potential benefits to other sectors. Policies designed to foster tourism—by improving security, stability, and political openness—can enhance growth in other sectors and distribute wealth more widely. Given that tourism is consumed on-site, it has significant spillover effects for local economic development. Policies to create an enabling environment for private sector investment in tourism and other sectors are crucial, as chapter 7 illustrates. The chapter also highlights the need of integrating tourism into economic diversification policies.

How Can Heritage Investment Be Financed?

There are a number of successful models, with an increasing integration of public and private financing.

Development is by nature a joint public and private effort. Besides traditional heritage investment entirely driven by public funds (grants, loans, or incentives), there are other approaches blending public and private financing. It is clear that, given the public good characteristics of heritage assets, historic city cores, and underutilized land of heritage value, the economic justification for public sector investment is well established. But it is unreasonable to expect the public sector to be the sole investor. On the other hand, the private sector alone is likely to provide suboptimal redevelopment and underprovision of investment due to the presence of risks and externalities, sometimes due to coordination problems among private agents. The solution is to have a combination of public and private investment, with a balance between the two that varies depending on the project scheme and context.

Four financial models have been applied successfully. They are presented below and discussed in detail in chapter 8.

Public-private partnerships. There are three types of public-private partnership (PPP) contracts used in projects dealing with historic city cores and underutilized land of heritage value: rehabilitate, operate, and transfer (ROT); build, rehabilitate, operate, and transfer (BROT); and rehabilitate, lease, and transfer (RLT). In most cases, these projects are implemented through a special purpose vehicle (SPV), which is typically a consortium of financial institutions and private companies responsible for all PPP activities, including the coordination of financing and service delivery.

Land value finance mechanisms. The basic approach of land value finance (LVF), also called land value capture finance, is to recover the capital cost of the investment by capturing some or all of the increments in land value increases resulting from the investment. The increases in land value may be captured directly or indirectly through their conversion into public revenues as fees, taxes, exactions, or other fiscal means.

Urban development funds. There has been a significant rise in the number of urban development funds (UDF). These funds have provided the vehicles for a range of investors to gain exposure to real estate markets by committing incremental investment. The funds focus on all forms of urban investment; they operate in diverse geographic areas and have different maturity dates that offer considerable choice to investors.

Impact investment funds. In recent years, a new form of investment, known as impact investment funds, has emerged in the market. The impact investment funds are designed as a socially responsible investment not driven exclusively by profit and generally targeted toward addressing heritage, environmental, and social issues. Impact investment is defined as actively placing capital in businesses and funds that generate social or environmental good and a range of returns to the investor.

What Has the World Bank Done?

The World Bank finances an increasing number of heritage projects[6] and has developed a three-pillar approach to ensure sustainable results.

The World Bank's support for heritage began with the reconstruction of post-war Europe. It included investment to conserve individual war-damaged heritage assets and landmarks in cities and significant natural heritage sites. As the rebuilding of Europe was completed, the Bank turned its attention to the needs of developing countries and the severe problems of poverty. Subsequently, investment in heritage was driven by the need to conserve and upgrade specific endangered assets in the phase of rapid urbanization, and to prevent and mitigate the possible adverse impacts of large infrastructural projects.

More recently, the Bank developed a new approach to heritage investment as part of its agenda for inclusive green growth and sustainable development. Heritage investment promotes an efficient use of built assets and land, maximizing the benefits of adaptively reusing assets that would otherwise be neglected or underutilized. It also encourages housing in dense, historic urban neighborhoods, walkability, and in general a low carbon development model. The three-pillar approach to heritage investment is explained with practical examples from Bank-supported projects (illustrated in boxes throughout the book). This approach consists of investing in:

1. Heritage asset conservation and management;
2. Housing (including security of tenure and access to finance), infrastructure, and service delivery to involve local communities living in the surroundings of heritage assets; and

3. Institutional strengthening, capacity building, and promoting an enabling environment for job creation and local economic development.

What Are the Key Messages?

Balance conservation with an acceptable degree of change. The far-reaching governance of projects dealing with heritage, historic city cores, and underutilized land calls for striking a balance between conserving and promoting a compatible and sustainable reuse—i.e., managing an acceptable level of change (adaptive reuse). To meet such an overarching objective, consensus must be reached among the stakeholders on the relative weight of the different values and the trade-offs between conservation and inclusive development.

Promote a blend of regulation and incentives. Measures to conserve historic city cores and heritage assets are not limited to rules and regulations that restrict activities. Incentives are also essential for achieving integrated conservation. Incentives can be regulatory or non-regulatory and comprise a wide range of policies and tools. Regulatory incentives are based on provisions for conservation areas, which can include waivers of minimum standards to facilitate adaptive reuse, special limits to plot ratios or zonings, and bonus floor area. In other cases, transferable development rights have been used, creating a market for conservation. Additional regulatory measures include contributions and consent fee waivers. At the other end of the spectrum, non-regulatory incentives comprise heritage grants and loans, mortgage rates relief, and tax relief. Cities have also applied with success public purchase and revolving acquisitions and funds, insurance rebates, and even events and promotion.

Ensure a dialogue between public and private sectors. In the initial stages of the urban regeneration process, policies focus on the legal and regulatory framework to identify and list heritage assets, defining the regulation to protect them. However, the bulk of responsibility for maintaining them is left mostly to the private owners. In a second stage of the process, the public sector supports the conservation process proactively, bringing into the task a wide variety of stakeholders with their financial resources and management capabilities, including capital investment on assets and infrastructure, and incentives for private owners. The most advanced stage of the process is reached when the reuse of heritage assets meets sustained demand, for which the private sector takes the lead under a consolidated and sustainable mix of regulations and incentives, often financed through revolving mechanisms.

Notes

1. In this book, "heritage" refers to assets having the following characteristics: (1) physical and/or non-physical assets inherited from past generations; (2) significance to community groups; and (3) being uncommon, rare, or unique. Heritage can include man-made physical assets, such as landmarks, historic city cores, urbanscapes, land with assets embodying ways of living or producing, isolated sites, uncommon immovable and movable properties, and cultural landscapes. Heritage can also include non man-made physical assets, such as fauna, flora, geology, landscape, landforms, parks, reserves, any natural resources with non-ordinary features (from a rock to a beach), and natural landscapes. Thirdly, heritage can also include non-physical assets, also defined as intangible heritage, such as traditions, customs, habits, production methods, and any other expressions of creativity that distinguishes a community group from another.
2. For a complete bibliography, see the end of each chapter, as referenced in the overview. The concept of integrated conservation has been systematized by the ICOMOS International Scientific Committee on the Economics of Conservation, led by Luigi Fusco Girard, based on the pioneering work that Nathaniel Lichfield carried out in Campania in the 1980's, and it is closely linked with the efforts undertaken by UNESCO with the Historic Urban Landscape Recommendation and by the Council of Europe under the Heritage and Beyond initiative.
3. Use value: The use value is the easiest to be assessed. It can include, inter alia, rents, ticket revenues, and any other cash flow that can be captured in market transactions.
4. Non-use value: Heritage yields public good benefits that can be classified in the same ways as environmental non-market benefits. Three types of non-rival and non-excludable public good benefits are presumed to exist for heritage, relating to its existence value (people value the existence of heritage even though they may not enjoy its services directly themselves), option value (people wish to conserve the option that they or others might enjoy the asset services at some future time), and bequest value (people may wish to bequeath the asset to future generations). Non-use value is not observable in market transactions, since no market exists on which the rights to them can be exchanged.
5. Cultural value: The third category of value, the cultural value, is the least apparent to be assessed, and it can be identified through both the revealed preferences and the stated preferences of individuals. Cultural value can includes aesthetic, symbolic, spiritual, social, historic, authenticity, and scientific value.
6. A recent portfolio review targeting cultural heritage, natural heritage, and sustainable tourism has shown that the World Bank Group has a growing portfolio in these three areas. Since the 1970's, the Bank has financed through its International Development Association (IDA) and International Bank for Reconstruction and Development (IBRD) about 320 projects (components of larger investments, stand-alone projects) and technical assistance activities for a commitment of US$7 billion. Moreover, the International Finance Corporation (IFC) has financed since the 1950's approximately 280 related projects for a commitment of US$2.5 billion. The total for the World Bank Group is US$9.5 billion in some 600 projects. Currently, IDA and IBRD have about 110 operations under implementation covering these three areas, for a commitment of US$3.5 billion; IFC has about 60 operations, for a commitment of US$600 million.

Livable Historic City Cores and Enabling Environment: A Successful Recipe to Attract Investment to Cities

John O'Brien

Head of Business Strategy, Industrial Development Agency (Ireland)

This chapter outlines the economic and social benefits of investing in historic city core regeneration and cultural heritage conservation, focusing on their role to define urban livability and attract investments for job creation. Touching tourism, but also going beyond it, the chapter begins by quoting Nobel Prize Laureate Robert Solow on the importance of identity and livability for places to succeed economically. Then, the content of the other chapters of the book is briefly presented, followed by an analysis of the role of cities in modern economies and the huge potential of foreign direct investments for job creation. Subsequently, Richard Florida's concept of the creative class is introduced, and heritage is described as a differentiator to ensure city livability and attract talents to cities. The successful story of Dublin is presented as a case study, describing it as a city that has successfully leveraged its historic city core to create a "talent hub"—attracting world leaders in knowledge industries to establish operations there while at the same time becoming a hotspot for indigenous entrepreneurial development. The chapter explains how the linkage between a livable historic city core and a city's ability to attract business is not confined to businesses that locate in or near the core. In the case of Dublin, proximity to a livable historic city core has also proved to be important for knowledge-intensive companies located on the periphery.

Introduction

This book takes inspiration from Nobel Prize Laureate Robert Merton Solow's quotation: "Over the long term, places with strong, distinctive identities are more likely to prosper than places without them. Every place must identify its strongest, most distinctive features and develop them or run the risk of being all things to all persons and nothing special to any. […] Livability is not a middle-class luxury. It is an economic imperative."

The positive influence of cultural heritage on livability, economic growth, and local economic development has been increasingly studied and discussed in the last few decades. Building on concepts springing from biodiversity and natural heritage conservation, cultural economists have been developing their arguments about the economic importance of cultural heritage assets. This book presents the latest contributions on this topic, including methods of assessing the economic values of cultural heritage and ways to apply these findings to the practical issues faced by policy makers confronted with explosive urban growth—one of the defining characteristics of this century. The authors argue that it is vital for policy makers and other stakeholders to appreciate the important role that cultural heritage can play in generating employment and sustainable economic development, and then incorporate this understanding into urban planning and development policies. This must be done to ensure that rapid urbanization, particularly in the developing world, is not accompanied by the destruction of much of our heritage.

Urbanization and the Jobs Crisis

The recent economic and financial crisis of the 2000s has resulted in job losses in both developing and developed economies. The International Labor Organization (ILO 2012) notes that, despite economic recovery since 2009, particularly in high-growth emerging economies, there are still 27 million more unemployed workers worldwide than at the start of the crisis, while the employment-to-population ratio showed the largest decline on record between 2007 and 2010. The ILO report estimates that the world faces an "urgent challenge" to create 600 million jobs over the next decade and that "job creation in the real economy must become our number one priority."

Paradoxically, in the midst of a global jobs crisis, businesses continue to have major concerns about their ability to attract sufficient talent to drive growth and development. A recent survey of about 350 senior business leaders worldwide (Deloitte Consulting 2010) found that "high unemployment rates in the U.S. and abroad have not created the talent surplus that many would have predicted. On the contrary, many executives predict talent shortages across key business units."

Furthermore, 41 percent rated competing for talent globally as one of their most pressing employment concerns. Resolving this paradox in a manner that provides increased employment opportunities across a range of skill levels and socioeconomic groups will require a multifaceted approach that will vary depending on many factors, such as a country's level of development and resource endowments. However, it is very clear that this challenge will have to be resolved in cities and that the bulk of the jobs will have to come from the private sector.

More than 50 percent of the world's people already live in cities, and they account for 70 percent of world gross domestic product. Furthermore, nearly 2 billion new urban residents are expected in the next 20 years, as people "vote with their feet" in search of opportunity. Most of these people will have to find jobs in the private sector, which is the engine of growth and employment accounting for about 90 percent of employment in developing countries.

The cities that will be most successful at meeting the jobs and growth aspirations of their inhabitants, while alleviating poverty and working toward social inclusion, will be those that employ all of their resources to promote a healthy environment for investment and talent. Among the resources these cities need to harness is their built cultural heritage.

Recent Trends in Foreign Direct Investment

The last two decades saw an explosion in the scale of worldwide foreign direct investment (FDI), with the annual flow growing from US$208 billion in 1990 to a peak of US$1,771 billion in 2008. The financial crisis caused a sharp fall in flows to a level of US$1,114 billion in 2009, having bottomed out in the latter half of 2009 before recovering modestly in 2010. The World Investment Report (UNCTAD 2011) anticipates a recovery in flows back toward the 2008 level by 2012, but cautions that prospects are still "fraught with risks and uncertainties, including the fragility of the global economic recovery."

Despite the recent short-term decline, FDI will continue to play a critical role in economic development. For cities in developing countries, this will be even more important given three factors:

- An increasing proportion of FDI is going to developing countries; 2010 was the first year ever that FDI flows to developing and transitional economies accounted for more than half the global total (UNCTAD 2011), and there is every sign that the importance of FDI there will continue to grow.
- Investment and trade in services in general, and in the creative industries in particular, are of growing importance in the world economy relative to manufacturing and extractive industries (UNCTAD 2004), and this has been reflected in global FDI flows.

- Creative industries are much more likely to locate in livable urban areas, and for that reason corporate location decisions will increasingly be based on the relative attractiveness of cities rather than of countries.

Cities Compete for Investment

In essence, all mobile investment decisions are based on three fundamental considerations:

- Access to markets;
- Costs; and
- Access to resources.

In most instances, it is a combination of all three, with the dominant consideration being a function of the nature of the business or sector, the function to be carried out at the given location, and the sophistication of the market to be served. Some of the factors that may influence location decisions (such as taxes and tariffs) will be determined by central government, and while the city may influence these, it does not control them. Furthermore, if the city is competing for investment with other cities in the same jurisdiction, then that city will be offering broadly the same advantages (and indeed disadvantages).

This similarity of factors may not just apply to the same jurisdiction; it may also apply across the entire region where cities have broadly equal labor costs for similar skill levels, offer much the same development incentives in terms of local tax relief and serviced sites, and may have similar connectivity. This is to some extent the "flat world" envisaged by Thomas Friedman in his book *The World is Flat* (Friedman 2007). However, evidence would suggest that the world is not flat, but is rather punctuated by "spikes" around which economic activity clusters, and that these spikes are cities or city regions. These cities compete for investment across a range of factors. A recent study (EIU 2012) ranked the competitiveness of 120 cities across the world, taking into account eight factors: economic strength, physical capital, financial maturity, institutional effectiveness, social and cultural character, human capital, environment and natural hazards, and global appeal.

The study found that U.S. and European cities are the world's most competitive ones today, despite concerns over ageing infrastructure and large budget deficits. The most significant advantage that these developed cities hold is their ability to foster and attract the world's top talent. It also noted that a "middle tier" of mid-size cities is emerging as a key driver of global growth; and that while infrastructure development would continue to drive Asian growth, "one of the most pressing challenges for emerging market cities in the decades ahead will be whether they can focus their development not just on skyscrapers, rail links and other infrastructure, but also on the softer aspects that will be crucial to their ability to attract and develop tomorrow's talent—including education, quality of life, and personal freedoms, among other things."

It is important to note the emphasis on attracting (and retaining) talent as well as developing it. This requires a much broader strategy than simply investing in education; it will require investing in shaping a city that will be attractive to what the urban economist Richard Florida has named the "creative class."

Talent and Urban Development

Richard Florida, in a number of works, particularly *The Rise of the Creative Class* and *Cities and the Creative Class* (Florida 2002, 2004), argues that this creative class is the key driving force in modern economic development. He defines this class or group as being made up of those whose job is to "create meaningful new forms." He divides the creative class into two categories:

- A super-creative core of that accounts for about 12 percent of the current U.S. workforce and comprises a group of highly educated professionals in areas such as science, engineering, research, and the creative industries such as arts, design, and media, who are fully engaged in the creative process.
- Creative professionals who are the classic knowledge-based workers including those in healthcare, business and finance, the legal sector, and education and who draw on complex bodies of knowledge to solve specific problems.

He claims that the creative class constitutes close to 40 percent of the population in the United States, that they predominantly live in cities, and that there is a strong correlation between how densely packed cities are with such people and the economic success of those cities. He further puts forth that successful cities of the future will be those that can best attract such workers; these workers, in turn, are attracted to places that have the three Ts: Talent, Tolerance, and Technology.

Florida's arguments have been controversial in the United States, but there is little doubt that at their core is the essential truth that talented people are relatively mobile and that they wish to live in interesting places where they can combine their professional activity with a varied lifestyle. However, such people want an environment that goes well beyond pure functionality: they want to live in an interesting and authentic place.

Indeed, much of the criticism of Florida's work has less to do with its fundamental hypothesis than with its facile application by developers whose idea of creating a cultural center is to add an art gallery/antique shop to an otherwise ugly mall. This misguided approach was recognized by the Organization for Economic Cooperation and Development (OECD 2007), which noted that in some cases planners, in their desire to appeal to a stereotyped image of the tastes of knowledge workers, had seriously undermined the local distinctiveness and uniqueness of their cities and instead created "analogous cities"—cities that are so generic it is difficult to differentiate one from another.

Any good strategist will attest that the key to a successful strategy is to positively differentiate your product from your competitors, and that such "me too" efforts are therefore wasteful and self-defeating. The key to successful differentiation is to build on urban assets that are unique to the city. In most cases, this will involve regeneration of historic core areas of the city in a manner that is sensitive to their cultural heritage. This will ensure that the city will have an authentic sense of place that contributes greatly to attracting talent on a sustainable basis, and which, in turn, will be a magnet for business. As Michael Bloomberg, mayor of New York City, put it recently: "I've always believed that talent attracts capital more effectively and consistently than capital attracts talent" (EIU 2012).

Implications for Urban Development Strategies

The above analysis and the case study of Dublin presented next suggest that urban regeneration strategies that build on the city's heritage and preserve its best features can provide the differentiation that can underpin a city's overall economic development strategy. In particular, the city's heritage character can contribute to its ability to attract investment for knowledge-based businesses.

This is not to suggest that this is the sole or primary reason for preserving our built and cultural heritage. But this significant benefit is a complement to others that are described in the chapters by Throsby, Rama, Nijkamp, and Rypkema. It is, of course, somewhat more difficult to make a direct connection between an urban regeneration/preservation project and a city's ability to later attract talent and business investment—harder than, for example, showing how a regeneration project has attracted tourists and their spending. As with assessing the value of future tourism earnings, an evaluation model to assess the value of attracting business investment would require assumptions about the value of likely investment flows in terms of their direct contribution to the local economy, as well as any spillovers and deadweight effects. Nevertheless, the potential for such positive results is very real.

The link between a livable urban core and a city's ability to attract business is not confined to businesses that locate in or near the core. In the case of Dublin, proximity to a livable city center has also proved to be important for knowledge-intensive companies located on the periphery. When these companies recruited employees with specialized skills and languages from outside Dublin, many of these people chose to live in the center and reverse commute. They clearly wanted to live in a genuine urban environment. This demonstrates the need to provide housing that allows people from a range of socio-economic backgrounds to continue to live in the core, and to ensure that the core offers a vibrant community setting with access to a range of goods and services. This highlights the need both for social (low income) and affordable (lower middle income) housing to be available and for local people to be genuinely involved in the development of their city.

As Rojas points out in his chapter, the evidence worldwide suggests that a successful project combining conservation and regeneration must have structures that respond to community interests and mobilize community support. For example, the Dublin docklands development provides for both social and affordable housing, and its overseeing authority devotes considerable resources to promoting community involvement.

It is also important to understand that the implication of the analysis is not confined to the attraction of high-tech activities. As the OECD (2006) states: "Not all metro-regions will become world leaders in high tech-activities. There is a need to search for strong viable niches outside this range." However, it is still probable that any sector that is likely to be globally competitive in the future will rely on the city's ability to attract and retain talent. Furthermore, as Arezki et al. point out in their chapter, while there are real benefits to be had from exploiting the tourism potential of conservation or regeneration projects, tourism alone will not generate sustained growth but rather needs to be combined with the development of other sectors. There are obvious overlapping benefits from urban renewal projects designed to attract knowledge workers and industries and those designed to attract tourism. An example is the Digital Hub in Dublin, which is close to and in the same regeneration area as the restored Guinness' Storehouse, the most visited attraction in the city.

Some of this analysis may seem esoteric to urban policy makers in rapidly developing cities facing the pressure to create jobs both for existing inhabitants and for the almost daily influx of new people. The policy makers' priority in such cities may, correctly, be the development of large industrial parks on the periphery that will, they hope, attract companies with thousands of assembly line jobs. However, it is essential to realize that such projects represent the start, not the end, of the city's job development process. As these cities are successful, they will seek to move up the value chain and attract and develop more sophisticated investments. At that point the city will need to be able to differentiate itself from others as an attractive place for talented people. It is also the case that this transition from manufacturing and extractive to knowledge-based jobs tends to happen much more rapidly than it used to, given the speed at which new competitors for basic processes emerge.

It is therefore important that the development and preservation of valuable cultural heritage be built into development plans from an early stage, to avoid what Rama describes as "the frantic transformation of centuries-old [...] cities into soulless agglomerations of generic architecture." This is especially vital, he continues, because "there is an element of irreversibility in transformations of this kind, as recovering what was lost is enormously more expensive than it would have been to preserve it in the first place." The essential message is this: preserving what may prove to be an essential differentiator of the city must be built into that city's development plans from the start, not left until later when it will be certainly more expensive, and perhaps impossible, to regain what was lost.

Dublin, Ireland: "Talent Hub" Strategy Based on Livability of the Historic City Core

Dublin provides an interesting case study of a place that has leveraged its cultural heritage with other asset to create a "talent hub"—attracting world leaders in knowledge industries to establish operations there while at the same time becoming a hotspot for indigenous entrepreneurial development.

Over the last three decades, Ireland has been very successful in attracting FDI, which now plays a vital role in the economy, accounting for:

- 250,000 jobs directly and indirectly out of a total of 1.8 million in employment;
- US$150 billion in exports, or 80 percent of the country's total exports;
- 65 percent of Corporation Tax payments; and
- 68 percent of business expenditure on research and development.

This investment comes from the world's leading companies in information and communications technology, life sciences, financial services, and engineering, and increasingly from "born on the internet" content and service providers including companies such as Google, Facebook, Amazon, eBay, Blizzard, and Electronic Arts. Indeed, the "IBM Plant Location International Report 2011" ranked Ireland as the number one destination worldwide for foreign investment projects by value and number two worldwide for FDI jobs.

Ireland's Industrial Development Agency is the government body charged with attracting FDI to Ireland and working with existing investors to maximize their contribution to the economy. An important part of its job is to continually monitor trends in global investment and develop an appropriate response by government and other public bodies to these trends so that they can maximize the FDI contribution to the economy in terms of jobs and added value.

Activities increasingly depend on two critical factors: interconnectivity with the rest of the world, and, above all, the availability of talent. Ireland's competitive strategy is based on four Ts: Talent, Technology, Tax, and Track Record.

It became clear in recent decades that for many of the world's leading companies that rely on a high creative input, their choice of where to locate was boiling down to deciding on which city rather than which country. Therefore, while Ireland's Industrial Development Agency continues to promote balanced regional development in line with the government's National Spatial Strategy, for many key projects success would depend on the promotion of Dublin (the only Irish city classified by the OECD as a metro-region) as an attractive city location compared to other similar competing European cities.

Over the last 20 years, major conservation projects have been undertaken in Dublin, by both the state and city authorities, on important public buildings including the Royal Hospital (1684), Dublin Castle, Collins (Royal) Barracks (1709), Dr. Steevens's Hospital (1719), Custom House (1791), Kilmainham Gaol (1792), and City Hall (Royal Exchange) (1769). A works project has been ongoing in the Phoenix Park, including the reinstatement of the main entrance gates and the return of the Phoenix Monument (1747) to its original position on the main axis of the park. Conservation works have also been completed and new uses found for the former Bluecoat School (1773) and the churches of St. George (1802) and St. Catherine (1760).

But in the city as a whole, the track record on the survival and conservation of the historic urban fabric is more mixed, directly reflecting the changing social dynamics of the city, the conflicts of the early 20th century, and modern redevelopment. Some surviving properties, particularly on the north side of the city, lost original fabric and details when they were converted to tenement occupation (although this too is now an important part of their history). Private individuals and bodies have also done significant conservation work, particularly in the northern side of the city. One important example is the project on North Great George's Street, where conservation and new interventions to replace missing historical fabric have helped to revitalize and reestablish the integrity of the street. Dublin City Council has published a conservation plan for Henrietta Street and recently started a program of urgent conservation works on a number of properties in the street (UNESCO 2010).

The linking of investment promotion to a specific urban redevelopment project in Ireland started with the establishment in 1987 of the Customs House Docks Development Authority (CHDDA) as a statutory body to promote the redevelopment of historic but derelict inner-city docks areas of initially 11 hectares. It was envisaged that the economic basis for the redevelopment would be the establishment in the area of an International Financial Services Centre (IFSC), and incentives were put in place to both encourage redevelopment and entice international financial companies to locate in the center. While the CHDDA would be responsible for the development of the area, the government mandated that IDA Ireland promote the center to investors. The initiative proved to be very successful, and today there are 30,000 people employed in financial services and ancillary support activities in the IFSC. Dublin is now a center for international banking, funds management, and insurance, and the sector continues to grow despite the international financial crisis.

In 1997, the CHDDA was subsumed into the Dublin Docklands Development Authority (DDDA) with a broader mandate to promote the development of the entire Dublin docklands area consisting of 520 hectares. Since the DDDA's inception in 1997, the area under its control has attracted more than €3.35 billion of public and private investment and has seen the creation of 40,000 new jobs. The number of residents in the area has grown from 17,500 to 22,000, and 11,000 new homes have been built, of which 2,200 are either social or affordable. In addition, the area has developed as a vibrant cultural center with a new theater and a new concert venue.

In 2003, as part of a further urban regeneration initiative, the government formed the Digital Hub Development Agency, an Irish state agency, to establish a digital hub in the historic Liberties area of the city. Its role is to provide incubator space and support for largely indigenous, small and medium-size enterprises while promoting the broader social and economic regeneration of the area. It currently houses more 90 such enterprises developing products ranging from mobile apps to online games.

Dublin, as the major urban center in the country, had always attracted a significant share of FDI into Ireland. By the mid-1990s, it was already attracting major investments from an impressive range of international companies, including Intel, Microsoft, Oracle, IBM, and SAP, as well as major financial institutions such as Citicorp, Merrill Lynch, Deutsche Bank, and HSBC. (See figure 1.1.) IDA Ireland recognized that this established track record, combined with the exciting urban redevelopment of the city core, provided the opportunity to promote Dublin as a "talent hub" that would attract the web-based knowledge industries of the future as well as encourage the existing technology and financial services companies already established there to deepen their investment and add more knowledge-based activities.

To succeed with this endeavor, it was evident that Dublin would need to have state-of-the-art data interconnectivity with the rest of the world. While this would be largely supplied by the private sector, it was clear that some pump priming would be needed, so IDA Ireland sought and received government funding to invest in a project, called Global Crossing, that connected Ireland to the transatlantic fiber network between the United Kingdom and the United States and thus to the rest of the world. This made Dublin a credible location for investment projects that require the speedy and secure transmission of high volumes of data at a competitive cost.

FIGURE 1.1

Historic Core of Dublin: Home to the Digital Hub, the IFSC, and Leading Online Players

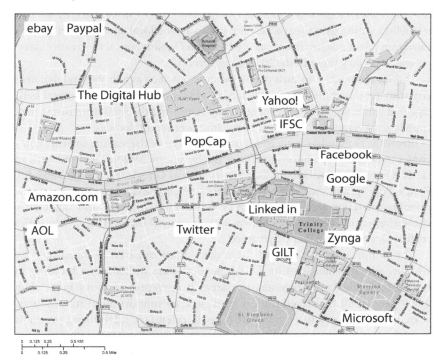

Source: Copyright Map Resources.

A basic pillar for the promotion of Dublin as a talent hub was the concentration of higher education institutions in the city. These include three universities (Trinity College in the city center and University College Dublin and Dublin City University just outside the center); the Dublin Institute of Technology, also in the city center; and the National College of Ireland that relocated its campus to the heart of the IFSC as part of the urban redevelopment project. These institutions educate 65,000 undergraduates and postgraduates in the full range of disciplines, with a strong focus on technology and business. They also conduct a wide range of research, with faculty and postdoctoral students drawn from varying backgrounds and nationalities; research activity has increased significantly since 2002 with the support of Science Foundation Ireland.

While having good higher education institutions locally can provide a stream of talent, it was clear that this, while necessary, was not sufficient to build a talent hub. Apart from the fact that (as has been pointed out by analysts such as Florida) not all cities with good universities retain their graduates, knowledge-based companies would only locate their regional base in a city that could supply people offering a wide range of skills and languages. Companies would need to feel that a Dublin location gave them access not just to a good local talent market but to a European talent market; this would be based on Dublin's appeal to "creative class" people, especially those in the 20 to 40 age group.

Dublin is attractive to such people because it is seen as a livable and dynamic city with good nightlife and leisure facilities but also with a strong cultural heritage that was reflected in a regenerated city center and the significant investment (public and private) in heritage conservation over recent decades.

Recently, Dublin has successfully attracted most of the leading internet companies to establish operations to service the European, Middle East, and African (EMEA) market from Dublin. Companies such as Google, Facebook, Linkedin, Zynga, Popcap, and Twitter have chosen to locate in the city center in or near the urban regeneration area. Others such as PayPal, eBay, Amazon, and Yahoo have chosen larger sites further out of town, as have many of the larger tech companies such as Oracle, HP, SAP, and Symantec.

The importance of talent to these companies can best be illustrated by Google, which established its EMEA headquarters in 2003 in a building in the Dublin docklands regeneration area. It currently employs more than 2,000 people, all higher-education graduates, to support all of its products: search engines, consumer products (Gmail, calendar), advertising products (Ad Words, Ad Sense), right through to business solutions for major corporations. It also undertakes new product development through a dedicated engineering team and provides central support for the finance, payroll, legal, and human resources functions. To do this effectively it operates in 45 languages and covers 65 countries.

It is also important to note that not all of the creative and innovative activity has been generated by FDI. The Digital Hub has been highly successful in nurturing and developing creative and innovative small and medium-size enterprises. The Digital Hub is currently home to more than 90 companies employing more than 500 people doing everything from developing apps for mobile phones to web design to computer games. This is only one manifestation of the strength of indigenous high-tech entrepreneurship in Dublin that feeds off the nexus of multinational corporations, innovative research in educational institutions, and the availability of venture capital.

The success of the talent hub approach can also be seen by the fact that in a recent survey called "Hotspots" (EIU 2012), which ranked the competitiveness of 120 major cities worldwide, Dublin ranked first in the Human Capital sub index and was tied for fifth (with Paris and Vienna) on the social and cultural sub index.

The following chapters give many more examples—from diverse places around the world facing varied economic and social challenges—that further demonstrate the role of heritage conservation as a major contributor to economic development.

Conclusion

In an increasingly urbanized world, cities are competing to attract more foreign direct investment and businesses, which will provide their citizens with jobs. To attract such businesses, which in turn will bring talent to the city, a city needs to provide an attractive and livable urban environment. The cities that will be most successful in creating jobs while reducing poverty will be those that use a variety of policies to utilize all their resources for creating a healthy environment for investment and talent. Historic city cores and their cultural heritage assets can have an effective role in differentiating a city from its competitors and in improving livability and attractiveness.

Dublin can be a good case study and an exemplary model for the integration of cultural heritage conservation in local economic development. Over the last 20 years, Dublin's stakeholders have undertaken major projects, in partnerships between the public and private sector. Dublin's ability to leverage its cultural heritage to create a "talent hub" is commendable and shows how cultural assets of a city have the power to attract knowledge industries and the creative class. While many of the world's cities are competing to attract more investment and create more jobs for their citizens, Dublin has positively differentiated itself from these competitors. The key to such successful differentiation is utilizing the urban cultural assets that are unique to the city and contribute to a livable environment. Dublin has successfully conducted regeneration activities in its historic core while ensuring the preservation of its authenticity and historic character.

The historic urban fabric of the city has also been well conserved through a mix of regulations and incentive programs. But Dublin has not stopped at just conserving its historic buildings. It has also invested in higher education institutions and revised its immigration policies and labor regulations to facilitate the influx of foreign companies and their employees. All in all, the conservation activities enhanced the city's identity as a livable and dynamic urban environment with good nightlife and leisure facilities, and a strong historic and cultural background. Such an image was instrumental in building a "talent hub" by attracting the young and creative class and the companies for which they work.

References

Deloitte Consulting LLP. 2010. *Talent Edge 2020: Blueprints for the New Normal.* http://www.deloitte.com/view/en_US/us/Services/additional-services/talent-human-capital-hr/Talent-Library/talent-edge-2020/index.htm.

Digital Hub Development Authority (DHDA). 2010. *Annual Report.* www.thedigital hub.com.

Dublin Docklands Development Agency (DDDA). www.ddda.ie.

Economist Intelligence Unit (EIU). 2012. *Hotspots: Benchmarking Global City Competitiveness.* Commissioned by Citicorp. http://www.citigroup.com/citi/citiforcities/pdfs/hotspots.pdf.

Florida, R. 2002. *The Rise of the Creative Class.* New York: Basic Books.

Florida, R. 2004. *Cities and the Creative Class.* New York: Routledge.

Friedman, T. 2007. *The World Is Flat: A Brief History of the Twenty-First Century.* New York: Farrar, Straus & Giroux.

International Labor Organization (ILO) Employment Sector. 2012. *Global Employment Trends 2012.* Geneva: ILO.

Irish Development Agency (IDA). 2010. *Horizon 2020: IDA Ireland Strategy.* www.idaireland.com.

Organization for Economic Cooperation and Development (OECD). 2006. *Competitive Cities in a Global Economy.* Paris: OECD.

———. 2007. *Competitive Cities: A New Entrepreneurial Paradigm in Spatial Development.* Paris: OECD.

Shimomura, T. and T. Motsumoto. 2011. *Policies to Enhance the Physical Urban Environment for Competitiveness: A New Partnership between Public and Private Sectors,* OECD Regional Development Working Papers 2010/11. Paris: OECD.

United Nations Conference on Trade and Development (UNCTAD). 2004. *Creative Industries and Development.* Sao Paolo: UNCTAD.

———. 2011. *World Investment Report.* Geneva: UNCTAD.

United Nations Educational, Scientific, and Cultural Organization (UNESCO). 2010. *The Historic City of Dublin: Submission of the Permanent Delegation of Ireland.* Dublin: UNESCO.

World Bank. 2012. *World Bank Innovations Influencing the Private Sector for Development.* Washington, DC: World Bank.

World Bank/International Monetary Fund. 2011. *Moving Jobs Centre Stage: A Discussion Note* Washington, DC: World Bank.

2

Investing in the Sense of Place: The Economics of Urban Upgrading Projects with a Cultural Dimension

Martin Rama
Director, World Development Report 2013, The World Bank

In a context of rapid urbanization, interventions to develop old cities emphasize infrastructure but often pay scant attention to the architecture of the buildings, or the social fabric associated with them. At the same time, the approaches used for heritage preservation are more relevant when trying to save an architectural or historic landmark than when dealing with the challenges of large-scale urbanization. This chapter provides simple analytical tools to discuss under which conditions it is socially desirable for urban upgrading projects to protect and renovate buildings and structures that do not qualify as heritage landmarks but are part of the soul of a place. Those tools clarify the conditions under which an intervention paying attention to aesthetic and cultural aspects results in net gains for local residents and outside investors, leading to higher financial returns than a standard urban upgrading project. The chapter discusses how a cultural component should be designed so as to align private incentives with the socially optimal outcome. It also analyzes the distribution of the gains between local residents and outside investors, and shows that standard approaches tend to favor the latter group and may result in the displacement of the original population. The chapter argues that these distributional issues need to be explicitly taken into account, and alternative arrangements be considered, including a "shareholders" approach in which long-time residents have a collective stake in the project.

Introduction

In a context of rapid urbanization, old cities struggle to modernize without completely losing their character. In the absence of a strategic public intervention to steer their transformation, many of them simply drift into a haphazard mix of demolition, new construction, and building upgrading. Their overall densification, which is certainly welcome from an economic point of view, is often accompanied by the displacement of the original population, which is more questionable from a social point of view. The level of economic activity these cities can sustain typically increases, sometimes substantially, but in the process these places also lose their distinctive traits and become less livable. This is not merely a concern of culture-loving intellectuals in the rich world, who may be too privileged to fully value the benefits of rapid urbanization. In many cases, the inhabitants of these cities also regret the loss of a sense of place and the disappearance of the physical markers of their identity.

Development interventions by local authorities (often with the support of international financial organizations) tend to reinforce this trend toward blandness. Those interventions emphasize access to water, sanitation infrastructure, or convenient commuting, all of which are commendable. But the interventions pay scant attention to the architecture of the buildings or the social fabric associated with them. They may include "livelihoods" components in addition to pipes and concrete, but the main focus of those components is on economic activity, not on aesthetics or culture. They often seek ways to compensate the original inhabitants for the property to be taken over by infrastructure and new construction; less frequently do they consider how to keep those original inhabitants in place. The frantic transformation of centuries-old Asian cities into soulless agglomerations of generic architecture is an obvious illustration of this trend. Moreover, there is an element of irreversibility in transformations of this kind, as recovering what was lost is enormously more expensive than it would have been to preserve it in the first place. Bringing back the original population is simply not possible.

Admittedly, there is also an increasing trend toward financing heritage projects, aimed at protecting and restoring unique buildings or architectural ensembles. These are the kind of structures that can aspire to join the United Nations Educational, Scientific, and Cultural Organization (UNESCO) World Heritage List, if they are not part of it already. They typically include landmarks and small historic centers of stunning homogeneity. Taking again Asia as an example, extraordinary towns such as Lijiang in China, Luang Prabang in Laos, or Hoi An in Vietnam fall in that category. While it is remarkable to see international financial organizations increasingly supporting projects of this sort, it is also clear that the heritage approach can only be marginally relevant when upgrading major cities and dealing with the challenges of large-scale urbanization.

What is missing is a workable approach to explicitly take into account the cultural dimensions of urban upgrading in agglomerations that have a history and (still) possess character, but would not warrant the type of intervention due to a designated heritage site. The question, then, is under which circumstances should standard urban upgrading projects include components aimed at protecting and renovating specific buildings and structures that do not qualify as landmarks but are part of the soul of a place. Answering this question requires assessing what the optimal intervention would be and identifying the ways in which private incentives need to be slanted to make the project viable. It also requires developing practical tools to appraise the costs and benefits of the intervention, so as to decide when laying pipes, pouring concrete, and supporting "livelihoods" is the only thing to do, and when to aim for more.

Those tools should also clarify the conditions under which paying attention to aesthetic and cultural aspects results in net gains for local residents and outside investors. It would be naive to assume that the preservation of urban ensembles that do not qualify as heritage sites can be conducted on a philanthropic basis. Therefore, an urban upgrading project with a cultural component should be designed in such a way that the private sector derives higher financial returns from the intervention than it would from a standard urban upgrading project.

Ensuring that the private sector benefits from the intervention raises the issue of how to distribute the capital gains between the local community and outside investors. Standard urban upgrading projects emphasize the importance of clear property rights, at the household level, to attract private investment. In doing so, they take an atomistic approach, relying on individual units rather than the collective. But an atomistic approach to property rights has important distributional implications, making it easier for outside investors to appropriate a larger share of the gains from upgrading. An atomistic approach to property rights also results in the displacement of the original population, hence undermining the sense of place that made the area special in the first place. Rethinking urban upgrading projects requires that these distributional issues be explicitly taken into account, and alternative property arrangements be considered, including a "shareholders" approach in which long-time residents have a collective stake in the project.

The objective of this chapter is to provide a simple analytical framework to think in economic terms about urban upgrading projects with a cultural dimension. Building on that framework, the chapter draws practical implications on a range of issues, from cost-benefit analysis to private participation to distributional impacts. The chapter does not include any conceptual innovation. Its main (if not only) contribution is to bring together the analytical toolkit of economists and the practical approaches of urban planners (Mason 2005, Rizzo and Throsby 2006). It is hoped that the chapter will serve as a guide for those involved in the preparation and appraisal of urban upgrading projects, supporting the broader trend toward rigorous economic analysis of development projects. It is also hoped that it can help local authorities in developing countries as they struggle to modernize their cities in ways that support economic growth without (completely) undermining cultural values.

Basic Concepts and Notation

To cover the entire spectrum of urban upgrading projects, it is convenient to consider an intervention area with a diverse set of features. Standard urban upgrading projects implicitly ignore architectural or cultural value, as if all the dwellings and buildings in the area were indistinct or generic. Most of the intervention area may indeed match this assumption. At the other end, heritage projects focus on landmarks of unquestionable historic, cultural, or architectural value. The typical intervention area may include one or several of such landmarks; for the purpose of this chapter, it could also include none. In between these two extremes, many old cities include dwellings and buildings that would not qualify for protection on their own merits, and individually do not make much of a difference, but taken collectively have enough character to be a recognizable feature of the intervention area. Continuing with the Asian examples, Haveli mansions in Ahmedabad and French villas in downtown Hanoi would fall into this category. A simplified representation of a typical intervention area can be found in figure 2.1.

FIGURE 2.1
Key Features of a Typical Intervention Area

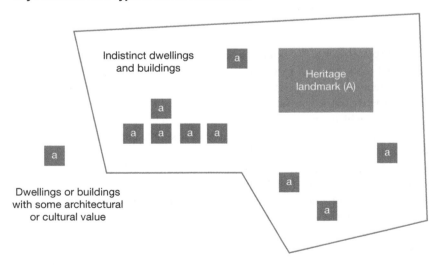

Source: Author.

Urban upgrading projects typically include several self-standing components, most of which require considerable investments for their implementation. The most common of those components is related to infrastructure development, for instance, in the form of improved access to water and sanitation or paved streets. Spending on this component is identified as U. While in some cases the individual beneficiaries of this component can be identified (such as households gaining improved sanitation or owning property on a newly paved street), for simplicity spending in urban infrastructure is treated here as a local public good, benefitting the area of intervention as a whole. It would be straightforward to distinguish between private and public gains, but that would not add much to the analysis and would make notation heavier.

A second component involves transferring resources to the local community, in the form of grants or loans to improve their dwellings or support their livelihoods. The net aggregate transfer to the community is identified as T. The allocation and use of resources under this component is at times managed by grassroots organizations involving the local population, in the form of community-driven development. Community participation of this sort may enhance the social capital of the intervention area, so that there is potentially a public good dimension to this second component. But again, for simplicity it is preferable to treat these grants and loans as transfers as if they accrued entirely to their ultimate beneficiaries, which are individual households.

Less conventional urban upgrading projects would include a third component; namely, the renovation of buildings or dwellings with cultural value. In the case of narrowly defined heritage projects, the renovation effort would focus on landmarks exclusively. But in the general case, renovation spending could also target dwellings and buildings with character, even if their intrinsic architectural or cultural value is not extraordinary. Aggregate spending on renovation is labeled R. Much the same as urban infrastructure, this component can be seen as a local public good, benefitting to various degrees all the inhabitants of the intervention area. An urban upgrading project will be said to have a cultural component if $R > 0$.

Finally, urban upgrading projects paying attention to the cultural aspects of the intervention may also include urban and architectural regulations, covering aspects such as construction heights, appearance of buildings, lighting and outdoor advertising standards, mobility, and the like. These regulations are more stringent than those applying to the intervention area before the implementation of the project and to surrounding areas afterward. For simplicity, it is assumed that there are no project costs associated with the setting of the standards. But those standards do affect the costs and benefits of the various investment choices faced by the local population and outside developers. For instance, lower authorized construction heights may make the option of demolishing a building with character and replacing it with a high-rise structure less appealing than renovating it.

Economic, Financial, and Private Returns

Economic returns are defined as the society-wide gains from the project compared to the situation that would prevail if the project were not undertaken. Considering society as a whole implies that the local residents are not necessarily the only beneficiaries. Households that do not live in the intervention area but value its architecture and culture are among those gaining from the project, as are outside investors who make a profit from it. When comparing expected project results with the situation that would prevail in the absence of the project, the relevant benchmark is not necessarily the situation that prevails when the project is considered. For instance, in the absence of the project, many buildings with architectural or cultural value could collapse due to disrepair or be replaced by more modern structures. In that case, the relevant comparison could be with a situation in which the architectural and cultural value of the intervention area is lower than at present or simply nonexistent.

The cost C of the project to society includes spending by the government, but also the spending I by local residents and outside investors induced by the project. Improved infrastructure, and potentially a greater heritage value of the area, could indeed encourage private sector efforts to upgrade existing properties and construct new buildings. Therefore, the cost C can be defined as:

$$C = U + R + I$$

Transfers T from the project to local residents are not counted as costs to society, as they basically involve a transfer between the government and the private sector. Much the same as taxes, they entail redistribution but not an additional pressure on resources.

Defining society-wide benefits is not that straightforward, as some of the ensuing gains are monetary while others are not. The non-monetary dimension is related to the value attached by society to aesthetics and culture, or heritage value H for short (Brueckner et al. 1999).[1] The monetary dimension concerns the market value V of all the properties in the intervention area, regardless of whether the owners are local residents. In algebraic form, the benefit B to society is the sum of the net gains from the project along the two dimensions:

$$B = \Delta H + \Delta V$$

ΔH is the change in the heritage value of the intervention area compared to a situation where the project would not be undertaken, and ΔV is the change in the value of all properties in the area.

Because some of the gains from the project are non-monetary, a clear distinction emerges between economic returns E and financial returns F. The former include the heritage dimension, whereas the latter do not:

$$E = B - C$$
$$F = \Delta V - C$$

The heritage dimension is relevant from the point of view of financial returns, but its role is indirect. The increase in the monetary value of the properties in the intervention area is affected by spending on the various project components, but it can also be amplified if the increase in the heritage value of the area is substantial. Typically, property in areas with architectural or cultural character is more expensive than similar property in generic areas.

An important connection between spending by the project and the increase in the value of properties in the area is spending I by local residents and outside investors on building improvements and new constructions. This spending can be partly funded by transfers T from the project. With this notation, private returns P to building improvements and new construction in the intervention area can be summarized as:

$$P = \Delta V - (I - T)$$

An urban upgrading project with a cultural component will have an economic justification if $E > 0$. However, as will be discussed below, assessing the non-monetary gains ΔH from such project is bound to be difficult. This is why financial returns may provide a safer benchmark. Indeed, provided that the project does not undermine the heritage value of the area ($\Delta H \geq 0$) a sufficient condition for it to be justified is $F > 0$. Last but not least, the project will succeed in attracting private investment if $P > 0$. In what follows, it is assumed that this condition is met. However, decentralized profit maximization by local residents and outside investors may not lead to the maximum collective profit, as will be discussed below.

Project Appraisal in Practice

A range of practical methods has been proposed to estimate the monetary and non-monetary gains from urban upgrading projects with a cultural dimension (Snowball 2008 and Nijkamp in this volume). At the risk of oversimplifying, they can be consolidated under two main conceptual approaches. One of them borrows from environmental economics, trying to attach a consumer utility to something that is intrinsically unique and hence has no market reference point for it. In the environmental literature, uniqueness can refer to a threatened species or a natural habitat, but in principle the method would be the same if it referred to a historic landmark or a distinct neighborhood. The other approach builds on urban economics, trying to assess how proximity to historic landmarks or to buildings with architectural value affects property prices. In this case, there is no attempt to attach a direct use value to aesthetics or culture, but rather to infer how they influence the price of assets for which a market does exist.

An Environmental Economics Approach

In the environmental economics approach, the value of protecting a historic land-mark or a neighborhood with character is generally assessed by seeking views from the population at large (Pagiola 1996, Navrud and Ready 2002). When this is done by asking a direct question, the method is called "stated preferences." When an indirect question is used instead, it is called "revealed preferences." The latter method is more reliable if respondents have an incentive to understate their subjective valuation; for instance, if they fear that expressing their fondness for a landmark would make them shoulder a bigger share of the associated mainte-nance costs. An example of a direct question is: "How much would you be willing to pay to protect and maintain this historic building?" The potential free-rider problem calls for questions such as "How much would you be willing to spend in travel to visit this historical building?"

While subjective valuations of this sort may yield some plausible figures for ΔH, they are not directly informative in relation to ΔV. Given the conceptual parallel between cultural and natural heritage, it is not surprising that those rely-ing on the environmental economics approach often think of the monetary gains from the project in terms of increased tourism revenue in the intervention area. Let ΔY_t be the additional tourism-related earnings local residents may derive for an urban upgrading project with a cultural dimension in year t, compared to their earnings in the absence of the project. In an efficient property market, the value of land and dwellings in the area should increase by the present value of additional tourism revenue over the years. Assuming a zero discount rate for simplicity, the proponents of the environmental economics approach postulate:

$$\Delta V = \sum_t \Delta Y_t$$

This is why several of the methods proposed in the literature focus on estimat-ing ΔY_t. The environmental economics approach is conceptually appealing, but it yields an underestimate of ΔV. The value of properties in the intervention area is likely to increase even in the absence of any additional tourism, because of the better urban infrastructure U provided by the project. Project-funded transfers T to local residents are also bound to result in improvements in the quality of existing dwellings as well as in some new construction, all of which would add to ΔV. Last but not least, tasteful architectural renovation and the successful preservation of a sense of place should make the intervention area a more pleasant place to live and work. This should also lead to higher property prices, even in the absence of any additional tourism to the area.

An Urban Economics Approach

The urban economics approach, on the other hand, relies on direct estimates of property prices (Ost in this volume). The unit of observation for the analysis is not the citizen's response to a questionnaire but the cadastral record. A typical cadastral record contains information on the main features of a land plot and the buildings standing on it, such as their commercial or residential nature, their estimated price, the land surface, the built surface, the number of stories, the nature of sanitation, and the like. Through the geo-referencing of records, it is also possible to estimate the distance of a plot to historic landmarks, to buildings with architectural value, and to a range of amenities. Even when cadastral records are not detailed or reliable enough, or are altogether missing, it is possible to collect this information through specially conducted door-to-door surveys.

Information from cadastral records or surveys can in turn be combined to generate hedonic price functions. These are statistical relationships between the price of a property, its own features, the nature of the infrastructure services available to it, the value of other properties in the area, and the like. In the context of urban upgrading projects with a cultural dimension, it makes sense to also link the price of a property to its own architectural value and to the heritage value of the area considered as a whole. Hedonic price functions are estimated through econometric analysis. Even if functions of that sort cannot be constructed for the intervention area, functions from suitably similar areas can be used for the analysis.

A hedonic price function allows simulating the effects of the project on the prices of properties in the intervention area. This can be done by modifying the level of key arguments in the function, including improved urban infrastructure, investments by local residents, and upgrading of historic landmarks and buildings with architectural value. Simulations should also involve estimating property prices in the event of a complete decay or disappearance of historic landmarks and buildings with architectural value if the project was not undertaken.

The simulations could be conducted for each property i in the intervention area, or they could consider relatively homogeneous groups of properties (such as single-dwelling buildings of generic architecture, decayed buildings with architectural value, or other). But even in this clustered version they would involve a considerable level of disaggregation, which is why exercises of this sort are called micro-simulations. Adding up the individual gains ΔV_i across all the properties in the area yields the aggregate monetary benefit from the project:

$$\Delta V = \sum_i \Delta V_i$$

The urban economics approach values the cultural component of the project through its contribution to property prices, but ignores its direct consumption value. However, both local residents and the population at large may derive subjective utility from knowing that a historic landmark they associate with their identity or value for its beauty is still standing and well maintained. Citizens who live outside the intervention area may still feel pleased if its character is preserved, even if they do not plan to visit often. This appreciation is independent of what renovating that landmark may do to property prices. From this perspective, the urban economics approach provides useful methods to estimate financial and private returns to an urban upgrading project with a cultural dimension, but it is not sufficient to estimate its economic returns.

In sum, the environmental economics approach is better at assessing non-monetary benefits from the project than it is at assessing its monetary benefits. Conversely, the urban economics approach is more effective at capturing the indirect effects of heritage on property prices but does not assess the nonmonetary benefits from the project. It is thus appealing to bring together the strengths of both approaches. From this point of view, project appraisal should combine stated or revealed preferences to assess ΔH, and hedonic pricing and micro-simulations to estimate ΔV.

Private Sector Participation

Economic returns of the project depend on how much is spent as part of the project on upgrading the infrastructure of the area, on supporting its population, and on renovating its historic landmarks and buildings with architectural value. But economic returns also depend on how the private sector reacts.

Private Investment Decision

If local residents and outside developers see the project as an opportunity to invest their own resources and make a profit, the increase in the value of the properties in the intervention area will be higher. In appraising an urban project with a cultural dimension it is therefore important to understand the behavior of the private sector and to take into account its investment response. This understanding can then be used to maximize the economic returns of the project.

The urban economics approach provides the basic model to value a property in the intervention area. A general expression is of the form:

$$\Delta V_i = f(I_i, \Delta H_i, U, \Delta \bar{V}, \Delta \bar{H})$$

The first argument in the hedonic price function above is total investment I_i on the property, some of which can be funded by the transfer T_i provided by the project. The second argument, ΔH_i, reflects the outcome of private decisions related to the heritage value of the property itself. In the case of generic buildings, there is no decision to be made: it can be safely assumed that their heritage value is nil both before and after investing, so that $\Delta H_i = 0$. The same applies to buildings with architectural value if their owners decide not to alter their character; on the other hand, demolition of the buildings or an intervention that substantially damages their key features would imply $\Delta H_i < 0$.

The last three terms in the hedonic price function embody what that well-known phrase "location, location, location!" means in real estate parlance. One of them captures the increase in the quality of the surrounding urban infrastructure, which is a function of project spending U on access to water, improved sanitation, and the like. The other two, common in the empirical literature on hedonic pricing, reflect the change in the average market price of properties in the area of intervention as a result of the project and the average change in their heritage value, $\Delta \bar{V}$ and $\Delta \bar{H}$, respectively. These two variables are directly related to the benefits of the project to society as a whole, ΔV and ΔH, with the bar on top of them simply indicating that they are computed as averages over all the properties in the area of intervention.

All partial derivatives of this hedonic price function are positive, which means that an increase in the value of any of the five arguments results in an increase in ΔV_i; conversely, everything else being equal, a decline in the heritage value of a property reduces its market price. The second derivative of the function with respect to I_i is supposed to be negative. This means that spending twice as much on a property does not result in a doubling of the associated capital gains.

Local residents and outside developers have to choose the value of their spending I_i that maximizes their profit P_i, taking the net transfer T_i from the project as given. Those with property rights on buildings with architectural value also have to decide whether to preserve them or to demolish them (or undermine their historic character in some other way). The expression of profits at the individual level is the same as the expression of private returns P at the aggregate level:

$$P_i = \Delta V_i - (I_i - T_i)$$

However, there is an important difference between maximizing private returns at the aggregate level and maximizing profits at the individual level. That difference stems from the fact that individual investors take the change in the property and heritage values of the neighborhood, ΔV and ΔH, as given. In doing so, they neglect the impact of their own investment and demolition decisions on other properties around theirs. This coordination failure implies that, in general, the combination of all private investment decisions will not maximize the sum of private profits.

Under relatively general assumptions, it can be shown that decentralized decisions result in both an insufficient volume of investment and an excessive amount of demolition. The word "insufficient" has a precise interpretation here. It means that if a single investor had to decide about the aggregate level of private spending I in the intervention area, he or she would go for a larger figure than the sum of all spending I_i by local residents and outside developers. Similarly, if the intervention area includes n properties with architectural value, a single investor who owned the entire area would possibly choose to renovate and preserve k of them (with $k \leq n$). But decentralized decisions by local residents and outside developers would result in fewer (and possibly none) of the properties surviving.

First Externality: Insufficient Investment

Ignore for a moment the fact that some properties in the intervention area have architectural value, and assume that all of them are generic buildings. The value of each of those properties increases by f'_I units for each unit of investment in the property itself, and by f'_V units when the average value of properties in the area goes up by one unit (the notation f'_X is used to indicate the partial derivate of the hedonic price function $f(.)$ with respect to argument X). Because decentralized investors take the average value of properties in the area as given, they only expect the value of their property to increase by f'_I units if they invest one unit. But a single investor spending a unit on all properties in the area would internalize the fact that property prices are bound to increase by $(1 + f'_V) \times f'_I$. Because the expected monetary gain is bigger in the single investor's case, he or she can be expected to spend more on each property.

This point is made diagrammatically in figure 2.2. The assumptions made on the first and second derivatives of the hedonic price function $f(.)$ imply that ΔV_i can be represented as a concave function of private investment spending I_i. Each individual investor, taking the decisions of others as given, spends so as to maximize the net gain $\Delta V_i - I_i$. In figure 2.2, this net gain is represented by the vertical distance between the function ΔV_i and the 45° line. The optimal spending, from a decentralized point of view, is therefore I_i^1. This spending yields a profit P_i^1, represented by the solid bold line. It is assumed that project spending U on infrastructure makes this profit strictly positive.

However, with all individual investors making a similar decision, property prices increase not just by ΔV_i but by $(1 + f'_V) \times \Delta V_i$. Once all private decisions are taken into account, profits are maximized for an investment level $I_i^* > I_i^1$. This is the spending a single investor owning all the properties in the area would choose. Private profits would then be P_i^*. The windfall profit, unanticipated by decentralized investors, is represented by the dashed bold line in figure 2.2.

Second Externality: Excessive Demolition

Consider the decision faced by the owner of a building with architectural value. Preserving it would typically put constraints on altering the surface of the property. Buildings with architectural value usually date from a time when techniques only allowed going a few stories over the ground; those buildings would barely support a few additional stories without crumbling. Anyone interested in erecting a tall structure would therefore need to first demolish what was there. On the

FIGURE 2.2
Private Investments Increase the Value of Other Properties in the Area

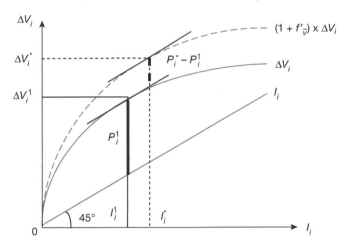

ΔV_i Increase in the value of the property as a function of private investment in it.
ΔV_i^* Increase in the value of all properties in the area when private investment decisions are coordinated.
ΔV_i^1 Increase in the value of all properties in the area when private investment decisions are decentralized.
P_i^* Joint profits by all owners and investors in the area when private investment decisions are coordinated.
P_i^1 Private profits from the investment project.
$f'_{\overline{v}}$ Increase in the value of an individual property when the average value of property in the area increases.
I_i Private investment spending.
I_i^1 Profit-maximizing level of investment when individual decisions are decentralized.
I_i^* Profit-maximizing level of investment when individual decisions are coordinated.
Source: Author.

other hand, an owner choosing to renovate a building with architectural value could secure a higher price per unit of built surface. This is because, for the same quality of construction, a building with character is more sought after. The owner of the property thus faces a choice between having a smaller building with a higher value per unit of surface and a larger building with a lower value per unit; or, in everyday speech, between "chic" and "big."

Choosing which way to go requires maximizing profits in each of the two options, and comparing the outcome. As before, profits are maximized for the level of private spending that yields the largest vertical distance between the ΔV_i function and the 45° line. Except that there are now two ΔV_i functions, depending on whether the original building is renovated or demolished. In figure 2.3, the profit-maximizing level of spending is I_i^H in the event of renovation, and I_i^0 in the event of demolition. The latter is larger than the former to reflect the assumption that the demolition option involves going "big." The expected profits in each of the two options are identified as P_i^H and P_i^0 respectively. These maximum profits are represented by the two solid bold lines in figure 2.3.

However, only one of these two options leads to equilibrium in the real estate market. To understand why, consider the case in which demolishing is the most profitable option for the owner of property i. If so, all other owners of buildings with architectural value would reach the same conclusion, and as a result the intervention area would lose character. As a result, $\Delta \bar{H} < 0$ and the function ΔV_i shifts downwards as shown by the dashed curve in figure 2.3. Therefore, once the behavior of other private players is taken into account the actual profit from demolition is not P_i^0, as originally anticipated, but P_i^*. The difference between both (the unanticipated loss) is represented by the dashed bold line. This problem does not arise when all investors choose to renovate, because in that case $\Delta \bar{H} = 0$ and the function ΔV_i is not affected.

Therefore, demolition may seem to be the most profitable option in a context of decentralized investment decisions, but may or may not be the option yielding the highest aggregate profits once all the owners of buildings with architectural value adjust their behavior. Because of this unanticipated loss, there will in general be more demolition than a single strategic investor owning the entire intervention area would have chosen.

Socially Optimal Preservation

The non-monetary gains from the project imply that its appraisal cannot be conducted on the basis of its financial returns F only. The financial returns ignore historic and architectural values, so that maximizing them could result in a suboptimal extent of preservation. This is why, provided that finance is not a

FIGURE 2.3

Private Demolition Reduces the Value of Other Properties in the Area

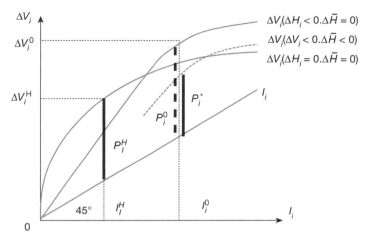

ΔV_i Increase in the value of the property as a function of private investment in it;

ΔV_i^0 Increase in the value of the property if existing buildings are demolished;

ΔV_i^H Increase in the value of the property if existing buildings are preserved;

ΔH_i Change in the heritage value of the property (= 0 if existing buildings are preserved, negative otherwise);

$\Delta \bar{H}$ Change in the heritage value of the average property in the area;

P_i^* Private profits when all investors choose to demolish the existing buildings;

P_i^H Private profits when all investors choose to preserve the existing buildings;

P_i^0 Private profits by an investor who demolishes existing buildings when nobody else does so;

I_i Private investment spending;

I_i^H Private investment when existing buildings are preserved; and

I_i^0 Private investment when existing buildings are demolished.

Source: Author.

constraint for the government, the decision to renovate landmarks and buildings with architectural value has to be taken on the basis of economic returns *E*. But in addition, the two externalities from private investment imply that in general private sector profit *P* will not be maximized on the basis of decentralized investment decisions by local residents and investors either. This results in a complex problem for the authorities, which have to decide on the project features leading to the highest possible economic return *E*, taking the private-sector response into account.

Heritage as an Economic Concept

What makes this a tractable problem is that it can be solved sequentially. The key assumption in this respect is that the renovation of a landmark, if there is one in the intervention area, has priority over the renovation of other buildings with architectural value. In other words, if there is only one building that will be preserved, it should be the landmark. With this assumption, the question for the authorities is whether to renovate no building, to renovate just the landmark, to renovate the landmark and some of the other buildings with architectural value, or to save all of them at once. In answering this question, authorities have to take into account that local residents and outside investors will also spend resources on the upgrading of properties, and that this spending will increase over time as each of these residents and investors factors in the implications of spending by the others. But authorities also need to consider that without any further incentives or constraints, local residents and outside investors could demolish some or all of the buildings with architectural value.

If the optimal choice from a social point of view is to save none of the buildings with historic or architectural value, the intervention is a standard urban upgrading project, involving infrastructure and livelihoods components, but having no cultural dimension. If the decision is to save only the landmark, the intervention becomes a traditional "heritage" project, in which the cultural dimension is geographically circumscribed. In between these two extreme cases, when it is socially optimal to preserve some or all of the other buildings with architectural value, the intervention becomes one of the increasingly common urban upgrading programs with a cultural dimension.

Because all of these choices could in principle be optimal, the notion of heritage becomes relative in the context of urban upgrading. In other words, the decision on what to preserve is influenced not only by historical or architectural criteria but also by economic considerations. For example, the landmark building could be on (or potentially eligible for) the UNESCO World Heritage List, and yet the socially optimal decision could be not to spend resources on renovating it. Conversely, the other buildings with architectural value may never make it to the UNESCO list or to any other major registry of historic buildings, but from an economic point of view, it could still be worth preserving them. Moreover, the optimal number of buildings with architectural value to be preserved could vary from a few to all of them, even if they were all physically identical. Which again shows that historical and architectural criteria matter, but may not be the main determinants of the social decision on what to preserve.

A Diagrammatic Representation

The sequential nature of the solution to the problem faced by the authorities is easier to grasp in diagrammatic terms. Consider an area of intervention including one historic landmark and n buildings with some architectural value. The number of buildings to preserve, represented in the horizontal axis of figure

2.4, ranges from 0 to $n + 1$. The social cost and benefit of the project, C and B respectively, are measured in the vertical axis. Both the cost and benefit can be expected to increase as the number of valuable buildings preserved increases, but the increase is not linear.

Consider the C function first. For simplicity, it can be assumed that the cost of upgrading urban infrastructure U is independent from the level of spending on renovation R. The latter, in turn, increases with the number of buildings with architectural value preserved by the project. If no building with architectural value is preserved, then $R = 0$. If only one building is preserved, that is by assumption the landmark, which is presumably an expensive undertaking. Subsequent increases in R, as more buildings are preserved, should be more modest. If all the buildings with architectural value (other than the landmark) were physically identical, it could be argued that in the range of 1 to $n + 1$ renovation spending R is indeed a linear function of the number of buildings preserved.

However, renovation also affects the level of private investment I in building upgrading and new construction. Because $\Delta \bar{H}$ increases with architectural preservation, the hedonic price function $f(.)$ shifts upwards, and the optimal level of spending by local residents and outside developers increases too, as shown in figure 2.2. This means that private investment I "jumps" as the landmark is renovated and keeps increasing as more and more buildings with architectural value are preserved. As a result, even if spending in urban infrastructure U is constant, and renovation spending R only increases linearly, the total project cost $C = U + R + I$ is a convex function of the number of buildings renovated (again, in the range of 1 to $n + 1$). This convexity of project cost is a diagrammatical way to state that architectural preservation can be an expensive proposition.

The social benefits B from the project also increase with preservation efforts, but they can be either a concave or a convex function of the number of buildings covered by the project's cultural component. Much the same as the cost function, B experiences a discontinuous increase when the landmark is renovated. This is because of the ensuing impact on the heritage value of the area ΔH, which in turn has a positive impact on the value of properties in the area ΔV. This impact is enhanced by the greater level of private spending in building upgrading and new construction spurred by the preservation of the landmark, already discussed above. But from then on, as more buildings with architectural value are preserved, determining whether ΔV grows (more or less than) proportionally to the renovation effort would require additional assumptions about the hedonic price function $f(.)$.

Advocates of cultural interventions would, in principle, be more inclined to believe that the social benefits are a convex function of renovation efforts. A critical mass of buildings with architectural value may indeed be needed before an area can be said to have character. On the other hand, those concerned with the perils of preservation may claim that the benefit function is concave, as renovation efforts are bound to suffer from decreasing returns at some point. In the end, whether B is convex or concave over the range of 1 to $n + 1$ buildings with architectural value preserved is an empirical issue, one that it could be very difficult to settle in practice. In what follows, to preempt any suspicion of cultural bias, it is assumed that those concerned with the perils of preservation are right. In figure 2.4, B is thus represented as a concave function of the number of buildings preserved. But even with this assumption, partial or even total renovation can still be the socially optimal decision.

FIGURE 2.4
Factors Determining the Optimal Extent of Renovation

A. Situation when saving one landmark leads to only small gains in overall value of the area, and renovating other buildings with architectural value leads to even smaller gains

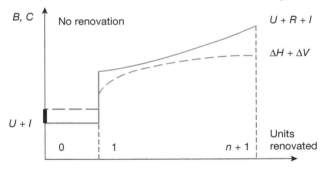

B. Situation when saving the landmark leads to large gains in overall value to the area, but renovating other buildings with architectural value only contributes marginally

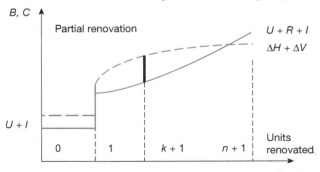

(continued next page)

FIGURE 2.4 *continued*

**C. Situation when saving the landmark leads to a large increase
in the value of the area, and renovating other buildings with
architectural value substantially amplifies the gains**

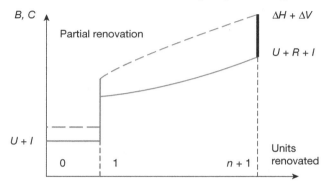

B	Benefit to society.
C	Cost to society.
U	Infrastructure upgrades.
I	Private investment.
R	Spending on renovation.
ΔV	Change in property value of the area.
ΔH	Change in heritage value of the area.
k	Number of buildings with architectural value preserved (apart from the landmark).
n	Total number of buildings with architectural value (apart from the landmark).

Source: Author.

Depending on how large the monetary and non-monetary gains from reno-vation are relative to project costs, three cases can be distinguished. They cor-respond to the three panels in figure 2.4A, B, and C. For simplicity, the figure assumes that undertaking a standard urban upgrading project is warranted, implying that the cost in the absence of renovation $C = U + I$ is less than the resulting change in the heritage and property values of the area of intervention, $\Delta H + \Delta V$. The change in the heritage value of the area ΔH can actually be negative if the absence of a cultural component in the project leads to the demolition of properties with architectural character. But the change in the property value ΔV is positive. In the figure it is supposed to be large enough to offset any possible decline in the heritage value, and also large enough that the net benefit from the project exceeds its cost to society. The only difference between the three panels thus concerns the relative increase in costs and benefits from the project as more and more properties with architectural value are renovated.

In figure 2.4A, "saving" the landmark does not result in large gains to soci-ety, and renovating each of the other buildings with architectural value even less so. Therefore, the social benefit $\Delta H + \Delta V$ does not increase much. Because it remains below the social cost C for any extent of renovation, economic returns are maximized when $R = 0$, as shown by the bold vertical line in the figure. The optimal decision is to ignore cultural aspects when designing the project and just do standard urban upgrading. Figure 2.4A thus corresponds to a standard project, in which no attention is paid to cultural issues.

At the other end, in figure 2.4C, "saving" the landmark results in a substantial increase in the heritage and property values of the area, whereas the cost to society of renovating the landmark is not that high. The sizeable gains from "saving" the landmark are reflected in the large "jump" of the B function; the relatively modest increase in cost translates into a smaller jump of the C function. Moreover, renovating some of the properties with architectural character adds to the overall value of the area but remains affordable. As a result, the gap between the benefits to society and the project cost keeps growing as more buildings with architectural value are renovated, implying that the optimal economic decision is to "save" all of them.

In between these two extremes, the intermediate figure 2.4B assumes that "saving" the landmark still leads to large gains to society, but renovating other buildings with architectural value only contributes marginally to the overall value of the area. The panel also assumes that project costs (included the induced investment decisions by the private sector) would increase substantially as more and more buildings with architectural value are preserved. In the example chosen for this panel, the gap between the social benefit function B and the social cost function C is widest when k buildings with architectural value are "saved" ($0 < k < n$). In this case, which might be the most relevant in practice, partial renovation is the socially optimal decision.

It is worth noting that the main difference between figure 2.4B and figure 2.4C does not lie on the intrinsic historic or architectural value of the buildings but rather on the shapes of the cost and benefit functions. As figure 2.4B shows, it could be worth preserving only some of the buildings with character (apart from the landmark), even if they were all strictly identical from an architectural or historic point of view. Conversely, figure 2.4C shows that under certain circumstances it could be justified to preserve all of the buildings with architectural or cultural value, even if none of them were extraordinary on their own.

Rationale for Public Intervention

Whatever the socially optimal preservation decision is, externalities from private sector investment imply that decentralized decisions may not be sufficient to implement it. When designing an urban upgrading project with a cultural dimension, it is thus important to include mechanisms to align private incentives with social objectives.

Externalities, Self-Correcting and Otherwise

As shown above, decentralized investment decisions lead to insufficient investment and excessive demolition. While the first externality can somehow take care of itself, the second one is bound to lead to a socially suboptimal outcome. The self-correcting externality concerns the level of private spending on upgrading or replacing properties without architectural value. As discussed above, this spending gradually converges to the level that maximizes collective profits. Initially, local residents and outside investors spend less, because they take spending by others as given. But eventually, as others upgrade their properties and construct new buildings, they also adjust their own spending level upwards. In terms of the analysis above, their individual spending gradually increases from I_i^1 to I_i^*. It is important for the authorities to take this gradual increase in private investment into consideration when appraising an urban upgrading project, but unless they want to speed up the convergence process, they do not need to take action.

On the other hand, there is no self-correcting mechanism in the case of renovation. While the socially optimal choice may involve preserving some or all of the buildings with architectural value, this is unlikely to happen spontaneously. The local residents and outside investors who own those buildings face no incentive to preserve and renovate them. They might not have considered spending any resources on them in the absence of the project. But the prospect of improved urban infrastructure and the finance provided by transfers T_i from the project may lead them to invest. Their investment could well include demolishing old structures and replacing them with newer ones, or altering the old structures in ways that undermine their character. Therefore, even if substantial spending R on renovation is foreseen by the authorities, by the time the project reaches the implementation phase there could be no buildings with architectural value left to be renovated.

The second externality from private sector behavior could be overcome if there were a single investor for the entire area, who would then internalize the effects of demolition. Unfortunately, there are not many examples of this happening in practice. The SoHo (South of Houston Street) neighborhood in New York and the Art Deco district in Miami are among the few coming close. In both cases, a single outside investor (Tony Goldman) bought a critical mass of property, which supported an unusual combination of architectural preservation and profit maximization. In recognition for this accomplishment, the National Trust for Historic Preservation awarded him its highest distinction in 2010. But even in those two relatively extreme examples, the mass of property bought by the investor amounted to only a fraction of the area. Given the shortage of known precedents elsewhere, it seems unlikely that local residents and outside developers will manage to preserve on their own a sufficient number of buildings with architectural value.

Investment Irreversibility and Its Implications

In practice, the justification for public intervention is even stronger than the discussion above suggests. This is because the simple model used to motivate the analyses in this chapter ignores uncertainty. The model assumes that the authorities can determine in a precise way whether the socially optimal decision is to preserve none, some, or all of the buildings with architectural value. But this may be unclear before seeing how the private sector reacts to the project, how property prices in the area evolve, and how sensitive those prices are to the heritage value of the area. Therefore, it may take years before there is clarity on whether all, some, or none of the buildings with architectural value should have been saved in the first place.

With this uncertainty, mistakes are bound to happen, although some mistakes are reversible while others are not. If an excessive number of buildings with architectural value are preserved, and subsequently it turns out that those buildings do not influence property prices in the area much, they can be replaced by modern construction. Amending a regulation on preservation may be laborious, but it is in principle feasible. On the other hand, after a building with architectural value has been demolished and a bigger and more modern structure has taken its place, going back in time may not be an option anymore. This is why, in a context of irreversible investments, it is sensible to protect a greater number of buildings with architectural value than would be optimal if there were certainty on how the area will evolve.

In financial terms, there is an option value in preserving buildings with important architectural or historic features. Keeping them amounts to refraining from making a profit in the short term in the expectation of making an even bigger profit in the future. Demolishing them is relinquishing this option. Estimating how much short-term gain should be foregone to exercise this option may, of course, be difficult in practice. But it is clear that in a context of uncertainty, more buildings with architectural value should be preserved than the discussion in the previous section implies.

Design of Cultural Component

While the renovation of a landmark is typically led by a team with historical and architectural expertise, the preservation and renovation of other buildings with architectural value is often in the hands of property owners or outside investors who may lack the specialized knowledge to do respectful and tasteful work. This raises coordination issues involving the amount of resources to be spent by these owners and investors. Coordination is also needed regarding the aesthetic and architectural criteria for them to follow.

Regulation, Incentives ... or Both?

The most straightforward way to align private incentives with the socially optimal preservation decision is regulation. Banning the demolition or alteration of all the buildings worth preserving would ensure that the social optimum is attained. However, this approach could face resistance. In terms of figure 2.3, the owner of a building with architectural value would expect a profit P_i^H in the event of preservation and a presumably larger profit P_i^0 if the building were demolished and replaced by new construction. The analysis above shows that this presumably larger profit is overestimated in a context of decentralized investment decisions, because it ignores the impact of the decision on the heritage value of the area. From the owner's point of view, regulations preventing demolition result in a relinquished profit $P_i^0 - P_i^H$. Because regulations do not apply to neighbors with properties of lesser architectural value, this approach would be perceived as unfair.

In the absence of regulations on preservation, aligning private decisions with the social optimum would require ensuring that the owners of buildings with architectural value would be indifferent concerning the choice to demolish or renovate them. In practical terms, in addition to the transfer T_i, the owners of those buildings should be confronted with additional resources R_i if they agree to preserve and renovate the building. This bonus should be equal to the expected foregone profit $P_i^0 - P_i^H$. The slope of the cost function C in figure 2.4 is determined by the size of this renovation bonus. In the simplest case, in which all properties with architectural value are similar, the bonus is the same for all of them and the cost function C is linear. Figure 2.4 was drawn under this assumption.

However, determining the level of the transfer R_i that would lead to indifference between demolition and renovation in each case may be difficult in practice. There is too much uncertainty on future property prices for this to be a workable solution. Moreover, expectations on future property prices may differ substantially among property owners. This is why it might be necessary to reach an explicit agreement with the owners. One way to do this is to establish a preservation easement, whereby the right to demolish or alter the property is bought by the project. In this case, a negotiation between the project and individual owners is needed to determine the level of the transfer R_i that would make each of them agree on the preservation of the property. Under a preservation easement, this agreement takes the form of a legally binding set of constraints on the allowed modifications to the property, by either its current or its future owners.

Providing financial incentives R_i to offset $P_i^0 - P_i^H$ may be questionable, however, as the relinquished profits from preservation are smaller than owners anticipate. In terms of figure 2.3, once the impact of preservation on the heritage value of the area is taken into account, the foregone profit from renovation is $P_i^* - P_i^H$. This is not only less than $P_i^0 - P_i^H$ but it could actually be a negative amount (meaning that renovation is actually more profitable than demolition). From this point of view, using economic incentives to support preservation would result in a windfall for the owners of buildings with architectural value. An alternative might be to set the incentive at its long-term equilibrium level $P_i^* - P_i^H$, but few owners would voluntarily agree to participate in a preservation easement in that case, and regulation would be needed to enforce preservation.

The Need for Architectural Standards

Sound architectural standards are also needed to maximize the value of properties in the area of intervention, regardless of whether incentives are sufficient for the owners of buildings with architectural value to voluntarily participate in the renovation effort. Those owners may not fully recognize which features of their buildings need to be protected to preserve their character and enhance the heritage value of the area. Even with the best intentions, their spending on preservation could do more harm than good. If renovation is conducted in a decentralized way, strict standards are needed regarding which features of the buildings with architectural value can be altered and which ones have to be kept. Those participating in the preservation easement should be required to strictly adhere to those regulations and face penalties if they do not abide.

In practice, financial incentives and construction standards may also be needed for the properties surrounding buildings with architectural value. For instance, creating or retaining a plaza around a set of buildings with architectural value—providing pleasant views from surrounding terraces, retail shops, and office building—may do more to maximize economic returns than allowing a crowded layout, in which the renovated building ends up choked by new construction. The decision to preserve a given number of buildings with architectural value should therefore be accompanied by land-use decisions and construction regulations to make the most out of these assets. The maximization of economic returns may require a combination of financial incentives R_i and architectural standards not just on buildings with architectural or historic value but also on surrounding properties. Such a combination should be an integral part of project design.

A Dubious Alternative: Property Reclamation

Many urban upgrading projects involve the reclamation of property to build infrastructure, and a similar approach could be envisioned to handle architectural preservation. In that case, the properties with architectural value to be preserved according to the socially optimal decision could be purchased from their owners, and their renovation be directly undertaken as part of the project itself. This approach is appealing because it is less costly than providing incentives for the owners to agree to the renovation, and it does not require that their investments be monitored for compliance with architectural standards. But property reclamation is fraught with problems in standard urban upgrading projects, and the analytical framework in this chapter helps understand why this is so. The same problems are bound to plague property reclamation for architectural preservation.

Those problems have their roots in the terms under which the local population is compensated in the event of property reclamation. In project jargon, those terms are covered under the project's "social safeguards," which are an integral part of any urban undertaking of this sort. The basic principle of social safeguards is that residents are entitled to receive the full market price of the property they occupy, regardless of whether they have legal rights to it. The market price used for compensation under the basic safeguards principle is the one prevailing before the project is implemented.

However, the analytical framework in this chapter makes it clear that the market price of properties in the intervention area will increase by ΔV_i^1 in the short term, and by ΔV_i^* in the longer term (see figure 2.2). Local residents who are compensated by the project are bound to see this outcome—maybe not on their own properties (if they are demolished to make way for infrastructure) but at least on those of their neighbors. And the local residents whose properties have been expropriated would not be totally wrong to think that whoever designed the project (and its safeguards) was fully aware that this property appreciation was bound to happen. Admittedly, part of the appreciation is a reflection of additional spending on the properties. But still, being compensated at the market price prevailing before the project is implemented amounts to foregoing a profit P_i^1 in the short term, and P_i^* in the longer term. It is not surprising, then, that so many urban upgrading projects lead to social conflict concerning the amount of compensation provided.

The same logic applies in the case of property reclamation for architectural preservation, and it makes it easy to understand why this is less expensive than providing incentives for local residents to renovate their properties. Indeed, if the project undertakes the renovation of properties with architectural value and then sells them, or leases them on a long-term basis, it makes a profit P_i^H on each them (see figure 2.3). If it provides incentives for their owners to undertake the renovation on their own, it needs to spend $T_i + R_i$ on each of them. However, these savings simply reflect a distributional issue. An urban upgrading project is typically a source of windfall profits for those owning property in the area of intervention, but unfortunately project preparation seldom devotes attention to who will appropriate those profits. The basic principle underlying social safeguards implies that those whose property is reclaimed should not be among the beneficiaries.

Distributional Effects and Property Rights

The idea that investment projects and policy reforms can create winners and losers is well understood in development economics. It has therefore become common practice to supplement their preparation by analyses of their potential distributional impacts. In the jargon of development economics, those analyses are known as Poverty and Social Impact Assessments (or PSIAs). The discussion of distributional issues has so far emphasized the difference between those whose property is reclaimed for architectural preservation (or infrastructure upgrading) and those who can fully enjoy the windfalls created by the project. However, there is another potentially important distributional issue that needs to be considered, and it concerns the difference between local residents as a group and outside investors.

Social Impact Assessments

When considering development policies or programs, PSIAs are often used to design complementary measures aimed at mitigating adverse impacts on the poor. From a political economy perspective, they may also justify measures to redistribute some or all of the gains from the winners to the losers from projects and reforms, regardless of whether the losers are poor or not. PSIA work is not common in the case of urban upgrading projects, however, because the expectation is that those projects can only create winners. Only in the case of property reclamation is there a concern about social impacts, and this is where safeguards kick in. The discussion of the pitfalls of relying on reclamation for the renovation of properties with architectural value challenges this expectation, as it shows that important distributional issues arise even when no one loses in absolute terms. Given how much social conflict has been associated with property reclamation for urban upgrading projects, perhaps distributional issues deserve a more careful analysis than is done in standard practice.

Hedonic price functions make the implementation of PSIAs relatively straightforward. As discussed above, rigorous project appraisal would require estimating the capital gains ΔV_i for each property or type of property in the area of intervention. The socially optimal decision on which properties with architectural value to preserve allows refining the estimates, directly in the case of those properties and indirectly in the case of other properties benefitting from the increase ΔH in the heritage value of the area. Therefore, the micro-simulations needed for rigorous project appraisal already contain some of the most important information needed for a rigorous PSIA. The only element missing is information on the socioeconomic status of the owners of the properties in the area. But that information can be collected as part of project preparation.

Even a cursory PSIA would provide useful guidance regarding property reclamation. If the expected capital gains ΔV_i from the project are modest, relying on standard social safeguards should not be a source of major social tension. On the other hand, if the expected ΔV_i is large, denying this windfall to a subset of local residents may be problematic.

Local Residents versus Outside Investors

Another potentially important distributional issue to consider is the relationship between local residents and outside investors. Standard urban upgrading projects assume that individual property rights are a prerequisite of efficiency. By allowing local residents to sell their properties to outside investors, individual property rights ensure that investment can be attracted to the area of intervention. Because transactions are on a voluntary basis, property rights also ensure that local residents are adequately compensated if they decide to transfer their buildings to outside investors.

However, there are two reasons why actual outcomes may not be ideal: these are access to finance and asymmetric information. If successful, the project should lead to a short-term increase ΔV^1 in the prices of properties in the intervention area, and to an even larger increase ΔV^* as private spending levels converge to their equilibrium level. This appreciation in property prices will be greater than what is spent on upgrading, demolishing, and rebuilding, as reflected in the positive profits P^1 and P^*, respectively. Thus, if outside investors have better access to finance than local residents, they may be in a better position to appropriate the profits from urban upgrading. If local residents do not have enough clout to understand the implications of the project, they may exercise their property rights too early for their own good.

The neglect of this distributional issue could be justified in the case of standard urban upgrading projects on the grounds that the transactions involved are voluntarily. But it is questionable in the case of projects with a cultural dimension. In the latter, the sense of place associated with the area of intervention is typically related to its local population, its culture, and its economic activity, as much as it is to the architectural value of its buildings. That sense of place can be lost if outside investors move in first and chase local residents away thanks to their better understanding and deeper pockets. Put differently, for the same level of private spending I^*, keeping local residents in place ensures a higher heritage value ΔH than bringing in outside investors does.

Community consultations can be used to provide information to local residents on the windfall they could make by sticking to their property (that is, the option value of waiting before selling). However, the livelihood component of standard urban upgrading projects is usually focused on helping local residents secure better earnings, rather than on helping them maximize the value of their property. Similarly, social safeguards aim at ensuring that local residents whose property is reclaimed for the project get compensated at "fair" market prices. But those are the prices prevailing before the project is implemented and windfall gains materialize. "Fairness" does not typically involve compensating for those windfall gains. The numerous demonstrations and protests by local owners of expropriated properties, as the implications of urban upgrading projects become apparent, suggest that this is not merely a hypothetical concern.

Conclusion

Unfortunately, there are no obvious alternatives to the standard practice. In a world of perfect information, local residents could be offered access to finance for an amount equivalent to I_i^*, or they could be compensated for their properties at the going market price plus P_i^*. But there is usually too much uncertainty on the outcome of the project for this to be a workable alternative. Even very competent project teams would have a hard time deciding what the "right" levels of I_i^* and P_i^* are in a specific context. In light of such uncertainty, any property transaction at an early stage of the project is bound to result in serious regret by one of the two parties involved. This likelihood suggests that, in spite of the emphasis put by urban upgrading projects on individual property rights, facilitating property transactions at an early stage may not be socially desirable.

An alternative to address this fundamental uncertainty is to shift the risk from local residents to urban authorities. This is the equivalent of transforming those residents into shareholders of the urban upgrading project, with the value of their property V_i as their equity in it. Like shareholders, local residents participating in the project would have a say on the broader strategy for the area of intervention. Once the strategy is approved, however, decisions would be in the hands of the project managers. This arrangement has similarities with the consultations typically preceding the implementation of urban upgrading projects, but it also puts more constraints on the project.

A local resident endorsing the project would accept the implications for his or her own property. Investments in renovation and new construction could still be conducted in a decentralized way, but the work done would need to follow the architectural standards set by the project. If the resident were to sell his or her property, the new buyers would be bound by the same standards, as in the case of preservation easements, but the resident would be able to choose if and when to sell the property, which means that he or she would be able to fully appropriate the capital gain ΔV_i. This amounts to keeping an option to claim deferred compensation on the property, but only at a time when the uncertainty about the consequences of the project has been removed.

Note

1. The notion of culture as an asset can be traced to Throsby 2001, but the idea that cultural amenities have an economic impact has been part of urban analyses for much longer.

References

Brueckner, J. K., J. F. Thisse, and Y. Zenou. 1999. "Why Is Central Paris Rich and Downtown Detroit Poor?" *European Economic Review* 43: 91–107.

Mason, R. 2005. *Economics and Historic Preservation: A Guide and Review of the Literature.* Washington, DC: The Brookings Institution.

Navrud, S., and R. C. Ready, eds. 2002. *Valuing Cultural Heritage: Applying Environmental Valuation Techniques to Historic Buildings, Monuments and Artifacts.* Cheltenham: Edward Elgar.

Pagiola, S. 1996. *Economic Analysis of Investments in Cultural Heritage: Insights from Environmental Economics.* Washington, DC: World Bank.

Riganti, P., and P. Nijkamp. 2007. "Benefit Transfer of Cultural Values: Lessons from Environmental Economics." *Journal of Environmental Policy and Law* 2: 135–148.

Rizzo, I., and D. Throsby. 2006. "Cultural Heritage: Economic Analysis and Public Policy." In *Handbook of the Economics of Art and Culture Vol. 1,* ed. V. Ginsburgh and D. Throsby, 984–1016. Amsterdam: Elsevier/North Holland.

Snowball, J. D. 2008. *Measuring the Value of Culture: Methods and Examples in Cultural Economics.* Berlin: Springer Verlag.

Throsby, D. 2001. *Economics and Culture.* Cambridge: Cambridge University Press.

3

Heritage Economics: A Conceptual Framework

David Throsby
Distinguished Professor of Economics, Macquarie University (Australia)

This chapter outlines a conceptual framework that integrates various strands from the discussion of heritage economics and provides an interpretation of some of the major issues of concern. The chapter is structured as follows: first, the basic concept of heritage as asset is discussed, placing it clearly into the context of capital theory. This leads, in the section on sustainability, to a consideration of the parallels between heritage as cultural capital on the one hand and environmental resources as natural capital on the other. These parallels have implications for the sustainability of the cultural and natural resources involved. The central issue in heritage economics is the question of value, discussed in detail further in the section on value and valuation; the analysis here divides the value embodied in or generated by heritage assets into economic and cultural components, and considers the critical issue of measurement. In the next section, the framework is extended to the policy arena, with a discussion of the major economic instruments for the implementation of heritage policy. The final section describes a case study of the application of some of the principles of heritage economics to a cultural investment project developed in Skopje, capital of FYR Macedonia, assisted by a World Bank project.

Introduction

As a specialist area of interest to economists, the economics of heritage is of relatively recent origin. This is not to say, however, that earlier concerns with the conservation of heritage and with heritage policy ignored economic aspects. For example, heritage figured prominently in discussions about the links between cultural policy and economic development in UNESCO in the 1960s and 1970s. Further initiatives in the 1970s and 1980s, such as the establishment of the World Heritage Convention and the use of the Burra Charter for heritage significance assessment in many countries, recognized that resources would be required for the implementation of heritage protection measures. But it was not until the 1990s that discussion began about the possibilities for formal application of the theory and practices of economics to the analysis of heritage decisions.

A leader in arguing the case for the development of an economics of heritage has been the renowned British economist Sir Alan Peacock. In a paper first published in 1995, Peacock pointed to the simple economic principle of opportunity cost as a constraint on resource allocation to heritage projects. At that time, given the budgetary constraints, more often than not, heritage projects received lesser funds from administrators in comparison to other projects on the scale of priorities. Since in most cases it was public funds that were being deployed, Peacock argued that public preferences should be taken into account in the decision-making process. These suggestions drew a spirited response from the heritage profession, whose members feared that their expert judgments on the cultural significance of heritage items would soon be displaced by crude financial criteria and lowest-common-denominator popular opinion in decisions concerning the allocation of heritage resources (Cannon-Brookes 1996).

Since then, a clearer understanding has evolved about the uses and limitations of economics in the cultural arena, to the point where economists are now often brought into heritage decision-making processes, especially where resource constraints are critical. At the same time, research and scholarship in the economics of heritage have led to an ever-expanding body of theoretical and applied literature in the field (Hutter and Rizzo 1997; and Schuster et al. 1997; Throsby 1997a; Rizzo and Towse 2002; Mason 2005; Peacock and Rizzo 2008; Benhamou 2010). This chapter outlines a conceptual framework that integrates various strands from the discussion of heritage economics and provides an interpretation of some of the major issues of concern.

Heritage as Asset

In referring to cultural heritage as a component of lending projects, the World Bank often describes heritage as an asset, whether it exists in the tangible form of buildings, sites, historic city cores, or open public spaces, or as intangible cultural phenomena such as festivals, dance, rituals, traditional knowledge, and so on. Such terminology is appropriate, considering that Bank lending projects in any area typically involve investment in capital facilities that are expected to be long lasting and to yield a rate of return over time.

The theoretical basis for treating heritage as an asset lies in capital theory, which has been fundamental to the interpretation of production processes in economics for more than two centuries. Capital can be defined as durable goods that give rise to a flow of services over time that may be combined with other inputs such as labor to produce further goods and services. Economists conventionally distinguish between different types of capital, including physical or manufactured capital, human capital, and natural capital. Recently, the concept of capital has been extended into the field of art and culture, in an effort to recognize the distinctive features of certain cultural goods as capital assets, and to capture the ways in which such assets contribute, in combination with other inputs, to the production of further cultural goods and services. Thus the economic concept of cultural capital has taken shape (Throsby 1999, 2001; Ulibarri 2000; Shockley 2004; Cheng 2006; Wang 2007; Bucci and Segre 2011).[1]

Why should a heritage item such as a historic building be placed into this specific category of cultural capital, rather than being simply regarded in the same terms as any other capital asset such as a power station or a commercial office building? The answer lies in the types of value to which the heritage building gives rise. It may have a potential sale price as real estate and a non-market value measured, for example, by the willingness of people to pay to see it preserved. But these measures of its economic value may be incapable of representing the full range and complexity of the cultural worth of the building: It may have religious significance that cannot be expressed in monetary terms; it may have had an influence over time on the development of a new urban plan, an engineering concept, or an architectural style; it may serve as a symbol of identity or place; and so on.

All these and many more are elements of what might be termed the building's unique cultural value, a multidimensional representation of the building's cultural worth assessed in quantitative and/or qualitative terms against a variety of attributes such as its aesthetic quality, its spiritual meaning, its social function, its symbolic significance, its historical importance, its uniqueness, and so on. Many of these characteristics will influence the economic value of the building and of the services it provides, such that an economic evaluation would be expected to capture much of the cultural importance of its heritage qualities. However, there are likely to remain some elements of the cultural value of the asset that cannot reasonably be expressed in financial terms yet are important for decision-making. If this is so, a justification for the treatment of heritage as a particular form of capital asset, different in the above respects from other forms, is established. In the section "Value and Valuation" below, a more detailed treatment of heritage value and valuation is presented.

As noted above, cultural heritage exists in both tangible and intangible forms; indeed there are now World Heritage conventions dealing with each type separately. Both tangible and intangible forms of cultural capital exist as a capital stock held by a country, a region, a city, or an individual economic agent. This capital stock could be assigned an asset value in both economic and cultural terms at a given point in time. The net effect of additions to and subtractions from the capital stock within a given time period indicates the net investment/disinvestment in cultural capital during the period, measurable in both economic and cultural terms, and determines the opening value of the stock at the beginning of the next period. Any holding of cultural capital stock gives rise to a flow of capital services over time which may enter final consumption directly, or which may be combined with other inputs to produce further cultural goods and services. Therefore, for example, a historic building may provide commercial office or residential space or may be a site providing cultural experiences for tourists.

Heritage investment projects typically provide for a range of activities; namely, the preventive maintenance, conservation, upgrading, or adaptive reuse of the heritage item or items involved. Economic evaluation of such capital expenditures can use standard investment appraisal techniques such as cost-benefit analysis. (See box 3.1.) The fact that the assets involved are items of cultural capital indicates that, in addition to its economic payoff, the project will produce cultural benefits whose value should also be assessed. The measurement concept and instruments in use are dealt with elsewhere in this chapter.

Sustainability

Interpreting cultural heritage as cultural capital has a clear parallel with the economic interpretation of natural heritage as natural capital (Throsby 2005; Rizzo and Throsby 2006). Both cultural and natural capital have been inherited from the past, will deteriorate or degrade if not maintained, and impose on the present generation a duty to care for the assets involved so they can be handed down to future generations. The long-term management of both cultural and natural capital can be cast in terms of the principles of sustainable development. When applied to natural capital, sustainable development implies management of natural resources in a way that provides for the needs of the present generation without compromising the capacity of future generations to meet their own needs; that is, the principle of intergenerational equity (World Commission on Environment and Development 1987). Another key element of sustainability in natural capital management is the precautionary principle that argues for a risk-averse stance in

---

BOX 3.1

Cost-Benefit Analysis Confirms the Cultural and Economic Value of Conservation in Zanzibar

Tanzania, Zanzibar Urban Services Project (Project number 111155)
Total Project Cost: US$38 million
Total Loan Amount: US$38 million
Approved: February 2011 – Ongoing

The government of Zanzibar and the World Bank have prepared a project that aims to improve access to urban services and help conserve Stone Town's traditional seafront, thereby safeguarding its World Heritage status. The World Bank loan will support the rehabilitation of Stone Town's sea wall and refurbishment of the adjacent Mizingani Road, which are both in danger of collapse. Investments also include improving key infrastructure below the roadbed and creating a pedestrian promenade with landscaping, street lighting, and street furniture along the sea.

Direct benefits are: (1) preserving the value of the historic sea wall and properties in the immediate area; and (2) avoiding replacement costs by preventing collapse of the sea wall, the road, and other key infrastructure. Indirect benefits are calculated based on the continued growth in revenue from Zanzibar's tourism. The analysis estimates that investing US$8.3 million in this work yields a net present value of US$15 million at a discount rate of 12 percent. The internal rate of return, 47 percent, indicates that it is desirable to invest in the rehabilitation of the sea wall and road. Non-quantifiable benefits include the enhanced urban aesthetics due to improvements along the sea wall and promenade and the development of a dual-lane road that will reduce the likelihood of accidents.

Source: Tanzania, Zanzibar Urban Services Project Appraisal Document.

---

decision making when irreversible consequences such as species loss are possible. Both of these principles are relevant to cultural heritage sustainability. Because the stock of cultural capital, both tangible and intangible, embodies the culture we have inherited from our forebears and which we hand on to future generations, it is inevitable that questions of intergenerational equity are raised; heritage decision making is constantly faced with the long-term implications of strategies for conservation, upgrading, and adaptive reuse of buildings and sites. Similarly, the precautionary principle can be invoked when demolition of a historic building is threatened; once gone, such unique cultural heritage cannot be replaced (World Commission on Culture and Development 1995; UNESCO 1998; Throsby 2003).

Indeed, we can go further in drawing the parallel between the sustainability of natural and cultural capital by suggesting that the concept of ecologically or environmentally sustainable development (often referred to as ESD) has a counterpart in culturally sustainable development, a proposition that foreshadows the possibility of identifying culturally sustainable growth paths for the economy. When applied to heritage, cultural sustainability implies assessing conservation investment projects against a set of criteria that might include:

- Efficient generation of material and non-material well-being for stakeholders;
- Serving principles of intergenerational equity by taking due care of the heritage in the interests of future generations;
- Ensuring equitable participation in the benefits of the heritage among members of the present generation;
- Observing the precautionary and safeguard principles; and
- Paying explicit attention to the long-term maintenance of the cultural values inherent in the heritage and in the services it provides.

An important aspect of sustainability is the maintenance of capital stocks. In discussions concerning the sustainability of natural capital, the question of substitutability or replacement between different forms of capital has arisen. Can a decline in the stock of natural capital in the economy be compensated for by an increase in the stock of physical capital, such that the economy's aggregate capital stock is maintained? If natural and human-made capital are perfect substitutes in the production of consumption goods and in the direct provision of utility for both present and future generations, it doesn't matter if the present generation uses up exhaustible resources as long as sufficient new physical capital can be provided to future generations by way of compensation. This is termed "weak sustainability." On the other hand, "strong sustainability" regards natural capital as being strictly non-substitutable for human-made capital; in other words, the strong sustainability paradigm assumes that the functions of natural capital are so unique to global air, land, and water systems that they cannot be replicated by any type of manufactured capital, no matter how spectacular future technological advances might be (Pearce and Turner 1990; Barbier et al. 1994; Neumayer 2003).

How do these sustainability paradigms apply to cultural capital? Using cultural heritage as our touchstone, we can see that the purely physical functions of heritage assets that generate the assets' economic value could be readily provided by manufactured capital. For example, the services of shelter and amenity that are provided by a historic building could as well be provided by another structure that has no cultural content. However, since by definition cultural capital is distinguished from physical capital by its embodiment and production of cultural value, one would expect that there would be zero substitutability between cultural and physical capital in respect to its cultural output, since no other form of capital is capable of providing this sort of value; the new building cannot replicate the historical content of the old. Thus, in regard to historic heritage, the strong sustainability principle would seem to apply.

Nevertheless, there may still be the possibility of sustainability within forms of cultural capital. For example, is new cultural capital substitutable for old? If so, the loss of heritage items by destruction or neglect could be substituted for by the creation of new cultural assets which themselves will embody or generate new cultural value in due course. For example, Baron Hausmann's bold plan for the redesign of Paris in the mid-19th century involved the demolition of many buildings that would presumably have had some cultural value at the time of their disappearance, and would possibly continue to do so today if they were still there. Yet the urban complex resulting from Hausmann's actions yielded a modern urban environment—with buildings set along broad tree-lined boulevards and a system of new parks—which, with the passing of time, are now regarded as having considerable cultural value in their own right. In addition, Hausmann's successful urban renewal project for Paris soon became an international reference—an innovative model for modernizing old cores of important metropolitan cities, which was emulated by, among others, Barcelona, Buenos Aires, and Rio de Janeiro. The difficulty here, of course, is that a recognition of cultural significance may take some time to evolve; who is able to predict which urban interventions or modern buildings, large or small, will be regarded as culturally important a century or so from now?

Recent application of the sustainability principle in development programs is, in a way, how planners and economists deal with the value of tangible cultural heritage over longer periods of time. Moreover, heritage policies are being increasingly integrated with urban regeneration strategies, tourism activities, cultural industry, community education and participation in programs, and even in regional planning as in the case of London's "Historic Environment" initiative. In this case, enhancing the sustainability of the natural and built environment, including important urban heritage sites, is sought through the formulation of a framework for action containing a coherent tourism and cultural strategy.[2]

Value and Valuation

The question of value is a core issue in heritage economics in both theoretical and practical terms. In the theory of cultural capital, it is the existence of cultural value that differentiates this form of capital from other forms. In the practical world of heritage decision making, assigning an appropriate value to heritage assets and to the services they provide is an all-pervading problem, whether the value sought is economic, cultural, or a mix of the two.

The distinction put forward earlier between the economic and the cultural value of heritage can now be elaborated in more detail.

Economic Value

As is the case with valuation of natural environments, it is customary in identifying the economic value of heritage assets to distinguish between use and non-use values, that is, between the direct value to consumers of the heritage services as a private good and the value accruing to those who experience the benefits of the heritage as a public good. Sometimes these effects are referred to, respectively, as market and non-market value.

The *use value* of a heritage building is observed in several ways. The building may provide office, retail, or other space to occupants who use the building for commercial purposes, in which case the actual or imputed rents paid serve as an indicator of the building's value in use. Likewise the heritage asset may be a domestic dwelling where again rental rates or their equivalent are a measure of the private-good value of the services provided. In the case of heritage buildings and sites that are visited by tourists, use values are reflected in the individual benefits that tourists enjoy as a result of their visit.

A monetary indicator is provided by the entry price paid, enabling aggregation of a total use value generated by the building or site over a given period of time. Although such a calculation yields an estimate of financial return, a complete account of the economic use benefits to tourists would need to include their consumer's surplus as well. In addition, for many heritage sites visited by tourists, the use benefits would also include revenue from the commercial exploitation of the site via visitor centers where cafes, restaurants, and gift shops are located.

Occasionally, a distinction is drawn between active use of a heritage building or site, such as those uses discussed above, and passive use that arises as an incidental experience for individuals, such as when pedestrians enjoy the aesthetic qualities of a historic building or site as they happen to pass by. This type of benefit is classed as a positive externality. Although in principle a monetary value could be assigned to it, in practice it is usually ignored in any calculation of the economic value of cultural heritage because of difficulties in defining appropriate populations of beneficiaries and in identifying the willingness to pay (to protect or enjoy the asset) in valid terms.

Turning to *non-use value,* we can observe that cultural heritage yields public-good benefits that can be classified in the same ways in which the non-market benefits of environmental amenities such as forests, wilderness areas, marine parks, and so on are determined. Three types of non-rival and non-excludable public-good benefits are presumed to exist for a cultural heritage asset, relating to its *existence value* (people value the existence of the heritage item even though they may not consume its services directly themselves), its *option value* (people wish to preserve the option that they or others might consume the asset's services at some future time), and its *bequest value* (people may wish to bequeath the asset to future generations). These non-use values are not observable in market transactions, since no market exists on which the rights to them can be exchanged.

The similarity between environmental and cultural assets (in other words, between natural and cultural capital) has meant that the methodologies developed for estimating the non-use values for environmental assets have been readily transferable to the heritage context (Pagiola 1996; Navrud and Ready 2002). (See box 3.2.) In particular, applications of contingent valuation methods, and more recently discrete choice modeling techniques, to evaluation of the non-market benefits of cultural heritage investments have grown rapidly in the last five to ten years (Santagata and Signorello 2000; Pollicino and Maddison 2001; Alberini et al. 2003; Dutta et al. 2007; Kim et al. 2007; Kinghorn and Willis 2008).

BOX 3.2

Environmental Economics Provides a Model for Estimating the Value of Investments in Heritage Conservation

As early as 1996, a World Bank paper entitled *Economic Analysis of Investments in Cultural Heritage: Insights from Environmental Economics* drew on advances in the field to discuss cost-benefit analysis for Bank-supported projects at cultural heritage sites. Bank staff Stefano Pagiola describes methodologies for estimating the use and non-use values of cultural assets. The author discusses the application, data requirements and limitations of contingent valuation, travel cost, hedonic, and market-price methodologies for evaluating cultural heritage investments. Pagiola points out that the choice of technique depends on the specific problem being studied. He also states that: (1) except in very simple situations, it is likely that a variety of techniques will be necessary to estimate the full range of benefits; and (2) where substantial investments are contemplated, it may be desirable to cross-check estimates by deriving them from multiple sources.

Source: Pagiola, S. *Economic Analysis of Investments in Cultural Heritage: Insights from Environmental Economics.* 1996. Washington, DC: World Bank.

These and other methods of assessing the economic value of heritage are discussed in detail in Peter Nijkamp's chapter in this book.

Cultural Value

The economic values discussed above are relatively easy to measure, at least in principle. Cultural value, by contrast, has no such unit of account. So how is it possible to express it? An initial step in constructing a theory of cultural value can be made by recognizing that it is a concept reflecting a number of different dimensions of value; not all of them may be present in a particular case, and their significance may vary from one situation to another. If so, it might be possible to disaggregate the cultural value of some cultural good or service into its constituent elements. To illustrate, we could deconstruct the cultural value of a heritage building or site into the following components (Throsby 2001; Avrami et al. 2000; De La Torre 2002; Mason 2008. See also O'Brien 2010). (See box 3.3).

- *Aesthetic value.* The site may possess and display beauty in some fundamental sense, whether that quality is somehow intrinsic to the site or whether it only comes into being in the consumption of it by the viewer. Under the general heading of aesthetic value we might also include the relationship of the site to the landscape in which it is situated; that is, all the environmental qualities relevant to the site and its surroundings.
- *Symbolic value.* The site may convey meaning and information that helps the community in which the site is located to interpret that community's identity and to assert its cultural personality; for example, the site may symbolize some event or experience of historical or cultural importance. The value of the site as a representation of meaning may be particularly important in its educational function, not just for the young but also for advancing the knowledge base and level of understanding of the whole community.
- *Spiritual value.* Spiritual value conveyed by the site may contribute to the sense of identity both of the community living in or around the site and also of visitors to the site. It may provide them with a sense of cultural confidence and of connectedness between the local and the global. Spiritual value may also be experienced as a sense of awe, delight, wonderment, religious recognition, or connection with the infinite. In addition, the realization that similar spiritual value is created by other sites in other communities may promote intercultural dialogue and understanding.
- *Social value.* The interpretation of culture as shared values and beliefs that bind groups together suggests that the social value of the heritage site might be reflected in the way it contributes toward social stability and cohesion in the community. The site may impinge upon or interact with the way of living in

---

BOX 3.3

Sites in Honduras Illustrate a Wide Range of Cultural Values

Honduras, PROFUTURO: Interactive Environmental Learning and Science Promotion Project (Project number 057350)
Total Project Cost: US$9.3 million
Total Loan Amount: US$8.3 million
Approved: June 1999 – Closed: October 2005

The PROFUTURO project's objective was to help the Honduran government expand that country's scientific, environmental, and cultural knowledge and management in the context of the country's sustainable development needs and ethnic diversity. A target area for the project was the Archeological Park of Copan, which was declared a World Heritage site in 1980, due to its ensemble of Mayan monuments and unique ceremonial sites. In the nearby municipality of Copan Ruinas, the project worked with local leaders to design and develop an interactive learning center to encourage the local community's understanding of the biodiversity, history, and cultural characteristics of the region, especially the scientific knowledge, sustainable development practices, and building techniques of pre-Hispanic cultures that are demonstrated in the area's archeological parks.

Source: PROFUTURO Project Assessment Document and Implementation and Completion Report.

---

the community, helping to identify the group values that make the community a desirable place to live and work.
- *Historic value.* This value, however it is received, is inarguably intrinsic to the site, and of all the components of cultural value it is probably the most readily identifiable in objective terms. Perhaps its principal benefit is seen in the way in which historic value assists in defining identity, by providing a connectedness with the past and revealing the origins of the present. This value is manifested by the celebration of the culture and its artifacts that we inherit from the past. As UNESCO points out: "Our cultural and natural heritage are both irreplaceable sources of life and inspiration."[3]
- *Authenticity value.* The site may be valued for its own sake because it is real, not false, and because it is unique. An important concomitant characteristic is

that the site has integrity, variously defined in different circumstances, which must be safeguarded. Protection of the site's integrity, however interpreted, may be a significant constraint imposed on project decision making when cultural value is taken into account.

• *Scientific value.* The site may be important for its scientific content or as a source or object for scholarly study.

The above approach to identifying cultural value as a multidimensional concept is not unlike Lancastrian demand theory in economics, in which goods are defined as a set of characteristics that may take different weights in different people's preference functions. It is plausible to propose that the various elements contributing to cultural value could be similarly weighted, providing a basis for aggregation to an overall indication of the cultural value of particular heritage assets or of the services they provide.

Nevertheless, difficulties of measurement need to be overcome. If one takes a lead from economic theory, one could propose that cultural value might be identified through both the revealed preferences and the stated preferences of individuals. In the former case, some indication of the overall cultural worth of a heritage item is expressed over time in the judgments of heritage experts and of members of the public. In due course, it may be possible to arrive at some aggregate consensus as to the item's cultural value. Such a consensus underlies the assertion of the cultural value of iconic heritage assets nominated for inclusion on the World Heritage List. Similarly, judgments as to the significance of heritage items for inclusion on lower-level lists or registers reveal something of the items' cultural value as assessed by the decision makers.

Alternatively, or in addition, stated preference methods might be applied, for example by asking individuals directly for their assessment of the value of a heritage item according to the various criteria of value listed above. This approach can be implemented using a Likert scale, which calibrates a respondent's agreement or disagreement with a series of qualitative statements about the heritage item. Under appropriate assumptions as to the relative strengths of different levels of agreement/disagreement, a numerical score can be assigned to responses. If weights can be allocated to the various components of cultural value specified, a weighted aggregate cultural value measure can be obtained. Similar procedures, including conjoint analysis, can be used to derive rankings rather than ratings for the cultural value elements.

Finally in this discussion of cultural value, it should be noted that the interpretation has emphasized the positive aspects of the values yielded by heritage. Nevertheless it has to be acknowledged that from time to time heritage, as a symbol of a given culture, has been invoked to foment social and cultural intolerance and hostility, and its tangible forms even targeted for desecration and destruction.

The demolition of the Bamiyan Buddhas by the Taliban in Afghanistan in 2001 is a well-known recent example. Another case is the destruction of ancient Armenian burial monuments (khachkars) during the armed conflict in Azerbaijan in the 1990s (Maghakyan 2007). Despite these extreme acts arising from political intolerance, however, the role of cultural heritage in normal life circumstances indicates that it is the beneficial characteristics of heritage as described above that are of primary significance.

Relationship between Economic and Cultural Value

What can we say about the relationship between economic value and cultural value when both are defined in the above-mentioned terms? Because as a general rule the more highly people value things for cultural reasons the more they will be willing to pay for them, we would expect some relationship between some aggregated measure of cultural value and the assessed economic value of a particular heritage asset or of the services the asset provides. Indeed, an appeal to the standard neoclassical economic model of individual utility maximization in a general equilibrium framework might suggest that the relationship should be a perfect one, thus rendering a separate account of cultural value unnecessary.

However, broadening our view to a more comprehensive notion of value would indicate that the correlation between economic and cultural value over a range of heritage items is not at all likely to be perfect, since there are some aspects of cultural value that likely cannot be rendered in monetary terms. For example, a moment's reflection would suggest that it makes no sense to use a financial yardstick to express the value of a sense of cultural identity to individuals or communities, or to measure the collective benefits of cultural diversity. Likewise, it is difficult to imagine that the spiritual value of a religious shrine could be adequately represented as a monetary amount.

If it is true that heritage yields these two distinct types of value, both of which are desired, the question arises as to how they are to be traded against one another in decisions for which more of one means less of the other. This is a familiar problem in the practical arena of heritage decision making. Some heritage buildings or sites may have high cultural value but relatively little economic value, even when the latter includes non-market benefits. Others may be exactly the reverse. In such a situation the choice between them, if there is a choice, entails some trade-off. How much economic value are we, as individuals or as a society, prepared to give up to secure a given level of cultural value, or vice versa? The answer depends on identifying the preference pattern for the individual or for society between the two types of value.

It is theoretically plausible to specify an individual or aggregate utility function with economic and cultural value generated by a heritage project as the arguments, implying the existence of a set of indifference curves between the two items of value that would enable marginal rates of substitution to be identified. We are still some way from being able to apply such a theoretical proposition in practice, although research in health economics does offer some ideas on how this trade-off can be represented in practical terms. An indicator called QALY (Quality-Adjusted Life Years) has been developed to confront the problem of choice for an ill person between a longer life with lower quality of life or a shorter life at a higher quality. It may be possible in due course to devise an indicator similar to a QALY to encapsulate the equivalent trade-off between economic and cultural value in regard to alternative cultural projects (Mason et al. 2009; Smith et al. 2009; O'Brien 2010).

Heritage Policy

The economic ramifications of cultural policy have become more prominent in recent years as a result of the growth of interest in the cultural and creative industries as a source of innovation, growth, and dynamism in the macroeconomy. Heritage services are one component of the cultural industries' outputs and as such are implicated in any consideration of the economic basis for cultural policy delivery (Throsby 2010). The range of activities that may be undertaken in regard to a heritage asset in public or private hands includes the following:

- *Preservation*: ensuring the continued existence of the asset;
- *Conservation*: caring for the asset and maintaining it in proper condition according to accepted professional standards;
- *Renovation or restoration*: returning an asset that has deteriorated to its original condition;
- *Adaptive reuse*: ensuring continuity of use through minimal changes to the asset; and
- *Area conservation planning and historic environment initiatives*: these ensure the value of historic buildings and sites to the economic buoyancy of whole areas, as is now receiving due attention in the United Kingdom through the London Historic Environment initiative.

Public authorities may undertake these activities on their own behalf, or may provide assistance or incentives to private individuals or firms to undertake them. They may also constrain private action in these areas in various ways.

The primary objectives of heritage policy are to promote efficiency in the production of both economic and socio-cultural benefits through heritage conservation, and to protect the public interest in regard to the various aspects of the public-good benefits of heritage. A number of different instruments are available for these purposes, including regulatory and fiscal interventions.

Regulation

Regulation is the most common form of government intervention in the heritage arena around the world. (See box 3.4.) Mechanisms include the setting of criteria to determine which heritage items are sufficiently significant to warrant some public control over their use, and the laying down of standards for the ways in which heritage buildings and sites can be protected, conserved, restored, altered, or adaptively re-used. A distinction can be drawn between "hard" and "soft" regulation when applied to the built heritage (Throsby 1997b).

Hard regulation comprises enforceable directives requiring certain behavior, implemented through legislation, and involving penalties for non-compliance. Such regulation includes preservation orders; constraints on the appearance, function, or use of buildings; land-use zoning; imposition of process requirements for development applications; and so on. Soft regulation on the other hand

---

BOX 3.4

Regulatory and Legislative Initiatives Support Heritage in Albania

Albania Institutional Development Fund (IDF) Grant for Cultural Heritage
Total Project Cost: US$172,000
Total Loan Amount: US$172,000
Approved: November 1993 – Closed: March 1996

This World Bank Institutional Development Fund Grant provided the resources required for Albania to take the critical first steps in preparing national legislation and decrees on cultural heritage protection, which were passed in 1994 and 1996, respectively. A major change under the new framework was that all ministries were required to report to the Ministry of Culture on any activity that might affect heritage sites. The grant also supported a national inventory, which registered some 20,000 items. The activities undertaken during the grant period helped create a consensus that conservation of cultural heritage deserves the full attention of the public sector and that it is appropriate to allocate public resources (according to national standards) for its protection. Since the project closed, Albania's legislation and regulations have been expanded and revised several times and are now closer to compliance with requirements for integration into the European Union.

Source: World Bank Operations Evaluation Department Cultural Heritage Database, 2001.

is not compulsory, but refers to unenforceable directives calling for or encouraging certain behavior, implemented by agreement, and not involving penalties. It includes treaties, conventions, charters, guidelines, codes of practice, and other instruments that operate through voluntary compliance rather than coercion (other than moral persuasion).

The obligations imposed by a public regulatory authority on those owning or managing heritage properties vary among and within countries, and may include:

- Restrictions on the extent to which the property can be altered;
- Requirements for maintenance of a property to ensure that it remains in good functional condition;
- A prohibition on demolition;
- Specification of types and quality of materials to be used in conservation or works for adaptive reuse; and
- Conditions attached to specific uses and functions of the heritage property, as well as restrictions on types of commercial transactions (rent, lease, or sale).

These public policies and regulations are usually legally binding, such that non-compliance will involve penalties. In some cases, public funding may be made available to assist private owners of heritage properties in their maintenance or restoration, in the form of incentives, as discussed further below.

As a policy device, regulation has a number of disadvantages familiar to economists. These drawbacks include the following:

- *Regulation may create inefficiency.* If a minimum amount of conservation is dictated by regulation that exceeds the private and social demand, a deadweight loss occurs. Moreover, regulation does not allocate resources between conservation projects in a way that would equalize the marginal benefits from each project.
- *Regulation involves administrative costs for formulating standards and for monitoring and enforcing them.* These are incurred by the public agency. It also involves compliance costs; that is, the expenditures incurred by firms and individuals to meet the regulatory requirements. The measurement of these costs may be elusive, since it may be that firms and individuals would have undertaken these expenditures anyway, and hence they could not be attributed directly as a cost of regulation.
- *Regulation offers no incentive to do better.* Although the specification of minimum standards of behavior (backed up by effective enforcement) provides an assurance that those minima will be met, regulation generally provides no incentive for firms and individuals to exceed requirements. This problem has been highlighted in the comparison between policy instruments in the environmental area, where it can be observed, for example, that maximum pollution limits for industry invite firms to pollute up to that level, and do not

encourage them to reduce their harmful emissions to lower levels than the specified maxima. In the urban conservation context, similar examples might be found; for instance, in the setting of maximum or minimum requirements for design standards, land or building usage, site coverage, and so on.

- *The regulatory process can be swayed by other influences.* Complaints are sometimes heard that heritage regulation processes can be subverted to serve sectional private interests rather than the public good. This may arise, for example, in the area of land-use zoning, where development controls may be weakened to allow demolition of centrally located heritage properties to make way for more lucrative new commercial buildings. Older buildings located in the historic city core, and occupying valuable parcels of land, have often in the past received rezoning to allow owners to recapture the market value of their property either through construction of new buildings or through participation in an urban renewal process.

Despite the interplay of advantages and disadvantages, regulation has some characteristics that make it attractive to heritage policy makers, including the following:

- *Heritage policy may involve all-or-nothing choices, such as the binary choice between preservation or demolition of a historic building.* In such circumstances, the use of instruments that allow gradations of behavior becomes inappropriate; the simplest way to ensure preservation of the building, if this is desired, is by the application of a regulation forbidding its demolition (provided, of course, that this is backed up with the power for monitoring and enforcement).
- *Regulations have the advantage of being direct and deterministic in their outcome.* In some cases, in the area of urban heritage preservation the social costs of individual action might be so great as to warrant outright prohibition of such action by regulation, rather than, say, allowing market forces to determine a solution. Regulation may also be indicated when the immediate public benefits from some action are judged to be so great relative to their costs as to warrant enforcing a regulation rather than simply encouraging the achievement of a goal. An example might be the requirement to provide certain levels of public amenities in urban redevelopment schemes involving heritage properties or precincts. Such amenities might be judged to provide such a high level of public benefit relative to their cost that it is more appropriate to secure them via regulation than to hope that other softer forms of intervention will yield the same result.
- *The previous justification for regulation is a particular case of a more general advantage*; namely, the fact that regulation, provided it can be enforced, delivers outcomes with certainty. In circumstances in which the public interest is best served by a clear and predictable outcome—not subject to negotiation, concession, or special dealing—then regulation may be indicated. This is relevant,

for example, in the area of design or safety standards governing public access to buildings and sites. In these situations, it may be desirable to leave nothing to chance, but rather ensure compliance for certain tough regulatory means.

• *Another advantage of regulations is that they may be invoked and removed relatively speedily.* Thus, direct controls may be a useful supplement to other measures, such as a system of charges, for the continuing maintenance of acceptable environmental conservation or preservation conditions. Their usefulness arises because of the inflexibility of tax rates and other instruments, and the relative ease with which certain types of regulatory controls can be introduced, enforced, and removed. Some crises can at best be predicted only a short time before they occur, and it may be too costly, for example, to keep tax rates sufficiently high to prevent such emergencies at all times. Therefore, it may be less expensive to make temporary use of direct controls, despite their static inefficiency. This point is acknowledged in the field of urban conservation through the use of temporary preservation orders; that is, controls that can be introduced at very short notice to forestall the demolition of historic properties until some due process of consultation or consideration can be pursued.

The principal regulatory device that governments or other public authorities use in the heritage arena is "listing"; that is, the establishment of lists of properties within a given jurisdiction—international, national, regional, or local—that are regarded as being of cultural significance. Criteria are generally laid down to specify the characteristics that define cultural significance such that any property meeting these criteria will be eligible for inclusion on a particular list.

In most jurisdictions, the inclusion of privately owned buildings or groups of buildings on an official, publicly sanctioned heritage list is compulsory, and the owners have no alternative but to comply with whatever requirements the list carries with it. In some cases, however, accession of properties to an official heritage list is voluntary; in these cases the representativeness and comprehensiveness of the list is dependent on the willingness of private owners to comply with the set of obligations the listing process imposes on them. In addition to lists maintained and enforced by public-sector agencies, there are often "unofficial" lists maintained by interest groups, nongovernmental organizations, and so on, such as National Trusts and local history societies.

Fiscal Incentives

Governments can also employ fiscal measures to implement heritage policy, using both direct and indirect means to do so. The most visible direct approach is through government financing of the conservation of heritage assets owned or controlled by public authorities at national or local levels, such as historic government buildings, public monuments, and so on. (See box 3.5.)

BOX 3.5

Direct Government Support for Heritage Protection Creates Visible Results in Romania

Romania Cultural Heritage Pilot Project (Project number 058284)
Total Project Cost: US$6.9 million
Total Loan Amount: US$5 million
Approved: December 1998 – Closed: December 2004

One component of this project was designed to test pilot conservation efforts in selected historic Saxon villages in Romania's Transylvania region. Works in the villages of Viscri, Biertan, and Mosna included emergency repairs to historic churches and surrounding fortified walls, rehabilitation of public squares and the facades of surrounding historic houses, and financing for community centers and information centers, as well as help for village museums. Based on a request from the government, project savings and further government contributions were used to complete additional conservation activities throughout the area.

Source: Romania Cultural Heritage Pilot Project Implementation and Completion Report.

In regard to privately owned heritage, direct fiscal intervention occurs via the payment of subsidies to ensure that the provision of the public benefits of heritage is encouraged. The rationale for such intervention is the standard case for collective action in the face of market failure. Of course, such collective action need not be confined to the public sector; voluntary organizations in the nonprofit sector, for example, may also provide such assistance. (See box 3.6.)

The implementation of heritage policy by indirect fiscal means occurs through the tax system. Nonprofit organizations engaged in heritage conservation and management reap the benefits of their not-for-profit status via tax exemptions of various sorts, including those allowed to philanthropic donors who provide them with financial support. Private owners of heritage properties may also be granted tax concessions, for example through remissions of property taxes and rates. Such benefits accrue particularly to owners of heritage houses, and to organizations such as churches and schools that are custodians of historic buildings and sites. In addition, corporate sponsorship of heritage conservation projects may in some jurisdictions be encouraged through tax breaks of various sorts.

Eligibility for incentives or for favorable tax treatment in any of the above situations may be contingent on the property involved being listed on an officially

---

BOX 3.6

A Comprehensive and Integrated Approach to Urban Regeneration in Vilnius

Lithuania, Vilnius Institutional Development Fund Grant
Grant Amount: US$225,000
Approved: June 1995 – Closed: December 1996

Working with the World Heritage City of Vilnius, the grant activities first developed an urban revitalization strategy which identified economic, social, cultural, and urban goals. The activity then helped organize the Old Town Development Agency to mobilize funds for the financing of revitalization projects, define priority investments for rehabilitation of essential infrastructure, and organize implementation. Guidelines were also developed for the role of private investment in building reconstruction, including taxes, special incentives, and architectural and building standards.

Source: World Bank Operations Evaluation Department Cultural Heritage Database, 2001.

---

recognized register. Occasionally, suggestions are made that listing of private properties should be voluntary, not compulsory, such that the eligibility for financial assistance could become a negotiated process between the owner and the regulatory authority. Such a process, it is argued, could provide a basis for determining the optimal amounts of financial assistance that owners could receive to help in their conservation efforts. A proposal for a negotiated procedure would rely on the well-known Coase Theorem, which requires three necessary conditions: that interested parties can be identified and property rights can be assigned; that transactions costs are negligible or zero; and that contracts can be enforced. It seems unlikely that a voluntary listing scheme would satisfy these conditions, because identifying the monetary value of the public interest via private negotiations would be hazardous, and the transaction costs of the whole process would be expected to exceed the costs of alternative ways of achieving the desired social outcome.

From Policy to Practice: Heritage in Economic Development

It has been known for some time that cultural heritage can play a significant role in economic development in many countries. Studies published by the World Bank and the Inter-American Development Bank pointed to the importance of heritage in sustainable development and the potential role of heritage assets in contributing to the economic revitalization of historic urban centers (Serageldin and Martin-Brown 1999; Rojas 1999; Serageldin, Shluger, and Martin-Brown 2001; Cernea 2001). Since that time, the World Bank has financed numerous heritage investment projects aimed at physical heritage conservation, local economic development, public infrastructure improvements, community development, and institutional capacity building in heritage management.

Particular attention has been paid to the integration of heritage buildings and sites into urban development projects, often involving adaptive reuse of historic buildings rather than their demolition and replacement with modern structures. In many cases, tourism is seen as an important source of revenue, providing an economic payoff to the original investment. Promotion of localized cultural industries has also been important, generating opportunities for commercial initiatives, business expansion, and employment growth as well as providing increased incomes and widespread community benefits.

Not a great deal is known about the economic and cultural impacts of these various investments in the years following project completion. If information about the medium and long-term impacts of heritage investment were available, it would be useful for providing feedback to improve the management of existing projects and to enhance the design and planning of new ones. Application of the methods discussed in this chapter could yield results that would assist the work of operational staff in the Bank and in government and nongovernmental agencies in borrowing countries.

Ideally, a retrospective economic impact analysis of an urban heritage investment project should attempt to undertake an ex post cost-benefit analysis (CBA) of the project, based on known financial flows since the project completion date. However, a serious constraint on any attempt to undertake a comprehensive ex post CBA is likely to be a lack of data to enable identification of the full range of market and non-market benefits and costs over every year since project completion; these data are also necessary to enable estimation of likely financial flows into the future. In these circumstances, a more practical approach may be to assemble a set of indicators of the economic impacts of the project, where an indicator is defined as any statistic that bears on some aspect of the possible economic effects of the project. Since the cultural impacts of the project are likely to be an important consideration in affecting the post-project sustainability of the investment, a set of cultural indicators can also be compiled. Indicators do not impose stringent data demands because their measurement and coverage can be tailored to suit whatever data are available.

In a recent study financed by the Italian government and implemented by the Bank, a retrospective assessment was undertaken of the economic impacts of an urban heritage investment project, which illustrates some of the concepts and principles discussed in this chapter (Laplante and Throsby 2011). The project involved the rehabilitation of heritage buildings in the historic center of the city of Skopje, FYR Macedonia, known as the Old Bazaar. Beginning in 2002, the World Bank provided funding of about US$4 million over four years to the government of FYR Macedonia for a wide-ranging project in community development and culture in all parts of the country. Further funds to the project were contributed by the Netherlands government. Of the total project funding, the amount directed to heritage-related works in the Skopje Old Bazaar was just over US$300,000. This injection of funds occurred in 2005 and it has resulted in further investments in heritage and infrastructure works in the site in subsequent years. Altogether an additional amount of more than US$2 million has been given by other donors following the initial stimulus provided by the Bank's investment.

The aims of the heritage rehabilitation project in the Skopje Old Bazaar were both economic and social. The primary monetary benefits of the project were expected to come from a revival of economic activity in the site, a stimulus to handicraft production, and increased tourist visits and expenditures. Social benefits were expected to flow from improved security in this sector of the Old Town in a neighborhood traditionally populated by a majority of ethnic Albanians; it was hoped that the rehabilitation of the area would improve relations between communities and enhance the multicultural quality of Skopje.

In the study, primary data collection based on surveys of selected groups of stakeholders enabled a number of indicators to be compiled covering tourism impacts, employment effects, property and rental prices, business activity, and other factors. It is important to note that in any retrospective impact analysis, trends in variables such as these need to be benchmarked against what they might have been in the absence of the project, so that the marginal effects of the investment can be isolated. One means for such benchmarking is to standardize the results for the project site by reference to a control site chosen to resemble the project site as far as possible but where no heritage investment has been undertaken. In the Macedonian study, the Old Bazaar in another town, Prilep, was chosen for this purpose; the same categories of data were gathered for this site as were collected for Skopje.

The economic indicators compiled for this research showed a range of positive impacts flowing from the heritage investment. For example, the number of customers to restaurants, cafes, and shops in the Skopje Old Bazaar increased by about 50 percent in the period since the heritage rehabilitation compared to the control site. Numbers of employees in local business enterprises grew by about 70 percent and workers enjoyed significant increases in real wages compared with their counterparts in Prilep. Overall, the economic indicators gathered in the study showed that an optimistic climate for business expansion had been created by upgrading of the area as a result of the heritage revitalization.

It was noted earlier that tourism is frequently looked to as one of the potential revenue sources to justify investment in cultural heritage in developing countries. In the Skopje case study, the numbers of foreign visitors to restaurants, cafes, and shops in the Old Bazaar almost doubled in the period since the heritage rehabilitation work, a faster rate of growth than experienced in the city as a whole; by contrast, numbers of foreign visitors in the control site in Prilep declined marginally over this time. Tourist expenditures per head per day also increased, indicating an improvement in revenues from this source. Because of its heritage characteristics, the Old Bazaar site is now featured prominently in tourist guides to Skopje; foreign visitors are drawn there by the social and cultural ambience of the site.

In addition to the economic indicators, an assessment was made of the cultural benefits produced by the project. In the section on "Cultural Value," above, this chapter discussed an approach to measuring the cultural value of heritage services in particular situations. The approach outlined there was applied in a survey of visitors to the Old Bazaar site. The survey was administered to a random sample of visitors in different parts of the site on different days. Constraints on research resources made it impossible to conduct a survey of the whole population of Skopje, to test how far perceptions of improvements to the Old Bazaar had spread to other parts of the city.

Nevertheless, the main group captured in the survey as it was carried out was residents from elsewhere in the metro area who happened to be visiting or passing through the project site. Respondents were asked the reasons for their visit to the site, the amount of time and money spent, their perception of the cultural value of the site, their willingness to contribute financially to help restore the heritage further, and their socio-demographic characteristics. The eventual sample size for the survey in the Skopje Old Bazaar was $n = 183$.

To provide indicators of cultural value yielded by the heritage investment, the following statements were presented to respondents in this survey and they were asked whether they agreed or disagreed:

- Restoring the Old Bazaar improves Skopje as a place to visit, work, live, or invest in (improvement in city livability, attractiveness, city branding);
- The Old Bazaar is an important part of Macedonian culture (symbolic/identity value);
- Investing in improvements in the Old Bazaar is a waste of money;
- The renovated buildings of the Old Bazaar are beautiful (visual/aesthetic value);
- The Old Bazaar gives me a sense of Macedonian cultural identity (symbolic/identity value);
- The Old Bazaar should be demolished and replaced with modern buildings; and
- I have learnt something about my cultural heritage from being here (educational value).

Table 3.1 shows the proportions of respondents agreeing or disagreeing with each statement.

These results indicate a positive attitude toward the heritage characteristics of the Old Bazaar. The role of the area and its heritage as important contributors to defining and celebrating Macedonian culture is clearly implied by the responses. Correspondingly, investing in improvements in the area is viewed as a sound use of resources. It appears that the strongest sense of the Old Bazaar's importance derives from its cultural relevance rather than from its visual appeal or its livability, although the latter factors are nevertheless seen in a positive light. There is unanimous agreement that the Old Bazaar is worth maintaining and that it should not be demolished to make way for modern development. This result can be compared with the views of visitors to the control site in Prilep, where no significant heritage investment has been undertaken; just over 20 percent of these visitors thought the Old Bazaar in that city should be demolished (Throsby 2012).

As already noted, conservation of cultural heritage assets in historic city cores is likely to give rise to significant non-market benefits. These benefits arise as public goods enjoyed in various ways by businesses, residents, and visitors both in the project site and in the wider urban environment. They may be related directly to the heritage assets themselves, or they may derive from a more general sense of improved amenity as a result of the project. In the former case, the non-market demand is likely to be based on perceptions of the existence, option, and bequest values of the heritage in question, as discussed earlier in this chapter. In the latter case, the increased livability is likely to be more diffuse in its origins. Whatever the source of these benefits, however, the demand for them can be assessed as willingness to pay among the relevant group of stakeholders.

Rigorous estimation of these benefits requires a carefully controlled contingent valuation or choice modeling study, which pays attention to:

- Defining the population of beneficiaries;
- Using appropriate procedures to ensure a valid random sample is drawn, if necessary stratified according to variables of interest;
- Designing a questionnaire that provides necessary information and realistic scenarios to respondents;
- Including questions that yield objective data on respondents' perceptions of the strength of the external or public-good effects under consideration;
- Controlling for biases in soliciting respondents' willingness to pay; and
- Specifying a feasible payment vehicle comprehensible to respondents.

Carrying out such a study would require research resources that typically are unavailable or cannot be easily mobilized in developing countries. It may nevertheless be possible to undertake a purely exploratory exercise to identify simply

TABLE 3.1

Perception of Cultural Benefits by Visitors to Skopje Old Bazaar, FYR Macedonia (percent)

	Strongly agree	Agree	Neutral	Disagree	Strongly disagree	Total
The Old Bazaar is an important part of Macedonian culture	79.2	13.1	5.5	2.2	0	100
Restoring the Old Bazaar improves Skopje as a place to visit or live in	23.0	61.2	10.9	4.9	0	100
Investing in improvements in the Old Bazaar is a waste of money	0	1.1	2.7	23.0	73.2	100
The Old Bazaar is a place that helps people come together	33.8	30.1	21.9	12.6	1.6	100
The renovated buildings of the Old Bazaar are beautiful	41.0	29.5	23.0	5.5	1.1	100
The Old Bazaar gives me a sense of Macedonian cultural identity	24.6	63.9	7.1	4.4	0	100
The Old Bazaar should be demolished and replaced with modern buildings	0	0	0	6.0	94.0	100
I have learnt something about my cultural heritage from being here	31.1	48.1	14.2	6.6	0	100

Source: Author.

whether any public-good effects are perceived and, if so, whether there is a positive or negative attitude toward paying for them.

This simplified approach was adopted in the Skopje study. The visitors' survey described above was used to assess respondents' willingness to contribute to further restoration work in the area. Interviewers asked them to indicate whether they would be willing to make a voluntary contribution to a fund to allow further heritage conservation work in the Old Bazaar to proceed and, if so, how much. Altogether, 90 percent of respondents said they would be willing to contribute, the majority indicating an amount of up to 500 Macedonian denar or MDen (roughly US$10), as shown in Table 3.2.

The survey that yielded these results and those concerning cultural impacts discussed earlier clearly does not meet the strict methodological requirements of a full contingent valuation study. Although a mean per capita willingness to pay of around US$6 per head could be calculated from these data under certain assumptions, the range of variability attached to such an estimate is so wide that it could not be used as a means of deriving an aggregate non-market benefit.

Despite this, however, the results can be used as a basis for drawing at least some broad conclusions about the non-market effects of the project. The questionnaire used in the survey did provide some indication of relevant stakeholders' perceptions of cultural benefits and their willingness to contribute to further heritage restoration, even if the amounts involved could not be taken as valid estimates of willingness to pay. The questions covered some important cultural outcomes and were comprehensible to respondents. The sample, though small, was randomly drawn from a defined group of beneficiaries. The results indicate an overall positive economic impact arising from the output of non-market benefits from the project.

As a tentative conclusion concerning the operational usefulness of the empirical approach adopted here as a basis for evaluating the non-market benefits of

TABLE 3.2

Visitors' Willingness to Make a One-Time Contribution to Heritage Restoration in the Old Bazaar in Skopje, FYR Macedonia

Amount willing to contribute	Proportion of respondents (%)
Zero	9.8
Up to 500 MDen	67.2
1000 MDen	16.4
1500 MDen	5.5
More than 1500 MDen	1.1
Total	100.0

Source: Author.

urban heritage projects in developing countries, it would appear that a simple data-gathering exercise such as this is capable of demonstrating with reasonable confidence whether a project has delivered some level of public-good benefits and whether these benefits are positively valued in economic terms. Such an approach is, of course, no substitute for a full-scale contingent valuation or choice modeling study, should one be possible in particular situations.

Altogether this case study of the application of an ex post economic impact evaluation to a Bank-financed heritage investment project in a borrowing country provides some quantitative evidence for the economic and cultural benefits arising from investment in cultural capital assets in historic cities. Although a full retrospective CBA was not possible because of data limitations, the indicators assembled showed positive impacts on the economic circumstances of the local businesses. A particular feature of this case study is its demonstration of the value of cultural impacts of the investment, with apparently significant non-market benefits. It can be noted that the observable willingness to pay could be converted into a tangible revenue stream for the municipal authorities or the national government if a suitable means for benefit capture could be found.

Conclusion

The aim of this chapter has been to draw together the principal strands of thinking in the application of economic theory and analysis to issues in heritage conservation. The fundamental concept of cultural capital as a means of representing the economics of heritage provides a means both for interpreting the properties of heritage as asset, and for identifying systematically the critical issues of valuation that attend any heritage-related decision. The non-market benefits of such assets are likely to be a significant component of the economic impacts of investment projects and should not be neglected in any evaluation. Much work remains to be done to develop robust assessment methods that can integrate economic and socio-cultural value into the appraisal of heritage investment projects such as those financed by the Bank in many parts of the developing world.

Nevertheless, the heritage valuation process in most countries is dealt with and circumscribed within the public policy realm. Societal agreement is of paramount importance in the identification and classification of cultural heritage assets to be preserved through the listing process and special administrative regulations. Tangible cultural heritage policies, regulation, and incentive instruments are meant to safeguard and protect the integrity of said assets; in turn, these can affect the performance of property markets and influence local development prospects and job creation opportunities. In investment operations, the economic outcomes are contingent on the adoption and proper use of a set of policy instruments (fiscal incentives, access to special credit lines, property tax deferment, or other) that may produce optimal economic returns and, at the same time, protect and preserve the non-market legacy value of cultural heritage assets.

Notes

1. Note that the concept of cultural capital in economics differs from that occurring in sociology, following Pierre Bourdieu.
2. See further in *Capital Values—The Contribution of the Historic Environment to London: A Framework for Action* (2012, London, UK). The report was commissioned by the London Historic Environment Forum and led by the London Cultural Consortium, comprising 14 members including, among others, representatives of English Heritage, Government Office for London, Heritage Lottery Fund, Royal Parks, and London Development Agency.
3. See UNESCO's website for further information: http://whc.unesco.org/en/about/.

References

Alberini, A., P. Riganti, and A. Longo. 2003. "Can People Value the Aesthetic and Use Services of Urban Sites? Evidence from a Survey of Belfast Residents." *Journal of Cultural Economics* 27 (3): 193–213.

Avrami, E., R. Mason, and M. De La Torre, eds. 2000. *Values and Heritage Conservation.* Los Angeles: Getty Conservation Institute.

Barbier, E. B., J. C. Burgess, and C. Folke. 1994. *Paradise Lost? The Ecological Economics of Biodiversity.* London: Earthscan.

Benhamou, F. 2010. "Heritage." In *Handbook of Cultural Economics,* 2nd ed., ed. R. Towse, 229–235. Cheltenham: Edward Elgar.

Bucci, A., and G. Segre. 2011. "Culture and Human Capital in a Two-Sector Endogenous Growth Mode." *Research in Economics* 65 (4): 279–293.

Cannon-Brookes, P. 1996. "Cultural-Economic Analyses of Art Museums: A British Curator's Viewpoint." In *Economics of the Arts: Selected Essays,* ed. V. Ginsburgh and P.-M. Menger, 255–274. Amsterdam: North Holland.

Carson, R. T., R. C. Mitchell, M. B. Conaway, and S. Navrud. 1997. *Non-Moroccan Values of Rehabilitating the Fez Medina.* Washington, DC: World Bank.

Cernea, M. 2001. *Cultural Heritage and Development: A Framework for Action in the Middle East and North Africa.* Washington, DC: World Bank.

Cheng, S. W. 2006. "Cultural Goods Production, Cultural Capital Formation and the Provision of Cultural Services." *Journal of Cultural Economics* 30 (4): 263–286.

De La Torre, M., ed. 2002. *Assessing the Values of Cultural Heritage.* Los Angeles: Getty Conservation Institute.

Dutta, M., S. Banerjee, and Z. Husain. 2007. "Untapped Demand for Heritage: A Contingent Valuation Study of Prinsep Ghat, Calcutta." *Tourism Management* 28 (1): 83–95.

Hutter, M., and I. Rizzo, eds. 1997. *Economic Perspectives on Cultural Heritage.* London: Macmillan.

Kim, S. S., et al. 2007. "Assessing the Economic Value of a World Heritage Site and Willingness-to-Pay Determinants: A Case of Changdeok Palace." *Tourism Management* 28 (1): 317–322.

Kinghorn, N., and K. Willis. 2008. "Valuing the Components of an Archaeological Site: An Application of Choice Experiment to Vindolanda, Hadrian's Wall." *Journal of Cultural Heritage* 9 (2): 117–124.

Laplante, B., and D. Throsby. 2011. *An Assessment of the Economic Impacts of Cultural Heritage Projects in Georgia and Macedonia.* Washington, DC: World Bank.

Maghakyan, S., 2007. "Sacred Stones Silenced in Azerbaijan." *History Today* 57 (11): 4–5.

Mason, H., M. Jones-Lee, and Donaldson, C. 2009. "Modelling the Monetary Value of a QALY." *Health Economics* 18: 933–950.

Mason, R. 2005. *Economics and Historic Preservation: A Guide and Review of the Literature.* Washington, DC: Brookings Institution.

Mason, R. 2008. "Assessing Values in Conservation Planning: Methodological Issues and Choices." In *The Heritage Reader,* ed. G. Fairclough, 99–124. Abingdon: Routledge.

Navrud, S., and R. C. Ready, eds. 2002. *Valuing Cultural Heritage: Applying Environmental Valuation Techniques to Historic Buildings, Monuments and Artifacts.* Cheltenham: Edward Elgar.

Neumayer, E. 2003. *Weak versus Strong Sustainability: Exploring the Limits of Two Opposing Paradigms,* 2nd ed. Cheltenham: Edward Elgar.

O'Brien, D. 2010. *Measuring the Value of Culture* (A Report to the Department for Culture, Media and Sport). London: DCMS.

Pagiola, S. 1996. *Economic Analysis of Investments in Cultural Heritage: Insights from Environmental Economics.* Washington, DC: World Bank.

Pagiola, S. 2001. "Valuing Benefits of Investments in Cultural Heritage: The Historic Core of Split." Paper presented at the International Conference on Economic Valuation of Cultural Heritage, October 19–20. Cagliari.

Peacock, A. 1995. "A Future for the Past: The Political Economy of Heritage." *Proceedings of the British Academy* 87: 189–243.

Peacock, A., and I. Rizzo. 2008. *The Heritage Game: Economics, Policy and Practice.* Oxford: Oxford University Press.

Pearce, D. W., and R. K. Turner. 1990. *Economics of Natural Resources and the Environment.* Baltimore: Johns Hopkins University Press.

Pollicino, M., and D. Maddison. 2001. "Valuing the Benefits of Cleaning Lincoln Cathedral." *Journal of Cultural Economics* 25 (2): 131–148.

Rizzo, I., and D. Throsby. 2006. "Cultural Heritage: Economic Analysis and Public Policy." In *Handbook of the Economics of Art and Culture Vol. 1,* ed. V. Ginsburgh and D. Throsby, eds. 984–1016. Amsterdam: Elsevier/North Holland.

Rizzo, I., and R. Towse, eds. 2002. *The Economics of Heritage: A Study of the Political Economy of Culture in Sicily.* Cheltenham: Edward Elgar.

Rojas, E. 1999. *Old Cities, New Assets: Preserving Latin America's Urban Heritage.* Washington, DC: Inter-American Development Bank and the Johns Hopkins University Press.

Santagata, W., and G. Signorello. 2000. "Contingent Valuation of a Cultural Public Good and Policy Design: The Case of 'Napoli Musei Aperti.'" *Journal of Cultural Economics* 24 (3): 181–204.

Schuster, J. M., J. de Monchaux, and C. A. Riley II, eds. 1997. *Preserving the Built Heritage: Tools for Implementation.* Hanover, NH: University Press of New England.

Serageldin, I., and J. Martin-Brown, eds. 1999. *Culture in Sustainable Development: Investing in Cultural and Natural Endowments.* Washington, DC: World Bank.

Serageldin, I., E. Shluger, and J. Martin-Brown. 2001. *Historic Cities and Sacred Sites, Cultural Roots for the Urban Futures.* Washington, DC: World Bank.

Shockley, G. E. 2004. "Government Investment in Cultural Capital: A Methodology for Comparing Direct Government Support for the Arts in the US and the UK." *Public Finance and Management* 4 (1): 75–102.

Smith, M., M. Drummond, and D. Brixner. 2009. "Moving the QALY Forward: Rationale for Change." *Value in Health* 12 (S1): 1–4.

Throsby, D. 1997a. "Seven Questions in the Economics of Cultural Heritage." In *Economic Perspectives on Cultural Heritage,* ed. Hutter, M. and I. Rizzo, 12–30. London: Macmillan.

Throsby, D. 1997b. "Making Preservation Happen: The Pros and Cons of Regulation." In *Preserving the Built Heritage: Tools for Implementation,* ed. J. M. Schuster, J. de Monchaux, and C. A. Riley II, 32–48. Hanover, NH: University Press of New England.

Throsby, D. 1999. "Cultural Capital." *Journal of Cultural Economics* 23 (1): 3–12.

Throsby, D. 2001. *Economics and Culture.* Cambridge: Cambridge University Press.

Throsby, D. 2003. "Sustainability in the Conservation of the Built Environment: An Economist's Perspective." In *Managing Change: Sustainable Approaches to the Conservation of the Built Environment,* ed. J.-M. Teutonico and F. Matero, 3–10. Los Angeles: Getty Conservation Institute.

Throsby, D. 2005. *On the Sustainability of Cultural Capital.* Department of Economics Research Paper No. 10/200, Macquarie University, Sydney.

Throsby, D. 2010. *The Economics of Cultural Policy.* Cambridge: Cambridge University Press.

Throsby, D. 2012. *Investment in Urban Heritage: Economic Impacts of Cultural Heritage Projects in Macedonia and Georgia.* Washington DC: World Bank.

Ulibarri, C. A. 2000. "Rational Philanthropy and Cultural Capital." *Journal of Cultural Economics* 24 (2): 135–146.

UNESCO. 1998. *World Culture Report: Culture, Creativity, and Markets.* Paris: UNESCO.

Wang, X. 2007. "An Analysis of Optimal Allocation and Accumulation of Cultural Capital." In *Departmental Bulletin Paper 2007-08-03,* 197–213. Kyoto: Graduate School of Policy and Management, Doshisha University.

World Commission on Environment and Development (WCED). 1987. *Our Common Future.* Oxford: Oxford University Press.

World Commission on Culture and Development (WCCD). 1995. *Our Creative Diversity.* Oxford: Oxford University Press.

4

Economic Valuation of Cultural Heritage

Peter Nijkamp
Professor of Regional Economics and Economic Geography,
Free University of Amsterdam (the Netherlands)

This chapter presents an overview of economic valuation methods in the domain of cultural heritage. After introductory and conceptual observations, a functional approach to heritage valuation is illustrated. Several issues are similar to environmental valuation, and a comparison between biodiversity valuation and cultural heritage valuation is presented. The chapter then looks at various classes of valuation methods, notably compensation, social cost-benefit, stated preference, and revealed preference methods. Compensation methods are linked to the applied welfare-theoretic methods and seek to find the sacrifices and revenues involved with a change in the availability or quality of a cultural asset. In the cost-benefit analysis tradition, a sophisticated toolbox has been developed over the years to deal with complex project evaluation issues, sometimes with large spillover effects. Stated preference analysis is essentially rooted in behavioral economics, but in the past decades it has found extensive application in the case of economic evaluation of non-market or quasi-market goods, when the essential evaluation concept centers on the individual willingness to pay. Revealed preference methods focus on market outcomes derived from real market transactions and include the travel cost method and the hedonic price method. The chapter argues that despite some important limitations, the use of hedonic price analysis may be promising for valuation of cultural heritage. Various applications and empirical illustrations of this approach are presented as well, followed by concluding remarks.

Introduction

Cultural heritage and local identity have become buzzwords in modern political parlance. These concepts clearly have social and historical roots, as they refer to local characteristic creative manifestations, accepted value systems, historic memory, language, literature, art, architecture, engineering, and urban planning. Cultural heritage is the result of cumulative human activity expressed and projected in a material sense (comprising historic city cores, built structures, iconic monuments, and landscapes) or in an immaterial sense (which includes music, dance, and literature). Cultural heritage may be seen as the legacy of physical artifacts and intangible attributes of a group (or society at large) that are inherited from past generations, maintained in the present, and bestowed for the future. Cultural heritage thus offers a focused and systematic lens to look from the present into the past, with a projection into the future.

To qualify as cultural heritage, goods ought to have historic significance and, more often than not, an intergenerational meaning and a sense of local identity (Coccossis and Nijkamp 1995). Clearly, cultural heritage includes an array of expressions, such as performing architectural heritage, archaeological sites, cultural landscapes, monuments, arts, literature, and so forth. Cultural heritage will be presented in this chapter as those parts of historic-cultural capital that have an explicit and recognized connotation to the past and may be seen as a self-identifying landmark of a place (Throsby 1999). Consequently, cultural heritage and identity are often closely interrelated concepts.

Part of our heritage is visible and tangible, and has a physical expression; for instance, the ensemble of a historic built environment comprising ancient temples, palaces, and gardens. It is noteworthy that the United Nations Educational, Scientific and Cultural Organization (UNESCO 1972) makes a distinction between cultural, natural, and intangible heritage (Arizpe et al. 2000; Klamer and Zuidhof 1999). Indeed, cultural heritage is a broad and heterogeneous concept, so that a comparative study of cultural heritage or an unambiguous economic evaluation is fraught with many difficulties, of both a methodological and empirical nature.

This chapter will focus on the physical and tangible artifacts created by humanity in the past. A significant share of these assets is part of our everyday living environment, both biotic and abiotic. The daily living environment thus encompasses a broad variety of collective or public goods, such as a quiet atmosphere, green urban areas, aquatic systems, and historic-cultural capital, as well as other forms of environmental capital.

Environmental capital, a concept that incorporates the set of all material and non-material collective assets around us, is clearly a broad and multifaceted ramification of goods that contributes to societal welfare or well-being, either by being enjoyed through consumption externalities, or by being used for economic purposes through production externalities. The same holds true for a subcategory of environmental capital, cultural heritage, which generate also in principle a variety of economic benefits that accrue to socioeconomic well-being through consumption and production externalities.

Cultural heritage should not be defined as a "soft" or "qualitative" good. It is observable, visible, and measurable in nature and should essentially be treated in the same way as "normal" economic goods. There is, however, in most cases an important difference with respect to normal goods on the market: cultural heritage is not strictly reproducible, as it refers to particular—sometimes unique— historic, cultural, political, or socio-economic events or goods. In many cases, it also refers to a common socio-cultural past. Since such unique commodity is not freely available on the market—and in many cases not traded at all; for instance, because of legal reasons—and yet because it is to be shared and used by many people, it usually belongs to the category of public goods. In light of the externalities involved—for instance, people watching the majestic view of the Acropolis from downtown Athens, or people in awe from having experienced the unforgettable beauty of the Taj Mahal complex in India—the economic meaning of such cultural heritage assets merits careful attention in both scientific research and policy making. It is noteworthy that cultural heritage may also promote many market benefits—such as an increase in tourism revenues, and spillovers to the hospitality and service sector—as well as non-market benefits—through externalities that bring benefits to an appreciative society in the form of livability, local attraction of investments and creative minds, self-esteem, and open-mindedness of the local population (Navrud and Ready 2002).

Frameworks for protecting cultural heritage have significantly improved over the past decades in scope, scale, and orientation. In many countries, they started as preservation planning, later on followed by conservation and adaptive reuse planning; witness, for instance, the recovery efforts for the historic city centers of European cities. However, the management of cultural heritage today goes much further, as cultural capital has to be positioned in the context of development planning of urban areas. Most metropolitan centers are currently going through a rapid transformation, in terms of urban regeneration and restructuring plans as well as urban expansion, especially in developing countries, and notably in Africa and Asia. Consequently, there is a risk that cultural heritage capital can turn into isolated islands of the past in wild seas of urban dynamics.

Even ancient "extramural" or rural cultural heritage amenities tend to become more and more encompassed by fast urban development. For example, the historic Giza pyramid complex in Egypt is increasingly becoming part of a dense and congested urban agglomeration, where a quiet and reflective atmosphere of these traditional holy places becomes illusory. Developmental planning for cultural heritage with a view to safeguarding historic-cultural and socioeconomic morphology in urban development thus becomes a major challenge. Creating a sustainable balance between different approaches to urban and land use calls for a systematic and operational evaluation of different development options (Choi et al. 2010). Especially in historic city cores, there is an increasing need for a solid assessment of the economic implications of the presence of cultural heritage assets.

This chapter includes a review of essential features of cultural heritage evaluation and a sketch of various functionalities involved, along with a broad overview of various methods and applications. This is followed by a section on the hedonic price, as the best possible market-based approach, provided that the necessary databases are available. Various empirical results are offered to illustrate the expounded cases.

Economic Valuation of Cultural Heritage

Cultural heritage has been redefined as an asset of historic, cultural, and socio-economic significance in a contemporary society (Hubbard 1993; Riganti and Nijkamp 2007). Cultural heritage management, including city monument conservation activities, cannot be adequately addressed as an isolated activity that is disjointed from broader urban or regional development policy, programs and projects (Coccossis and Nijkamp 1995). Urban development means the creation of new assets in terms of physical, social, and economic structures. Nevertheless, at the same time it should be recognized that each development process often also destroys traditional physical fabric, including social and cultural assets derived from our common heritage. Although not always immediately computable, all cultural heritage assets represent for society at large an economic value that ought to be properly incorporated into any urban transformation process. In practice, the inclusion of such assets in the planning process cannot be left to the market mechanism, as most urban historic-cultural assets represent "unpriced goods" characterized by external effects that are not included in the conventional metrics or "measuring rod of money" commonly used in assessing economic outcomes of investment.

An operational and reliable assessment of the socioeconomic and historic-cultural value of monuments, or cultural heritage in general—including the impacts of preservation policy—is fraught with many difficulties. Often experts rely on tourist revenues to reflect part of the interest of society in monument conservation and/or restoration, but in many cases this provides a biased and incomplete measure, so that preservation policy can hardly be solely based on tourism. On the contrary, in various places one may observe a situation in which large-scale tourism, sometimes marked by congestion, even affects the quality of or access to a cultural heritage asset, as in the cases of Venice, Florence, or Rome.

In recent years, this phenomenon has resulted in a wealth of studies on so-called crowding effects (Neuts and Nijkamp 2011b).

It is noteworthy that the socioeconomic and historic-artistic value of a cultural good is a multidimensional or compound indicator that cannot easily be reduced to one common denominator—as measured by monetary metrics. In fact, we are—from a planning viewpoint—much more interested in the "complex social value" of cultural resources (Fusco Girard 1987). This implies that the meaning of historic and cultural resources is not, in the first place, dependent on these assets' absolute quantities, but on their constituent qualitative attributes or features such as age, uniqueness, historical meaning, visual beauty, physical condition, and artistic value. For instance, cities such as Venice, Florence, Siena, or Padua would never have received international recognition, and even acclaim, without the presence of intangible values inherent in their tangle of cultural heritage assets as markers of their unique history, which imbue them with a sense of place.

The previous observations have to be interpreted against the background of rapid changes in urbanization patterns. With the advent of the 21st century as the urban century, the preservation and management of historic-cultural footprints endowed from the past has become a great concern and a challenge. The Bank's urban and local government strategy (World Bank 2009) highlights many of these trends and challenges, such as megacity and secondary-city development, persistent poverty in urban areas, dysfunctional land markets, slum development, and the need for new financial instruments. The persistent urbanization trends put severe stress on cultural heritage conservation strategies. Historic city cores house a wealth of architectural and cultural-physical assets that define their local identity. What is Rome without its Forum Romano, Campidoglio, and the Coliseum; Berlin without its Brandenburg Gate; New York without its Statue of Liberty, but also Rockefeller Center, Fifth Avenue, and Central Park; Moscow without its Kremlin and the Bolshoi theater; or Beijing without its Forbidden City? Worldwide, thousands of such ensembles of fine cultural heritage assets have become icons of international tourism and magnets for those seeking to experience past lifestyles and arts. A recent UNESCO document (UNESCO 2010) recommends that following issues be addressed in management of historic cities:

• System of values and meaning of historic city cores;
• Definition of historic urban landscape;
• Management of change;
• Sustainable social and economic development; and
• Updated tools for urban development management and historic city core conservation.

This chapter attempts to investigate and review economic valuation methods for highlighting the socioeconomic value of cultural heritage against the background of a broad valuation perspective. It should be noted that there is already a long tradition of the development of economic assessment tools dating back to the postwar period. The need for transparency in managing public expenditures has prompted the application of solid methods for estimating the benefits and costs of new policy, as applied in the areas of water management, infrastructure, and housing construction. (See box 4.1.) The 1960s showed a strong dominance of the use of economic evaluation tools in public planning; for instance, the application of cost-benefit analysis and cost-effectiveness analysis.

BOX 4.1

Cost-Benefit Analysis Is Useful in Considering Investments in Conservation and Tourism in Honduras

Honduras, Regional Development in the Copan Valley Project (Project number 081172)
Total Project Cost: US$13.4 million
Total Loan Amount: US$12 million
Approved: May 2003 – Closed: March 2009

The Copan project supported the Government of Honduras' efforts at promoting sustainable economic growth through tourism as a means to generate local employment opportunities, create investment opportunities for the private sector, and reduce poverty in one of the poorest regions of Honduras. The project invested in the creation of an archeological tourism circuit integrating emblematic parks and sites; supported sustainable tourism branding and strategic planning for pro-poor tourism development; strengthened the capacity of the private sector to provide quality services to visitors; supported indigenous and locally-owned enterprises; and enhanced national and local institutional capacities for cultural heritage management and planning.

The project's economic rate of return was analyzed by comparing the public investment cost of the project with the project's stream of expected net benefits in terms of additional net incomes to Honduran factors of production. In this variant of the analysis, the costs and benefits were all accounted for at their economic opportunity costs. The Net Present Value (NPV) for the medium-growth-in-demand scenario was US$9.4 million with a 20.5 percent Economic Rate of Return (ERR). Under a high-growth scenario, the NPV was US$32.4 million with a 78.5 percent ERR.

Source: Honduras, Regional Development in the Copan Valley Project Appraisal Document.

It was a widely held belief that a systematic application of rigorous economic thinking in evaluating and selecting public projects or plans would be a valuable tool for improving the performance of the public sector (Little and Mirrlees 1974; Renard 1986; Warr 1982).

However, a compound valuation of public capital goods—such as historic city cores, monuments, landmarks, palaces, parks, and landscapes—is far from easy and cannot be undertaken by the exclusive consideration of the tourist and recreation sector (Kalman 1980; Lichfield 1989). Especially in the Anglo-Saxon literature, the expenditures made in visiting recreational destinations are often used as a proxy value for assessing the financial or economic meaning of natural parks, palaces, and museums. The complicating problem here is that in geographic terms such recreational commodities and the various users are distributed unequally over space. This means that recreational expenditure are codetermined by distance frictions, so that the valuation of recreation opportunities is prominently determined by the transportation costs inherent in recreational and tourist visits. Consequently, the socioeconomic value of recreational opportunities is a function of their indigenous attractiveness and of their location in geographic space. However, the historic-cultural value of monuments may be invariant with respect to geographical location—apart from the scale economy emanating from a "socio-cultural complex"—so that we are still left with the problem of a compound evaluation.

It seems to make sense to adhere to the basic economic principle that the value of a good is dependent on the user perspective or orientation for that particular good. Therefore, in agreement with conventional multi-attribute utility theory, the value of a good—including a good in the realm of cultural heritage—depends on the functions offered to and the use of it made by the bidder, or by society at large in the case of public goods. Hence, in the next section a functional perspective that may form a systematic foundation for evaluating urban cultural heritage is presented.

A Functional Perspective on the Value of Cultural Heritage

The economic valuation of cultural heritage differs from the intrinsic meaning of a cultural asset but aims to assess the meaning of a cultural asset for society. Thus, the question is whether one can identify and estimate implications of the presence of or the use of cultural heritage for the broader local or regional economic system. Such implications may translate themselves into a multiplicity of effects, such as impacts on:

- Local production system (investments, consumption, and demand for products);
- Regional labor market (including new jobs and labor force participation);

- Local housing market (sale and rent);
- Transport and communications infrastructure (including mobility and accessibility);
- Public services (health care, education, and research);
- Financial-economic system (incentives, taxes, and distributional aspects);
- Effects on the physical environment (such as pollution, congestion, and energy use);
- Local social community (including security, social inclusion, and community bonds); and
- Cultural context (performing arts and citizen's participation in cultural manifestations).

In general, economic valuation refers to the use value of a good. Nevertheless, it ought to be recognized that in many cases there are also non-users—certainly in the case of externalities of goods—who may attach a possible value to a cultural asset, even though this asset is not actually visited by them. Economic actors may be willing to leave the option of use or enjoyment open, now and in the future. This has led to the notion of an option value (Weisbrod 1964); this concept may have various meanings (Hyman and Hufschmidt 1983):

- *Risk aversion:* potential visitors are not sure that they will ever visit a given heritage site or monument, but do not want to lose the possibility to visit it in the near or distant future;
- *Quasi-option demand:* potential visitors have an interest in visiting the recreational good concerned, but prefer to wait until sufficient information is available;
- *Existence value:* non-users attach a high value to the fact that the scarce sociocultural asset is maintained, even when they do not plan to visit it;
- *Vicarious use value:* non-users want to keep a certain public good intact because they like it when others can enjoy this good; and
- *Bequest value:* non-users see it as their moral responsibility to protect and maintain a certain public good for future generations.

It is noteworthy that the concept of option value is strongly related to the symbolic value of a good. It is also clear that there are many intangible elements involved with the specific kind of use associated with a historic asset. However, making a reliable monetary assessment of option values in the framework of monuments is far from an easy task (Greenley et al. 1981).

It is important to note that especially the potential and actual functions of cultural heritage assets—as far as they are perceived, appreciated, and lead to behavioral changes of economic actors—have influenced the economic valuation methods over the past decades. This has led to a wealth of approaches to valuation in economics. The methodology to take account of various—priced and unpriced, direct, and indirect—effects is clearly not straightforward. One may broadly distinguish three major assessment classes for cultural assets: (1) performance indicators analysis, (2) monetary analysis, and (3) decision support analysis.

Performance indicators analysis is a method that stems from the management literature and takes for granted that cultural heritage may be viewed, in the same way that a corporate organization is as an entity that may have to be judged on the basis of a set of predefined performance indicators. These indicators may refer to heritage quality indices, conservation or rehabilitation risks, natural landscape conditions (using aerial photography, for instance), architectural identity, accessibility, integration into the urban fabric, uniqueness of historic districts, and so on. Methods used in this context, to obtain a systemic comparative framework are benchmark techniques and balance-scorecard techniques.

Monetary analysis method has its origin in the applied welfare theory; it is based on the assumption that public policy serves to improve national welfare. To achieve this measure, public expenditures are to be made, but these expenditures are not aimed for general purposes but for specific goods and services in the framework of designated plans or projects. Thus, all cost components have to be measured as accurately as possible. Furthermore, the aim of national welfare is very broad and needs to be more focused, as usually not all individuals, groups, or regions in society will benefit to the same extent from a plan or project. Hence, plans or projects have to be evaluated with a view to their foreseeable impact on different groups or regions in a society; consequently, measurements of costs, of benefits, and of distributive effects are necessary.

The conventional economic evaluation of cultural heritage usually finds its origin in the notion of consumer surplus, by way of incorporating the so-called travel cost method. This consumer surplus represents the consumer's financial sacrifices—represented in terms of distance a visitor is willing to travel and time he is willing to devote, the so-called willingness to pay minus the actual costs of a visit. Usual research methods used to assess this willingness to pay are, among others, based on survey techniques and interviews. A major problem in this case is the specification of a demand function, because of heterogeneity among individual users, the importance of remaining (omitted) explanatory variables, synergetic effects caused by other recreation users (congestion, for example), the evaluation of time (or time preference), and the intangible nature of cultural heritage.

Finally, the decision support analysis method is based on an operations research type of approach. This strand of literature rests on the proposition that cultural heritage has multiple use dimensions and that its societal significance is hard to translate in a single and unambiguous common denominator such as a monetary dimension. Examples in practical valuation exercises can be found in community impact analysis (Lichfield 1989) and multicriteria analysis

(Nijkamp et al. 1990). In community impact analysis, effects of international policies regarding cultural heritage are mapped out for all relevant groups of society. This approach leads normally to the design of a comprehensive effect matrix, which also incorporates the distributive effects. Multicriteria analysis is a quantitative judgment method based on a multidimensional impact assessment. It has become a popular tool in many evaluation studies over the past decades. Seen from the viewpoint of conservation policies, there is a need for an integrated cultural and functional economic urban development strategy in which economic, social, architectural, and historic aspects of city life are dealt with in a holistic way.

In this perspective, it is insufficient to look at the cost side of cultural heritage policy. Cultural assets generate social benefit, the value (economic, social, and cultural) of which is related to the historic development of society and is perceived by the present generation—including all direct and indirect users factored in view of the future. These benefits are clearly multidimensional in nature. Here a parallel may be drawn with antiquities sold on the market. The value of an antique good (a painting, for example) depends on its age, its degree of uniqueness, its artistic quality, and its representation of a certain style period. The same holds true for cultural heritage, although here an additional important consideration plays a role; namely, its integration into the existing historic urban structure, also known as the "urban ensemble." (See box 4.2.)

The three described approaches are used in different stages of evaluation methods of cultural heritage assets. As mentioned before, the valuation of cultural

---

BOX 4.2

Contingent Valuation Estimates the Willingness to Pay of Both Tourists and Residents in Guizhou, China

China, Guizhou Cultural and Natural Heritage Protection and Development
Project (Project number 091950)
Total Project Cost: US$89.8 million
Total Loan Amount: US$60 million
Approved: May 2009 – Ongoing

Working with the government of Guizhou, this project is assisting the province in increasing economic benefits for local communities through improved tourism activities and better protection of cultural and natural heritage. The project focuses mainly on support for 17 ethnic minority villages, four ancient towns,

(continued next page)

> **BOX 4.2** *continued*
>
> and four national parks. Project activities include investments in infrastructure, housing, and income generation activities.
>
> A cost-benefit analysis was performed on several representative project sites. The non-monetized benefits (consumer's surplus) of heritage protection were estimated based on the results of a contingent valuation study that estimated the willingness to pay values of both tourists and residents for cultural heritage conservation. Monetized benefits were also estimated, including increases in admission fees, tourism taxes, and extra profits (or rents) captured by service providers due to the improved conservation provided by the project. Other indirect benefits, such as improvements in local public health and environmental protection, were real. Each individual site had a different economic internal rate of return, ranging from 13.7 percent to 19.6 percent. The variation is due primarily to the different nature and size of investments at the different sites. Sensitivity analysis—which assumed a 10 percent reduction in the number of visitors and a 10 percent increase in investment costs—showed that the analysis was robust.
>
> *Source:* Guizhou Cultural and Natural Heritage Protection and Development Project Appraisal Document.

heritage bears some resemblance to the valuation of environmental goods. In the next section, valuation issues in environmental economics, in particular biodiversity, are presented.

Lessons from Cultural Heritage Valuation and Biodiversity Valuation

There is a striking similarity in research approaches to the economic valuation of cultural heritage and that of biodiversity. Both domains make up the environmental context of mankind, and both domains are overloaded with spatial-economic externalities (Nunes and Nijkamp 2011). (See box 4.3.)

A prominent issue in recent discussions about sustainable development is concern over the loss of biological diversity (or biodiversity). Biodiversity requires research attention for two reasons. First, biodiversity provides a wide range of direct and indirect benefits to humankind, on both local and global scales. Second, many human activities contribute to unprecedented rates of biodiversity loss, and this threatens the stability and continuity of ecosystems, as well as affecting socioeconomic activities of humankind. Consequently, in recent years much

---

BOX 4.3

Contingent Valuation Is Used to Estimate Both the Cultural and Ecological Value of Lake Sevan in Armenia

Environment as Cultural Heritage: The Armenian Diaspora's Willingness to Pay to Protect Armenia's Lake Sevan

Lake Sevan is one of the largest high-altitude (alpine) lakes in the world. However, as of 2005, the level of the lake had dropped by 18 meters and its volume of water had fallen by more than 40 percent. These changes had various significant adverse effects on Lake Sevan's ecology. Perhaps more important was the threat to Armenian culture, in which Lake Sevan has figured prominently in history, art, poetry, and music over many centuries.

A study was undertaken of the Armenian diaspora in the United States regarding the willingness to pay to protect Armenia's Lake Sevan. Dichotomous choice-contingent valuation questions were asked by surveys to elicit respondents' willingness to pay for the protection of Lake Sevan. The results indicate that, on average, each household of the Armenian diaspora in the United States would be willing to provide a one-time donation of approximately US$80 to prevent a further degradation of Lake Sevan, and approximately US$280 to restore the quality of the lake by increasing its water level by three meters. At the time of its writing, the paper based on this research was believed to be one of the first willingness to pay studies in which a natural asset was also considered as a cultural site of interest. It also appears to be the first time that a diaspora constituted the target population.

Source: Development Research Group, World Bank, 2005.

---

attention has been directed toward the analysis and valuation of the loss of biodiversity, both locally and globally.

Economic valuation aims to provide a monetary expression of biodiversity values. The reason for this is that the theoretical basis of economic valuation is monetary (income) variation as a compensation or equivalent for direct and indirect impacts of a certain biodiversity change on the welfare of humans. Both direct and indirect values related to production, consumption, and non-use values of biodiversity are considered when pursuing the economic valuation of biodiversity. Explicit biodiversity changes, preferably in terms of accurate physical-biological indicators, should be assessed. Biodiversity changes must be marginal or small for economic valuation to make sense. The economic valuation of biodiversity changes is based on a reductionist approach to value. This means that the total economic value is regarded as the result of aggregating various use and non-use values, reflecting a variety of human motivations, as well as aggregating local values to attain a global value, in a bottom-up approach (Nunes and Schokkaert 2003).

Moreover, the economic valuation of biodiversity starts from the premise that social values should be based on individual values, independently of whether the individuals are knowledgeable about biodiversity-related issues or not. This can be considered consistent with the democratic support of policies.

Biodiversity—like cultural heritage—describes a complex system. Hence, it is not plausible that an unambiguous value indicator can be derived. Nevertheless, several partial studies help to reveal aspects of this multidimensional whole (Nunes and Nijkamp 2011).

Which lessons can we draw from a comparison with the biodiversity valuation? It is striking that the nature of the underlying issues are largely similar—such as long-term perspective, economic externalities, and psychological or spiritual attachment. In economic terms, it comes as no surprise that the array of evaluation methods used in both domains is quite similar. The costs of policy interventions in these domains are made up by direct capital outlays for the implementation, necessary wage costs, factor supply costs, overhead costs, opportunity costs, and social costs. Social costs may either be quantifiable or not, but refer to all costs incurred that are not reflected in the usual market mechanism. In all cases it is desirable to measure costs in terms of current factor input prices, among others, due to information comparison.

In the case of public projects, market prices for goods and services are usually not easily available, although for such cases proxy values for costs may be imagined and used, such as social marginal costs (for instance, a charge to the user of an output equal to the benefit received), shadow prices (based on a linear programming approach), and marginal costs (based on standard economic equilibrium assumptions). It is plausible to derive some important lessons from biodiversity economics, but it is also clear that cultural heritage has its own indigenous features that call for tailor-made valuation methods. These are discussed next.

The Economist's Toolbox

The economic valuation of cultural heritage projects essentially finds its roots in the evaluation of non-priced goods, in particular arising from evaluation of environmental goods. The overarching aim is to attach a price tag to such goods.

Cultural assets resemble environmental goods, though with a few distinctive features, such as their historical dimension, features of uniqueness, and often an abiotic nature. Despite these marked differences, several supporting pillars from the economics of environmental evaluation apply also to cultural goods, such as increasing scarcity, non-market values, and site specificity (Carruthers and Mundy 2006; Choi et al. 2010; Navrud and Ready 2002).

Cultural heritage assets are, in a way, a living presence of past human activities, with their presence in present time and space carrying a great historic value and a high degree of local specificity. In part, their long-term existence is the result of shared values held among residents, and sometimes a broader community—so that this type of good is emerging out of common values of society (Nijkamp and Riganti 2008, 2009). This holds true for historic landmarks and also for non-monumental buildings, which often have a symbolic value. Cultural goods usually embody a form (or sense) of creativity, a historic-symbolic meaning, and a reference to an important era, a style, a building innovation, or a celebrated event in the past (Throsby 2001).

Consequently, to judge the economic value of such a good is not an easy task, in particular if there is a need to maintain, preserve, or conserve cultural assets through public interventions. Are the costs justified in light of social and economic benefits? It should be noted that the benefits are usually not only related to the direct use value (such as in the form of tourism revenues) but also to the broader spillover effects (and externalities) on the entire urban fabric (the "urban ensemble"). This urban ensemble comprises a portfolio of physical historic-cultural assets that represent a delivery of cultural, artistic, or architectural values to society at large, such as museums (and objects therein), churches, castles, monuments, artistic expressions, historic districts, or even landscapes. From this perspective, cultural heritage is essentially a club good (that is, shared by many people in a large group) in the sense of Buchanan (Buchanan 1965).

The previous observations provide a context for assessing the economic value of cultural heritage, but the valuation task itself is fraught with many uncertainties and dilemmas. The economic literature offers a wide array of possible evaluation approaches (Mitchell and Carson 1989; Schuster 2003). These may range from preferences expressed by behavioral-oriented approaches based on often fictitious beliefs or legends to stated preference methods (such as contingent valuation analysis or conjoint analysis) to multi-attribute utility methods or market-based methods (such as travel cost methods or hedonic price methods). At this point a concise overview based on Lazrak is presented (Lazrak et al. 2011a). This work by Lazrak also offers a review of pros and cons of the array of methods in use, as well as of the conditions under which such methods may provide a meaningful evaluation. It should be added that most methods described here can be classified under the heading of "monetary analysis" (see previous section of this chapter) and partly also under the heading of "decision support analysis." "Performance indicators analysis" receives less attention here, as this is more of an engineering type of approach than an economic valuation analysis.

Compensation Methods

Compensation methods in the evaluation of cultural heritage are linked to the applied welfare-theoretic methods and seek to find the sacrifices and revenues involved with a change in the availability or quality of a cultural asset (Lazrak et al. 2011a). If a cultural good is demolished, then the financial compensation for the loss of this good may be estimated by assessing the costs of reconstructing the asset. This does not necessarily imply an actual physical rebuilding of the asset concerned, and hence a virtual compensation can also take place. It should be noted that a lost cultural heritage good may also be compensated for by the construction of another, new heritage good with at least the same cultural quality value. This approach is increasingly used in urban planning.

There are numerous examples of old buildings (including castles, mansions, and pavilions or even small towns; for instance, Bruges in Belgium, and Willemstad in Curaçao) that have been conserved, partly or entirely, after a period of decay. In such cases, the amount of money necessary to restore a physical cultural heritage good in its historic state provides a shadow price for that good that offers useful information for compensation costs in project evaluation. Hypothetically, it will then be worthwhile to rebuild or restore an asset when its social value is at least equal to its shadow price.

However, in many cases, also in valuing cultural heritage, it is hard to determine its shadow price or it is uncertain whether the social value will exceed its shadow price unless a further thorough investigation into the various use values of the good in question is undertaken. It is clear that an important limitation of any compensation method is the fact that it presupposes substitutability of the good concerned, either in physical terms or in monetary terms. If a good is seen as exclusive or even unique, then a major evaluation problem emerges, although the system of insurance values and insurance premiums offers some way out.

Social Cost-Benefit Methods

Social cost-benefit analysis has a long history in the economics of project evaluation methods. In the cost-benefit analysis tradition, a sophisticated toolbox has been developed over the years to deal with complex project evaluation issues, sometimes with large spillover effects. In the past decade, many attempts have also been made to incorporate intangible environmental effects into these calculation schemes. In the past decades, two complementary evaluation methods have emerged: economic impact assessment and multicriteria analysis.

From the perspective of cultural goods (Tyrrell and Johnston 2006), one can describe economic impact analysis as seeking "to estimate changes in regional spending, output, income and/or employment associated with tourism policy, events, facilities of destinations" (Tyrrell and Johnston 2006, 3). Economic impact studies can be used for valuing various types of cultural heritage, especially cultural heritage that attracts large numbers of tourists who spend money from outside the impact area (Snowball 2008, 33). Such impact studies try to monetize the direct and indirect effects of an event on an impact area. Snowball points out that these impact studies focus mainly on the private good character of the arts that is usually captured by market transactions instead of merit or public good characteristics. This is a limitation that is comparable to that of a compensation method, as described above. But it is clear that, especially at the interface of tourism and cultural heritage, cost-benefit studies have provided a meaningful contribution, often in combination with revealed or stated preference methods.

To measure directly net impacts of cultural heritage goals on user groups, it is important to identify the main spending groups in the impact region affected by the cultural asset concerned. Spending groups that otherwise would spend their money in another way in the impact area will have to be identified. It is important to take into account only the spending that otherwise would not have occurred. Next, indirect net impacts depend on chain effects or induced effects of direct net impacts for the impact area. Clearly, the amount of leakage in a multiplier sense depends on the size and nature of the impact area (Snowball 2008). Baaijens and Nijkamp offer an empirical meta-analysis approach with regard to those leakages in tourist regions and present a rough set analysis approach to estimate income multipliers for different characteristics of such impact areas (Van Leeuwen et al. 2006).

Economic assessment studies raise abundant methodological and conceptual concerns (Snowball 2008). A main criticism is that the demarcation of the impact area influences the outcomes of the study: there are alternative spending opportunities and, therefore, the size of the impact area influences the size of those alternatives. Another caveat is that redistribution issues usually remain implicit. Especially with regard to cultural events, rich residents usually profit more than poor residents (Richards 1996). Impact studies are also plagued by methodological issues in valuing the public good characteristics of cultural goods. Costs can be measured relatively easily, but when cultural goods are free of charge the benefits are hard to quantify. So there may be significant distributional consequences involved.

Another strand of the evaluation literature focuses on methods that do not require a monetary translation of relevant socioeconomic impacts, but that are able to capture in principle all relevant intangible effects. These methods are usually grouped under the heading of multicriteria analysis (Nijkamp et al. 1990). Research cases can be found to show how and where multicriteria analysis in the cultural heritage field may be applied (Coccossis and Nijkamp 1995). Multicriteria analysis offers an opportunity to assess and weight simultaneously qualitative and quantitative effects of plans or programs. Given the broad range of value-generating aspects of cultural heritage, multicriteria analysis allows one, in principle, to deal also with qualitative categorical information in economic evaluation and to address policy trade-offs by assigning policy weights to the different attributes of cultural heritage. Often multicriteria analysis is pursued on an item-by-item stated preference evaluation in regard to different policy criteria. Such criteria may not only relate to economic aspects but also to social, environmental, and broader cultural aspects.

This approach allows one to take account of distributional issues, by either including distributional elements explicitly in the evaluation criteria or by having such interests reflected in the weight vector in a multi-criteria analysis. The multicriteria approach is adequate in the case of the assessment of distinct alternatives to be decided on, but is less effective when it comes to a broader societal evaluation of cultural heritage.

Stated Preference Methods

Stated preference analysis is essentially rooted in behavioral economics, but in the past decades it has found extensive application in the case of economic evaluation of non-market or quasi-market goods, when the essential evaluation concept centers on the individual willingness to pay. For a market good, the marginal willingness to pay is equal to its price, which is clearly convenient for applied welfare analysis. However, many valuable goods are not traded on a market—and cultural heritage offers many examples, such as the benefits of living in historic city districts. An optimal design of public policies for cultural heritage calls for an estimate of the willingness to pay also for non-market goods.

In general, stated preference methods aim to uncover what individuals are willing to pay or are willing to accept in case of a change in the availability of a public good. This research is often conducted through the use of survey questionnaires. (See box 4.4.) Contingent valuation methods form an important subclass of preference elicitation methods and focus directly on willingness to pay by using open-ended questions (Mitchell and Carson 1989). A second subset of stated preference techniques is based on choice experiments, in which one tries to estimate the preferences of people from the choices they make between bundles of attributes that describe the good to be valued at different levels (Noonan 2003; Snowball 2008). Although conjoint choice analysis extracts the willingness to pay

BOX 4.4

A Variety of Techniques Are Used to Estimate the Benefits of Investments in Confucius' Hometown

China, Shandong Confucius and Mencius Cultural Heritage Conservation and Development Project (Project number 120234)
Total Project Cost: US$130.78 million
Total Loan Amount: US$50 million
Approved: May 2011 – Ongoing

The objective of the project is to assist Shandong province in enhancing cultural heritage conservation and tourism development in Qufu and Zouchen— the hometowns, respectively, of Confucius and Mencius, his disciple. The components include support for: (1) key conservation works; (2) improved signage, interpretation, and displays; (3) urban redevelopment and improvements for water supply and wastewater infrastructure; (4) conservation of historic houses; and (5) capacity building, including design of manuals and guidelines focused on historic city regeneration.

Three different valuation techniques were employed to estimate economic benefits of the project. Productivity change technique was employed to estimate incremental economic earnings from improved tourist services associated with the project. Hedonic valuation technique was employed to estimate increased value of land and real estate properties due to the project. Contingent valuation was applied to capture the tourist enjoyment of improved heritage values (or the consumer's surplus of tourist services). The final results of the analysis for Qufu can be summarized as follows. The present value of the total economic benefits (at a discount rate of 8 percent) amounts to CNY1,577.30 million, and the total cost in present value terms is CNY784.18 million. The economic internal rate of return on the investment would be 27.5 percent, with a net present value of CNY793.13 million (US$116.64 million) and a benefit-cost ratio of 2.01.

Source: Shandong Confucius and Mencius Cultural Heritage Conservation and Development Project Appraisal Document.

in a more indirect way than contingent valuation methods, the former's focus on concrete choices is generally regarded as an advantage because it reduces the risk that respondents indicate a willingness to pay on the basis of a subjective perception or a superficial impression of the nature of the good in question. Indeed, such methods may be very relevant for cultural heritage evaluation.

The ability of stated preference methods to identify quasi-market values for non-market goods has one major down side: the hypothetical character of the statements made by consumers raises questions about their methodological reliability in investigating and assessing the willingness to pay of the consumers in actual cases (Arrow et al. 1993; Hoevenagel 1994; Murphy et al. 2005; Snowball 2008). Several biases in stated preference methods have been identified in the literature (Kahneman and Knetsch 1992; Snowball 2008). In particular, it has been observed that the stated willingness to pay often differs significantly from the willingness to accept, as paying and receiving are not necessarily symmetric due to a ceiling caused by income availability (Kahneman et al. 1990, 1991; Morrison 1997a, 1997b).

Over the years, various amendments have been introduced that reduce the risk of some strategic biases in preference statements. Snowball (2008) also identifies various potential problems in the literature with regard to the conjoint analysis method, as there may be problems related to complexity and choice consistency as well as to individual valuation and summation. Snowball also mentions in the context of cultural goods two reasons why a mixed good—with both private and public goods characteristics—could cause a bias. In the first place, there is an incentive for users to overstate its non-use value (Throsby 1984). Secondly, willingness-to-pay studies may also capture expected economic benefits that do not only reflect present earnings but also bequest earnings (Seaman 2003). Nevertheless, it seems plausible that research conducted according to the United States National Oceanic and Atmospheric Administration (NOAA) recommendations[1] by Arrow et al. (1993) is more valid, more reliable, and reduces the size of a number of biases (Noonan 2003; Snowball 2008). Benefits or value transfers can be used if estimations in one context can be generalized to indicate values in other similar contexts. It is thus clear that the validity and reliability of contingent valuation methods—and stated preference methods in general—are still matters of debate (Diamond and Hausman 1994), especially in situations in which benefit transfers are harder to realize.

Over the years, there have been various applied studies using stated preference methods for the evaluation of cultural heritage assets. One of the first contingent valuations of cultural heritage is found in a study to value the Nidaros Cathedral in Norway (Navrud and Strand 1992). Subsequently, stated preference techniques for the evaluation of cultural heritage have been applied in numerous evaluation studies. Noonan (2003) offers a meta-analysis of this rich literature. Snowball (2008) provides an update of the contingent valuation literature, in which the application of conjoint choice experiments in the cultural economics field is also reviewed. More recent examples include a study by Alberini et al. (2003) on the value of the cultural and historical dimensions of a square in a city, done by comparing the actual square with a hypothetical square that is similar but without the same cultural and historical dimensions. The authors conclude that aesthetic and use attributes contribute to the explanation of the hypothetical choices individuals made.

An example of a conjoint choice experiment recently undertaken by Willis (2009) concerns a case study on the preferences of visitors in the management of Hadrian's Roman Wall (United Kingdom), with a particular view to the interaction effects between the attributes of an archaeological or heritage site. The study concludes that visitors to the Vindolanda site were clearly able to state their preferences for the future management of the archaeological site.

Finally, a very recent application of stated preference methods can be found in a case study (Neuts and Nijkamp 2011a) on the critical evaluation attributes of visitors of the historic city of Bruges in Belgium. This very popular tourist destination is faced with severe congestion effects during the tourist high season, which reduces visitors' appreciation of the city.

Revealed Preference Methods

The following methods focus on market outcomes derived from real market transactions. One important class is the travel cost method, based on the total cost people are prepared to pay to visit a particular cultural site. The hedonic price method is the price actors are willing to pay for real estate objects that are considered as cultural heritage or are located in the proximity of such objects (that is, an externality case). These two approaches will be discussed next.

Travel Cost Method

Visiting cultural heritage means that one has to travel to its location. The associated travel cost—the financial sacrifice to get there, including entry tickets and accommodation costs—acts as a price for the visit and indicates the consumer's willingness to pay for the cultural heritage good. The costs of visiting the cultural heritage good do not only refer to monetary outlays but also to the time spent at the site and all other costs that stem from that visit (Navrud and Ready 2002; Snowball 2008). The demand curve for the cultural heritage good can be derived from the differences in travel costs incurred by different classes of visitors. In this way, one can use a traditional demand analysis, even if there is not, strictly speaking, an unambiguous (ticket) price associated with the visit. The travel cost method has some intrinsic problems. In the first place, travel cost methods are faced with the problem of multipurpose trips. A tourist visiting several cultural heritage goods will find it hard to distinguish which part of the costs of the trip can be assigned to a particular cultural heritage good, as he buys essentially a non-separable bundle of goods. A related problem is that the visitor to a cultural heritage good can derive utility from the trip itself or from the company in which the journey occurs (social externalities). Secondly, the opportunity costs of a visitor are hard to estimate; currently, the visitor's wage is often used to value the opportunity cost (Navrud and Ready 2002). Thirdly, with travel cost methods, substitutes of cultural heritage can cause distortions and create difficulties to assess direct effects. Finally, when people who choose to live in the vicinity of cultural heritage have a high preference for cultural assets, the distance to the cultural heritage site itself is then a residential location factor, which may cause complications in estimating the related demand function as the basis for economic valuation.

The literature offers various examples of cultural heritage studies that aim to estimate the values of these assets by means of the travel cost method. These include the use of a site choice model to estimate the value of different Dutch museums (Boter et al. 2005) and the estimate of the consumer surplus of four cultural heritage goods in the Castilla y Leon region in Spain on the basis of a travel cost method (Bedate et al. 2004). Another study used methods that combine the travel cost with contingent valuation carried out to value cultural heritage in Armenia; this approach also offers interesting opportunities to separate use and non-use values (Alberini and Longo 2006). The approach of using travel cost studies has gained momentum in applied evaluation studies, despite the above-mentioned limitations.

Hedonic Price Method

The hedonic price method takes for granted that "goods are valued for their utility-bearing attributes or characteristics" (Rosen 1974). This approach is based on the idea that prices of heterogeneous goods stem from the characteristics of attribute variety. Although Rosen's original analyses were developed for a market with perfect competition, the method is applicable under alternative market conditions (Bajari and Benkard 2005; Rouwendal and van der Straaten 2008). Clearly, hedonic price methods carry some intrinsic weaknesses. For example, a study points out that the measurement of different attributes of the hedonic price method raises questions about the correct model specification (Jones and Dunse 1996).

In a later study, the same authors criticize the fact that the method reaches an equilibrium state throughout the property market and no interrelationship between the price of attributes is found (Dunse and Jones 1998). It is noteworthy that hedonic price analysis, in principle, may contain many variables that influence the value of real estate. In a conventional cross-section analysis, limited information on potentially relevant characteristics implies the risk of omitted variable bias. In addition, some other value determinants may be strongly correlated with the variable of interest; for instance, an architectural feature that is typical for a particular period or style.

Despite some important limitations, the use of hedonic price analysis may be promising for gaining a better understanding of the value of cultural heritage. In particular, the recently emerging availability of large databases—constructed, for instance, by the land registry or cadastral offices—may lead to detailed information on transactions in the real estate market. Such data systems are especially useful if they comprise disaggregated data on the characteristics of the properties sold. In this context, Geographic Information System (GIS) techniques often offer the possibility to further enrich such data with mapping of information about geographic neighborhood characteristics. With such data, the problem of omitted variables can be mitigated considerably, while the large number of observations enables the analyst to incorporate a satisfactory number of moderator variables.

The literature offers various hedonic price studies on cultural heritage, sometimes in relation to the designation of a building as cultural heritage through the "listing" process (Coulson and Lahr 2005; Leichenko et al. 2001). The first study estimating a full hedonic price function was undertaken by Ford in the American city of Baltimore (Ford 1989); in his reports, a positive impact of designation on property values was found. More recently, a study used a hedonic price function to estimate the market price difference between listed heritage and regular, unlisted houses in Sydney's upper North Shore (Deodhar 2004). A hedonic pricing method was also used to monetize housing value with respect to cultural heritage in the old Hanseatic town of Tiel in the Netherlands (Ruijgrok 2006). The author found that historical characteristics had a positive impact of almost 15 percent. Insights into the different effects that property designation and district designation have on property value is offered by Noonan (2007). He estimates a hedonic price function on data from the Multiple Listing Service of northern Illinois, United States, which includes Chicago. As explanatory dummy variables, an indicator for allocation in a designated historic district ("district") and an indicator for historic designation of an individual property ("landmark") are included. Prices of landmarks are higher than those of otherwise comparable houses, while for districts a smaller premium is estimated.

There are several hedonic studies that evaluate architecture and focus on architectural quality in a city (Hough and Kratz 1983; Ruijgrok 2006; Vandell and Lane 1989; Moorhouse and Smith 1994). Several authors have looked specifically at architectural style, details of façade features, historical or architectural quality, and similar factors. For example, in their study that asked "Can 'good' architecture meet the market test?" Hough and Kratz (1983) investigated the way the office market of downtown Chicago values "good" architecture and concluded that a considerable rent premium is paid for "good" new architecture, but not for "good" old architecture. Similarly, Moorhouse and Smith (1994) explained the original purchase price of houses related to relevant architectural characteristics identified through visual inspections of houses that were built between 1850 and 1874. Finally, there are also studies on the effect of churches on neighborhood quality. In particular, a regression of church amenities on transaction prices of neighborhood property allows one to assess the effect of the cultural heritage component of churches on house values (Carroll et al. 1996; Do et al. 1994). An overview of various hedonic price studies in the area of cultural heritage valuation is contained in table 4.1. There is indeed an increasing volume of hedonic price studies in the area of urban cultural assets. It appears, however, that a detailed analysis of spatial proximity and externalities related to cultural heritage is largely lacking. An illustration of the latter type of study will be offered in the next section.

A Spatial Hedonic Price Study on the Impact of Cultural Heritage on Real Estate Value

Hedonic pricing has been discussed in the previous section. Indeed, real estate prices in a city—especially in historic inner-city areas—are codetermined by the ambience of these neighborhoods, reflecting such features as cultural amenities, historic buildings, or the "historic-cultural ensemble" of the city as a whole. These amenities enhance the attractiveness of inner cities for residents, and hence tend to increase the value of real estate (Brueckner et al. 1999; Glaeser et al. 2001). These conditions may offer an interesting case for testing the empirical relevance of spatial hedonic pricing models in cultural heritage valuation.

This section will focus on an empirical example of the spatial-economic effects of the presence of cultural assets (namely, listed heritage assets) on the price of real estate in areas of the Dutch city of Zaanstad (Lazrak et al. 2011b).[2] This city is endowed with a wealth of cultural heritage originating from its prominent position as a seaport in the Dutch Golden Age. The basic assumption tested, as described below, is that cultural heritage offers net positive externalities.

The hedonic price study concerned uses a spatial econometric model to estimate (1) the direct effect of monument status on the market price of a given house, and (2) the indirect externality effect of urban monuments on the value of nearby property. The analysis is based on an extensive micro-data set regarding some 20,000 individual housing transactions over 22 years (1985–2007). The entire urban areas of Zaanstad contain 281 national monuments, 64 provincial monuments, and 150 municipal monuments. Complete

TABLE 4.1

Overview of Hedonic Price Studies with Regard to Cultural Heritage

Authors	Study	Study area	Key findings
Narwold et al. (2008)	Effect of designated historic houses on sale price	San Diego, California, U.S.	Historic designation of single-family residences creates a 16 percent increase in housing value, which is higher than the capitalization of the property tax savings due to designation.
Noonan (2007)	Effect of landmarks and districts on sale price	Chicago, Illinois, U.S.	Designated property has a positive effect on both itself and neighboring properties.
Ruijgrok (2006)	Effect of authenticity, ensemble, and landmark designation on house prices	Tiel, The Netherlands	Authenticity and façade elements account for 15 percent of sale prices in the Hanseatic city of Tiel.
Coulson and Lahr (2005)	Effect of district designation on appreciation rate	Memphis, Tennessee, U.S.	Appreciation rates were 14–23 percent higher when properties were in neighborhoods that were zoned historic. In this case, local designation proved to be more important than national designation.
Deodhar (2004)	Effect of heritage listing on sale prices	Sydney, Australia	On average, heritage listed houses commanded a 12 percent premium over non-listed houses. This premium is a combined value of the houses' heritage character, their architectural style elements, and their statutory listing status.
Coulson and Leichenko (2001)	Effect of designation on tax-appraisal value	Abilene, Texas, U.S.	Local historic designation raises value of designated property by 17.6 percent.
Leichenko et al. (2001)	Effect of historic designation on house prices	Nine different Texas cities, U.S.	Historically designated properties in Texas enjoy 5–20 percent higher appraised prices than other property.

Asabere and Huffman (1994a)	Effect of federal historic district on sale prices	Philadelphia, Pennsylvania, U.S.	Owner-occupied property located in national historic districts in Philadelphia sell at a premium of 26 percent.
Asabere and Huffman (1994b)	Effect of historic façade easements on sale prices	Philadelphia, Pennsylvania, U.S.	Condominiums with historic easements sell for about 30 percent less than comparable properties.
Asabere et al. (1994)	Sales effects of local preservation	Philadelphia, Pennsylvania, U.S.	Small historic apartment buildings experience a 24 percent reduction in price compared to properties not locally certified as historic.
Moorhouse and Smith (1994)	Effect of architecture on original purchase price	Boston, Massachusetts, U.S.	Architecture design was valued with a premium.
Schaeffer and Millerick (1991)	Impact of historic district on sale prices	Chicago, Illinois, U.S.	Properties with national historic designation have a premium and local historic designation have a discount over non-designated properties. Properties near a historic district may enjoy positive externalities.
Asabere et al. (1989)	Effect of architecture and historic district on home value	Newburyport, Massachusetts, U.S.	Historic architectural styles have positive premiums. The historic district of Newburyport does not have positive external effects.
Ford (1989)	Price effects of local historic districts	Baltimore, Maryland, U.S.	Historic districts do have higher prices than non-historic districts.
Vandell and Lane (1989)	Effect of design quality on rent and vacancy behavior on the office market	Boston and Cambridge, Massachusetts, U.S.	Design quality has a positive premium of 22 percent on rents, but there is a weak relationship between vacancy behavior and design quality.
Hough and Kratz (1983)	The effect of architectural quality on office rents	Chicago, Illinois, U.S.	Tenants are willing to pay a premium to be in new architecturally significant office building, but apparently see no benefits associated with old office buildings that express recognized aesthetics excellence.

Source: Lazrak et al. 2009; this includes sources for all studies cited.

GIS-based information on the nature and location of these cultural heritage assets is available on all items in this research, regarding the dwellings sales as well as regarding their features and their sales. The main question addressed is whether there is a significant difference between listed heritage and dwellings sold in a cultural, historic urban landscape as compared to other (comparable) dwellings sold.

For the spatial-econometric analysis of hedonic prices, the following model has been used:

- $\ln P = f$ (intercept, transactional attributes, structural characteristics, spatial features, and heritage characteristics) in which P is the market price of the dwelling sold. The determinants of the housing prices will be concisely described.
- Transactional attributes refer to leasehold conditions, to the question of whether the house is newly built, as well as to the selling conditions of the property.
- Structural characteristics comprise such factors as floor area, capacity, number of rooms, presence of gas heater, dwelling insulation, maintenance conditions (indoors and outdoors), existence of garden, presence of parking space, housing type, and year of construction.
- Spatial features are related to the location near a busy street, proximity to open water, population density, foreign population housed in the neighborhood, distance to city center, and nature of the village.
- Finally, heritage characteristics refer to the question of whether the property (building, monument in urban historic landscape) has relevance in terms of its architectural beauty, meaning for science, or historic-cultural value—in some cases defined as the building having a minimum age of 50 years.

It should be added that estimation of the above spatial hedonic model calls for proper spatial autocorrelation test statistics.

The impact of heritage housing can be assessed in a direct and an indirect manner. The direct estimation aims to assess the difference with otherwise comparable houses that are not listed, while the indirect effect aims to gauge the impact of the proximity of the listed heritage (within a radius of 50 meters) on the value of non-listed houses in the same area, as well as the impact that sold houses in a historic, protected urban landscape experienced compared to other sold houses. Admittedly, a listed heritage status also implies restrictions on the free use of the property, but the counter-side is that there is also a possibility to obtain subsidies or tax exemptions on a listed monument.

Several interesting results were obtained by applying two variants of the hedonic price model outlined above, particularly for variant 1 with a monument dummy and listed heritage in a 50-meter radius, but also for variant 2 with a monument dummy and location in a protected historic landscape.

Variant 1 leads then to the following empirical findings:

- A dwelling that is designated with a heritage status is worth approximately 21 percent more than a comparable house without a monument status (in monetary terms, €33,600).
- An additional house with a heritage status raises the average value of all other houses within a 50-meter radius by 0.24 percent (in monetary terms, €384 per dwelling).

Variant 2 offers the following results:

- A dwelling with the listed heritage characteristic has an additional value of approximately 19.5 percent (in monetary terms, €31,200).
- Any dwelling located in a protected historic urban landscape is worth approximately 23.4 percent more (in monetary terms, €37,400).

A subsequent question can be raised regarding how sensitive the results are to the assumed spatial distance parameter of 50 meters. This calls for an extensive sensitivity analysis. If we use a spatial-econometric hedonic price model, it has been estimated with a distance contiguity matrix of 1,000 meters. Using again the two variants outlined above, the following results are found.

Variant 1 provides the following estimated results:

- A house with a heritage status commands an additional value of approximately 26.9 percent (in monetary terms, €41,100).
- An additional house with a listed heritage character in an urban area raises the value of all other houses within the 50-meter action radius by 0.28 percent (that is, €430).

Variant 2 leads to the following findings:

- A dwelling with a listed heritage character has approximately 23.8 percent more worth (that is, €31,200).
- Any house in a historic, protected urban area gains an additional value of approximately 26.4 percent (that is, €42,200).

Based on the above presented empirical findings, the following overall conclusions can be drawn:

- A dwelling with a listed heritage status gains a direct value premium ranging from 19.5 to 26.9 percent;
- Any additional dwelling obtaining a monument status leads to an additional value premium of all houses in the vicinity (50-meter radius) ranging from 0.24 to 0.28 percent; and
- Dwellings in a protected historic-cultural area gain a 23.4 to 26.4 percent premium compared to dwellings outside this area.

This study (Lazrak et al. 2011b) has clearly demonstrated that: (1) dwellings on a heritage list capture a positive premium for their own value, (2) these heritage houses also generate positive premium effects for other dwellings in the 50-meter vicinity, and (3) dwellings located in a "historic-cultural ensemble" also capture an additional property value.

Conclusion

Cultural heritage is a broad concept that may have a multiplicity of meanings and perceptions. Sometimes it is conceived of as a nation's or city's collection of historic buildings, monuments, countryside, and landscapes that are—because of their socio-cultural and historical importance—worthy of preservation. Others may be inclined to interpret also a typical local ambience or atmosphere, a recognized cultural environment, or an artistic neighborhood as cultural heritage—all based on the concept of historic endowment that forms the historic environment. These two interpretations come close to the concept of cultural capital, as advocated by Bourdieu (1984).

The societal role attached to cultural heritage designation is reflected in the economic surplus value that accrues to urban land rent in a competitive urban economy. In particular, the premium on real estate located in historic-cultural districts or the direct premiums accrued for a house as a result of being listed as heritage offer a promising departure for a solid economic analysis of value capturing in historic sites. From the perspective of a market evaluation of cultural heritage, the hedonic pricing model offers great potential to assess the additional economic value of real estate in the case of its location being adjacent to cultural assets. This approach also offers many opportunities for value transfer of findings from a given case study to comparable sites or monuments. Needless to say, conducting a thorough economic investigation into the market aspects of cultural heritage—through advanced spatial hedonic price models—will pose a formidable challenge in the years to come.

Notes

1. The National Oceanic and Atmospheric Administration (NOAA) reviewed the use of contingent valuation and concluded that, if its guidelines and recommendations were followed, "contingent valuation studies can produce estimates reliable enough to be the starting point of a judicial process of damage assessment, including lost passive-use values" (NOAA, 1993, 24).
2. In this chapter it is presented in a summary form with the main methodology and results.

References

Alberini, A., and A. Longo. 2006. "Combining the Travel Cost and Contingent Behavior Methods to Value Cultural Heritage Sites: Evidence from Armenia." *Journal of Cultural Economics* 30 (30): 287–304.

Alberini, A., P. Riganti, and A. Longo. 2003. "Can People Value the Aesthetic and Use Services of Urban Sites? Evidence from a Survey of Belfast Residents." *Journal of Cultural Economics* 27: 193–213.

Arizpe, L., A. B. Preis, and M. Taurus. 2000. *World Culture Report 2000: Cultural Diversity, Conflict and Pluralism.* Paris: UNESCO.

Arrow, K., R. Solow, P. R. Portney, E. Leamer, R. Radner, and H. Schuman. 1993. "Report of the NOAA Panel on Contingent Valuation." *Federal Register* 58: 4601–4614.

Baaijens, S., and P. Nijkamp. 2000. "Meta-Analytic Methods for Comparative and Exploratory Policy Research: An Application to the Assessment of Regional Tourist Multipliers." *Journal of Policy Modeling* 22: 821–858.

Bajari, P., and C. L. Benkard. 2005. "Demand Estimation with Heterogeneous Consumers and Unobserved Product Characteristics: A Hedonic Approach." *Journal of Political Economy* 113: 1239–1276.

Bedate, A., L. C. Herrero, and J. Sanz. 2004. "Economic Valuation of the Cultural Heritage: Application to Four Case Studies in Spain." *Journal of Cultural Heritage* 5: 101–111.

Beer, S. 1971. "Questions of Metric." *Operations Research Quarterly* 22: 133–144.

Boter, J., R. Rouwendal, and M. Wedel. 2005. "Employing Travel Time to Compare the Value of Competing Cultural Organizations." *Journal of Cultural Economics* 29: 19–33.

Bourdieu, P. 1984. *Distinction: A Social Critique of the Judgment of Taste.* Cambridge, MA: Harvard University Press.

Brueckner, J. K., J. F. Thisse, and Y. Zenou. 1999. "Why Is Central Paris Rich and Downtown Detroit Poor?" *European Economic Review* 43: 91–107.

Buchanan, J. M. 1965. "An Economic Theory of Clubs." *Economica* 32: 1–14.

Carroll, T. M., T. M. Clauretie, and J. Jensen. 1996. "Living Next to Godliness: Residential Property Values and Churches." *The Journal of Real Estate Finance and Economics* 12: 319–330.

Carruthers, J., and B. Mundy. 2006. *Environmental Valuation: Interregional and Intraregional Perspectives.* Aldershot: Ashgate.

Choi, A. S., B. W. Ritchie, F. Papandrea, and J. Bennett. 2010. "Economic Valuation of Cultural Heritage Sites: A Choice Modeling Approach." *Tourism Management* 31 (2): 213–220.

Churchman, C. W. 1972. "On the Facility, Felicity, and Morality of Measuring Social Change." In *Accounting for Social Goals*, ed. J. L. Livingstone and S. C. Gunn, 17–22. New York: Harper & Row.

Coccossis, H., and P. Nijkamp, eds. 1995. *Planning for our Cultural Heritage.* Aldershot: Ashgate.

Coulson, N. E., and M. L. Lahr. 2005. "Gracing the Land of Elvis and Bells Street: Historic Designation and Property Values in Memphis." *Real Estate Economics* 33 (3): 487–507.

Deodhar, V. 2004. "Does the Housing Market Value Heritage? Some Empirical Evidence." In *Research Papers from Macquarie University*, Macquarie University no. 403. Sydney: Macquarie University.

Diamond, P., and J. A. Hausman. 1994. "Contingent Valuation: Is Some Number Better Than No Number?" *Journal of Economic Perspectives* 8 (4): 45–65.

Do, A. Q., R. W. Wilbur, and J. L. Short. 1994. "An Empirical Examination of the Externalities of Neighborhood Churches on Housing Values." *The Journal of Real Estate Finance and Economics* 9: 127–136.

Dunse, N., and C. Jones. 1998. "A Hedonic Price Model of Office Rents." *Journal of Property Valuation and Investment* 16: 297–312.

Eilon, S. 1972. "Goals and Constraints in Decision-Making." In *Accounting for Social Goals*, ed. J. L. Livingstone and S. C. Gunn, 218–230. New York: Harper & Row.

Ford, D. A. 1989. "The Effect of Historic District Designation on Single-Family Home Prices." *Real Estate Economics* 17: 353–362.

Fromm, G., and P. Tauber. 1973. *Public Economic Theory and Policy*. New York: MacMillan.

Fusco Girard, L. 1987. *Risorse Architettoniche e Culturali*. Milano: Franco Angeli.

Glaeser, E. L, J. Kolko, and A. Saiz. 2001. "Consumer City." *Journal of Economic Geography* 1: 27–50.

Greenley, D. A., R. G. Walsh, and R. A. Young. 1981. "Option Value: Empirical Evidence from a Case Study of Recreation and Water Quality." *Quarterly Journal of Economics* 95: 657–673.

Hagerhall, C. M. 2000. "Clustering Predictors of Landscape Preference in the Traditional Swedish Cultural Landscape." *Journal of Environmental Psychology* 20: 83–90.

Hoevenagel, R. 1994. *The Contingent Valuation Method: Scope and Validity*. Amsterdam: Vrije Universiteit.

Hough, D. E., and C. G. Kratz. 1983. "Can 'Good' Architecture Meet the Market Test?" *Journal of Urban Economics* 14: 40–54.

Hubbard, P. 1993. "The Value of Conservation." *Town Planning Review* 64 (4): 359–373.

Hyman, E. L., and M. M. Hufschmidt. 1983. "The Relevance of Natural Resource Economics in Environmental Planning." Working paper, The East-West Centre, Honolulu.

Kahneman, D., and J. L. Knetsch. 1992. "Valuing Public Goods: The Purchase of Moral Satisfaction." *Journal of Environmental Economics and Management* 22: 57–70.

Kahneman, D., J. L. Knetsch, and R. H. Thaler. 1990. "Experimental Tests of the Endowment Effect and the Coase Theorem." *Journal of Political Economy* 98: 1325.

Kahneman, D., J. L. Knetsch, and R. H. Thaler. 1991. "Anomalies: The Endowment Effect, Loss Aversion, and Status Quo Bias." *Journal of Economic Perspectives* 5: 193–206.

Kalman, H. 1980. The *Evaluation of Historic Buildings*. Ottawa: Ministry of Environment.

Klamer, A., and P. W. Zuidhof. 1999. "The Values of Cultural Heritage: Merging Economic and Cultural Appraisals." *Economics and Heritage Conservation: A Meeting Organized by the Getty Conservation Institute, December 1998*, ed. R. Mason, 23–61. Los Angeles: Getty Institute.

Lazrak, F., P. Nijkamp, P. Rietveld, and J. Rouwendal. 2009. "Cultural Heritage: Hedonic Prices for Non-Market Values." In *Markets and Politics,* ed. W. Schäfer, A. Schneider, and T. Thomas, 285–299. Maiburg: Metropolis.

Lazrak, F., P. Nijkamp, P. Rietveld, and J. Rouwendal. 2011a. "Cultural Heritage and Creative Cities: An Economic Evaluation Perspective." In *Sustainable City and Creativity, ed.* L. Fusco Girard, and P. Nijkamp. 225–245. Aldershot: Ashgate.

Lazrak, F., P. Nijkamp, P. Rietveld, and J. Rouwendal. 2011b. "The Market Value of Listed Heritage." Research Paper, Dept. of Spatial Economics, VU University, Amsterdam.

Leichenko, R. M., N. E. Coulson, and D. Listokin. 2001. "Historic Preservation and Residential Property Values: An Analysis of Texas Cities." *Urban Studies* 38: 19–73.

Lichfield, N. 1989. *Economics in Urban Conservation.* Cambridge: Cambridge University Press..

Little, I. M. D., and J. A. Mirrlees. 1974. *Project Appraisal and Planning for Developing Countries.* London: Heineman Educational Books.

Mitchell, R. C., and R. T. Carson. 1989. *Using Surveys to Value Public Goods.* Washington, DC: Resources for the Future.

Moorhouse, J. C., and M. S. Smith. 1994. "The Market for Residential Architecture: 19th-Century Row Houses in Boston's South End." *Journal of Urban Economics* 35: 267–277.

Morrison, G. C. 1997a. "Resolving Differences in Willingness to Pay and Willingness to Accept: Comment." *American Economic Review* 87: 236–240.

Morrison, G. C. 1997b. "Willingness to Pay and Willingness to Accept: Some Evidence of an Endowment Effect." *Applied Economics* 29: 411–417.

Murphy, J. J., P. G. Allen, T. H. Stevens, and D. Weatherhead. 2005. "A Meta-analysis of Hypothetical Bias in Stated Preference Valuation." *Environmental and Resource Economics* 30: 313–325.

Navrud, S., and J. Strand. 1992. "The Preservation Value of Nidaros Cathedral." *Pricing the European Environment,* ed. S. Navrud. Oxford: Oxford University Press.

Navrud, S., and R. C. Ready, eds. 2002. *Valuing Cultural Heritage: Applying Environmental Valuation Techniques.* Cheltenham: Edward Elgar.

Neuts, B., and P. Nijkamp. 2011a. "Strangers on the Move." Research Paper, Dept. of Spatial Economic, VU University, Amsterdam, 2011a.

Neuts, B., and P. Nijkamp. 2011b. "Crowding Perception in a Tourist City." Research Paper, Dept. of Spatial Economics, VU University, Amsterdam.

Nijkamp, P., and P. Riganti. 2008. "Assessing Cultural Heritage Benefits for Urban Sustainable Development." *International Journal of Services Technology and Management* 10 (1): 29–38.

Nijkamp, P., and P. Riganti. 2009. "Valuing Urban Cultural Heritage." In *Cultural Tourism and Sustainable Local Development,* ed. L. Fusco Girard and P. Nijkamp, 57–72. Aldershot: Ashgate.

Nijkamp, P., P. Rietveld, and H. Voogd. 1990. *Multicriteria Evaluation in Physical Planning.* Amsterdam: Elsevier.

Noonan, D. S. 2003. "Contingent Valuation and Cultural Resources: A Meta-analytic Review of the Literature." *Journal of Cultural Economics* 27: 159–176.

Noonan, D. S. 2007. "Finding an Impact of Preservation Policies: Price Effects of Historic Landmarks on Attached Homes in Chicago, 1990–1999." *Economic Development Quarterly* 21: 17–33.

Nunes, P. A. L. D., and E. Schokkaert. 2003. "Identifying the Warm Glow Effect in Contingent Valuation." *Journal of Environmental Economics and Management* 45: 231–245.

Nunes, P. A. L. D., and P. Nijkamp. 2011. "Sustainable Biodiversity: Evaluation Lessons from Past Economic Research." *Regional Science Inquiry* 2 (2): 13–4.

Poor, P. J., and J. M. Smith. 2004. "Travel Cost Analysis of a Cultural Heritage Site: The Case of Historic St. Mary's City of Maryland." *Journal of Cultural Economics* 28: 217–229.

Renard, R. 1986. "The Rise and Fall of Cost-Benefit Analysis in Developing Countries." Unpublished mimeograph, Department of Economics, Free University, Brussels.

Richards, G. 1996. "Production and Consumption of European Cultural Tourism." *Annals of Tourism Research* 23: 261–283.

Riganti, P., and P. Nijkamp. 2007. "Benefit Transfer of Cultural Values: Lessons from Environmental Economics." *Journal of Environmental Policy and Law* 2: 135–148.

Rosen, S., 1974. "Hedonic Prices and Implicit Markets: Product Differentiation in Pure Competition." *Journal of Political Economy* 82: 34–55.

Rouwendal, J., and W. van der Straaten. 2008. "The Costs and Benefits of Providing Open Space in Cities." CPB discussion paper No. 8, CPB, The Hague.

Ruijgrok, E. C. M. 2006. "The Three Economic Values of Cultural Heritage: A Case Study in the Netherlands." *Journal of Cultural Heritage* 7: 206–213.

Schuster, T. 2003. *News Events and Price Movements.* Finance 0305009, EconWPA.

Seaman, B. 2003. "Contingent Valuation vs. Economic Impact: Substitutes or Complements?" Paper presented at the Regional Science Association International Conference, Philadelphia.

Snowball, J. D. 2008. *Measuring the Value of Culture: Methods and Examples in Cultural Economics.* Berlin: Springer Verlag.

Throsby, D. 1984. "The Measurement of Willingness-to-Pay for Mixed Goods." *Oxford Bulletin of Economics and Statistics* 46: 279–289.

Throsby, D. 1999. "Cultural Capital." *Journal of Cultural Economics* 23: 3–12.

Throsby, D. 2001. *Economics and Culture.* Cambridge: Cambridge University Press.

Tyrrell, T. J., and Johnston, R. J., eds. 2006. "The Economic Impacts of Tourism: A Special Issue." *Journal of Travel Research* 45 (3).

UNESCO. 1972. *Convention Concerning the Protection of the World Cultural and Natural Heritage.* Paris: UNESCO.

UNESCO. 2010. "A New International Instrument: The Proposed UNESCO Recommendation on the Historic Urban Landscape." Paris: UNESCO.

Van Leeuwen, E. S., P. Nijkamp, and P. Rietveld. 2006. "Economic Impacts of Tourism: A Meta-analytic Comparison of Regional Output Multipliers." In *Tourism and Regional Development: New Pathways,* ed. M. Giaoutzi and P. Nijkamp, 115–132. Aldershot: Ashgate.

Vandell, K. D., and J. S. Lane. 1989. "The Economics of Architecture and Urban Design: Some Preliminary Findings." *Real Estate Economics* 17: 235–260.

Warr, P. G. 1982. "Shadow Pricing Rules for Non-traded Commodities." *Oxford Economic Papers* 34: 231–243.

Weisbrod, B. 1964. "Collective Consumption Services of Individual Consumption Goods." *Quarterly Journal of Economics* 78: 471–477.

Willis, K. G. 2009. "Assessing Visitors Preferences in the Management of Archaeological and Heritage Attractions: A Case Study of Hadrian's Roman Wall." *International Journal of Tourism Research* 11: 487–505.

World Bank. 2009. "Urban and Local Government Strategy—Concepts & Issue Note". Washington, DC: World Bank.

World Bank. 2010. "System of Cities: Harnessing Urbanization for Growth & Poverty Alleviation." Washington, DC: World Bank.

5

Heritage Conservation and Property Values

Donovan Rypkema
Lecturer in Preservation Economics, University of Pennsylvania (U.S.)
Principal, Place Economics

Most countries today have some form of identification of heritage buildings, often called "listing" or "designation." Often (but not always) that designation is accompanied by regulations that may limit what an individual property owner may do to his/her building. It is through these regulations that the public values of that heritage are protected. But when a certain category of properties are subject to regulations that do not apply to other properties, that can raise some legitimate concerns. In response to that basic issue, this chapter addresses five inter-related questions: (1) What is the meaning and impact of heritage designation? (2) How do researchers measure value change in the marketplace? (3) How does heritage designation influence the value of affected buildings? (4) Why is the marketplace willing to pay a premium for heritage properties? (5) How does a premium for heritage properties affect low-income households? In answering those questions, and based on analyses from around the world, it has been found that heritage designation and its accompanying regulatory protection not only does not have a negative effect on value, but often creates a market-assigned value premium for historic structures. Increased property values in neighborhoods designated as historic can, however, have a potentially negative impact on low-income households, particularly if they are renters. This chapter concludes that possible negative results need to be mitigated through public policies and actions early in the heritage designation process.

Introduction

The field of heritage conservation addresses many kinds of resources—sites, individual landmarks, structures, objects, monuments, collections of historic buildings, archeological digs, natural heritage, and landscapes. In addition to the category of tangible heritage there is also intangible heritage, such as language, music, dance, cultural traditions, oral history, indigenous crafts, and other forms of expression. But probably the largest share of any country's heritage assets is its collection of historic buildings and historic city cores.

What makes a building "historic"? Different countries have different definitions, but the most common criteria would typically include age, association with important people or events, aesthetic quality, character, and craftsmanship. In addition, buildings are often designated "historic" because they were the first, the most representative, or the best example of a building style, type of construction, or innovative engineering or construction technique.

When a building (or a group of buildings) is evaluated and meets one or more of the criteria as historic, commonly the property receives a designation as a heritage building (or site or district). Depending on the country, the heritage protection laws, and the relative significance of the building, that designation may mandate legal protections for the property. These protections can include restrictions on what can or cannot be changed and are often accompanied by a set of design and conservation guidelines specifying how alterations and maintenance are to be undertaken.

But in the end, four facts must be recognized about heritage buildings:

- There are far more heritage buildings worthy of preservation than can be made into museums or cultural centers.
- Not even the wealthiest of governments have the financial resources within the public sector to protect and maintain all of the heritage buildings.
- Heritage buildings are most at risk:
  - When there is no funding available, and
  - When there is an abundance of funds available.
- In essence, heritage buildings are real estate.

Since heritage buildings are real estate, they will be subject to the same set of influences as any other real estate, particularly in market and transitional economies. Real estate is peculiar in that it possesses certain characteristics unlike any other asset: (1) it is fixed in place; (2) every parcel is unique; (3) it is finite in quantity; (4) it generally lasts longer than any of its possessors; and (5) it is necessary for every human activity. Because of these distinctions, real estate has always been treated differently in law, in economic theory, in philosophy, in finance, and in public policy. In most countries, regardless of economic or political system, there is some basic concept of property rights that applies to real estate. It is within this property rights and public policy framework that heritage designation is applied.

Other chapters in the book discuss the principle that total economic value is made up of both use and non-use values. Within that framework, use value is further divided into direct use value (providing, for example, income, residential and commercial space, and industrial space) and indirect use value (contributing to environmental and aesthetic quality, national identity, community image and self-esteem, and social interaction). This chapter will focus exclusively on direct use value. It is the direct use value that is most apparent in the actions of the marketplace—by buyers and sellers, landlords, and tenants.

That is not to say that direct use benefits are more important than indirect benefits, or that the use values of heritage buildings are more important than their non-use values. And it is critical to understand that total economic value is the use value plus non-use values.

This chapter, in focusing on direct use values, will address five basic questions:

1. What is the meaning, and impact, of heritage designation?
2. How do researchers measure value change in the marketplace?
3. How does heritage designation influence the value of affected buildings?
4. Why is the marketplace willing to pay a premium for heritage properties?
5. How does a premium for heritage properties affect low-income households?

What Is the Meaning and Impact of Heritage Designation?

Why do cities and countries around the world designate and, through designation, protect historic properties? According to Robert Stipe (Stipe 1983), there are seven reasons, paraphrased here:

- Historic resources physically link us to our past;
- We save our architectural heritage because we have lived with it and it has become part of our reference and identity;
- Because we live in an age of rapid communication and technological transformations, in the face of the ensuing homogeneity, we strive to maintain difference and uniqueness;
- Historic sites and structures relate to past events, eras, movements, and persons that we feel are important to honor and understand;
- We seek to preserve the architecture and cultural landscapes of the past simply because of their intrinsic value as art;

- We seek to preserve our past because we believe in the right of our cities and countryside to be aesthetically pleasing; and
- We seek to preserve because we have discovered that preservation can serve an important human and social purpose in our society.

While two different countries may place slightly different emphases on the factors listed above, for the most part there would be broad agreement as to "why we preserve." What varies widely, however, is the matter of "how we preserve."

Designating a property or a group of properties as "historic" has different socio-cultural and economic implications in different parts of the world. No meaningful evaluation of the likely effect of heritage listing on real estate could be undertaken without knowing what the consequences of that listing would be. The differences found in just a small sampling of countries reflect the wide diversity of the impact and protection that heritage designation provides.

In Azerbaijan, for instance, historic properties are identified by the Department of Archaeology and Architecture of the Academy of Sciences. Heritage properties of national significance may only be owned by the state. While the demolition of heritage property is illegal, the law is rarely enforced. There are conservation zones covering groups of properties. The responsibility for the protection of Icheri Sheher (which means "inner city" in Azeri)—the historic core in the center of the capital, Baku—was transferred to the national government after the site was placed on UNESCO's list of World Heritage in Danger. (See box 5.1.)

In Brazil, since 1936 the heritage designated to be of national importance is listed by IPHAN—an acronym that stands, in Portuguese, for the national institute of historic and artistic patrimony, which is linked to the federal Ministry of Culture. Iconic buildings, historic towns, and historic city cores are protected under safeguard policy and specific regulations, including guidelines for maintenance and repairs. However, the listing status acquired by nearly 1,000 buildings and 50 historic city cores doesn't necessarily ensure that these places will receive public funds and resources for their routine maintenance or for repairs and capital improvement works. Most of the conservation and heritage building repair programs are currently financed by partnerships of state enterprises, private foundations, and local public funds (Taddei Neto 2001).

In Cuba, all buildings and neighborhoods built prior to 1930 in Old Havana are designated as a conservation zone. All of the properties are state-owned, although many are leased. Any changes of this regulation have to be approved by the Historian's Office of Havana.

In England, most pre-1830 buildings, high value structures built between 1830 and 1935, and exceptional structures built after 1935 are considered architectural heritage. There is both a national list, maintained by English Heritage, and local

---

BOX 5.1

Responsible Planning and Investments Restore the Walled City of Baku's World Heritage Listing

Azerbaijan Cultural Heritage Support Project (Project number 058969)
Total Project Cost: US$8.9 million
Total Loan Amount: US$7.5 million
Approved: May 1999 – Closed: June 2007

In 2003 Icheri Sheher, the Walled City of Baku, with the Shirvanshah Palace and Maiden Tower, was listed as a UNESCO World Heritage site. However, three years later UNESCO placed Icheri Sheher on the list of World Heritage in Danger, citing damage from a November 2000 earthquake, poor conservation, and dubious conservation efforts. The World Bank was already assisting the Azerbaijan government in designing a program of investments to better conserve several of the country's key monuments and strengthen the capacity of the agencies responsible for their protection. At that point, the Bank Project was restructured to earmark investments to be used not only to conserve the key landmark of the Walled city, namely the Shirvanshah Palace, but also to prepare and implement detailed plans for the conservation, use, and management of the entire Walled City. The conservation efforts and the preparation of the plans (that included also a tourist plan and an operation and maintenance plan) had an immediate impact on the number of visitors to the site, which had increased by about 35 percent in 2007. In 2009, two years after project completion, the World Heritage Committee praised Azerbaijan for its efforts to preserve the Walled City and removed it from the endangered list.

Source: Azerbaijan Cultural Heritage Support Project Appraisal Document, and Implementation and Completion Report.

---

lists, which are the responsibility of local governments—although anyone may nominate a building for inclusion on the lists. The protection measures, including statutory norms, safeguards, and laws for heritage buildings, are integrated into the local planning system. The law states simply that to be listed, a building must be of "special architectural or historic interest" (Cherry 2001).

In Italy and France, the national government (through the Ministry of Culture) and regional, department, and municipal governments identify heritage buildings. The protection policies, laws, and regulations for heritage buildings are on multiple levels, including master plans, zoning ordinances, and protected sector designation. Additionally, buffer zones are established around heritage districts to enhance their protection.

In the United States, at the national level there is the National Register of Historic Places. This listing includes buildings and groups of buildings that have national significance but also those whose significance is only regional or local. However, there is virtually no legal protection for properties listed on the National Register except from actions of the federal government itself. Nearly all significant protection applied to historic properties is found at the local level when a community has adopted a historic preservation ordinance. Like zoning, these ordinances are part of planning and land-use laws.

While there are obviously differences among the examples above, there are some common denominators:

- Historic structures can be listed individually (often called "landmarking") and as a group of buildings (often called a historic district, conservation area, or heritage zone).
- Often, but not always, heritage designation is accompanied by statutory protections of the building.
- Typically, these protections provide:
  - Prohibitions against demolition or a deferral of issuing a demolition permit.
  - Approval requirements for any exterior changes.
  - Approval requirements for any additions.
- In addition, some ordinances include:
  - Approval requirements for changes to significant interior features.
  - Standards for repairs and routine maintenance.
  - Prohibition against "demolition by neglect" precluding the owner from simply allowing a property to deteriorate to the point that it is no longer repairable.
- Many heritage protection agencies also provide design guidelines so that the property owner understands the grounds upon which approvals will be granted or denied.

How Do Researchers Measure Value Change in the Marketplace?

Among the reasons noted above for designating and protecting heritage resources, "increasing property values" is not a driving motivation. It is for aesthetic, cultural, environmental, and even sociological reasons that historic properties are first identified and then protected. But for a variety of economic, social, and political reasons, the interrelationship between heritage designation and property values has been the economic aspect of heritage studied most often. However, before discussing results of some of the research cited in this chapter, it may be useful to look at the ways that property values are measured.

When there is no market activity on which value estimates can be based, it is sometimes appropriate to use indirect assessment methods. Other chapters in this book explore an array of such methods, including the travel cost method, contingent valuation estimates, among others. These, too, can be used for estimating the value of individual heritage buildings or groups of buildings.

Among the wide range of heritage economic research being conducted, studying real estate transactions is the one approach that uses market data to estimate direct use value.[1] There are two types of market data that can be used as an indicator of economic use value—rents and sales prices. Where property taxes are levied on an "ad valorum" basis (i.e., in proportion to value), the assessed value for taxation purposes can be effectively used as a proxy for sales prices. For residential properties, using sales (or a proxy for sales) has been the favored approach. For commercial properties, using rental rates often provides greater reliability since there would usually be more data available about rental rates than about sales.

Whatever data are used, however, it is important to convert the information into a common unit of comparison. For sales data this might be dollars per square foot of usable space or euros per square meter of gross area. For rental data, a unit of comparison might be pounds per square meter per month in England, or pesos per square meter per year in Mexico. In Japan, commercial property is often quoted as yen per tatami, a tatami being a traditional module measuring approximately 0.9 meters by 1.8 meters (the size of a single straw mat traditionally used as floor covering). But whatever the currency and standard of measurement used, it is only by converting data into a unit of comparison that patterns, trends, and distinctions can be evaluated.

However, in most countries and cities it can be hard to obtain a sufficient quality and quantity of data upon which to make assessments and informed judgments. In that case, some market-based but indirect indicators can be used. While using these indicators may be less exacting than using sales or rental data, at least they can be useful references for identifying patterns of change over time. Among these alternative measures are:

- Property taxes generated from the district;
- Number of building permits issued;
- Vacancy or occupancy rates and their change over time;

- Amount of investment in buildings in the designated area;
- Condition of heritage buildings in the area and change in condition over time[2];
- Increasing frequency of sales; even if actual sales prices are not available, this is a good indicator of increased interest (and subsequently value) of a heritage area; and
- Information about how long a property remains on the market before being sold; although often difficult to obtain, this indicates the depth of demand for properties in the area.

But collecting usable data is just the first step. Then the question becomes, "What is it that should be looked at?" It is important to recognize that data itself in this context are relatively useless; they only become useful when some comparison is made. Depending on the availability of data and the specifics of the particular situation, there are several approaches to using the data for analysis, ranging from the very simple to the relatively complex. Below is a range of those approaches. In each case an appropriate unit of comparison should be used, for instance adopting U.S. dollars per square foot or euros per square meter.

- *Simple value comparison.* What is the difference in value between a property located in a heritage district and a similar property not in the district?
- *Before and after designation.* What was the average value of houses in the neighborhood before historic designation and after historic designation?
- *Appreciation compared to the local market.* At what rate did properties in the historic district appreciate (or decline in value) over time and how does that value change compare with that of properties in the local market that are not in a historic district?
- *Appreciation compared to a similar neighborhood.* At what rate did properties in the historic district appreciate (or decline in value) over time and how does that value change compare with that of properties in a similar neighborhood that is not a historic districts?
- *Resales of the same property.* If a property sold more than once during the study period, what was the value change and how does that value change compare to the appreciation rates for non-designated property?[3]

For commercial properties, the same approaches listed above can be used if there are sufficient sales data. If not, however, the same comparisons can be made using rents rather than sales.

The most elaborate analysis that has been used in heritage property value studies is known as hedonic pricing. This method attempts to identify the individual components of a property and each component's contribution to the overall property value. A study of historic neighborhoods in San Diego,

California, United States (Narwold et al. 2008), used a limited number of rather straightforward variables:

- Number of bedrooms;
- Number of bathrooms;
- Square feet of living area;
- Square feet of the parcel of land;
- Number of garage spaces;
- Availability of a swimming pool; and
- Age of the property.

Then, having calculated the relative contribution of each of those elements, a final distinction was made—historic designation. The assumption was that when the contributory value of all of the other variables is accounted for, any remaining difference in price was attributable to that designation.

Other studies have used a more comprehensive list of variables that have included such factors as distance to the city center, proximity to water, architectural style, condition of the building, character of the neighborhood, proximity to individual monuments, population density, and presence of a garden. To select which variables to use, one must know which variables are most significant to buyers and sellers in the market area under study.

But it bears emphasizing that whichever approach is used, to be meaningful the value of heritage property has to be compared to non-designated property, and ideally that comparison is made over time.

How Does Heritage Designation Influence the Value of Affected Buildings?

The impact of heritage designation on property values has been the most frequently studied aspect of the relationship between historic preservation and economics. Although this research has been conducted in different countries, using different methodologies (including those discussed above), at different times over the last 20 years, the results are remarkably consistent. The vast majority of the published research indicates that heritage designation has a positive impact on property value. While there are a few studies that show no impact and one or two that indicate a negative impact on value, more than 90 percent of the studies demonstrate that properties under the protection of heritage designation experience value enhancement.

This assertion is a bit counterintuitive. When heritage properties are protected through meaningful legislation, a set of restrictions applies to those buildings that non-designated properties are not subject to. Thus one may think, "more regulation means less value"—an argument frequently used by those who oppose heritage designation. In fact, the opposite has been proven to be true. Why? Later, this chapter will identify a number of likely contributing variables to this value premium, but the most basic reason comes from the real estate cliché: "The three most important things in real estate are location, location, location." But cliché though it may be, there is an underlying reality that makes this premise valid. Note that the cliché is not: "The three most important things are roof, walls, and floor." The majority of the economic value of a particular parcel of real estate comes not from within the property lines but from its context; that is, its location within a given neighborhood and its adjacent public facilities and natural and cultural surroundings. That is why identical houses in Mexico City, Hanoi, Prague, and Rabat will have dramatically different values. But the comparison doesn't have to cross international borders. As anyone who has bought, sold, or financed real estate knows, even within a small city, the same house in a different neighborhood will command a different, sometimes dramatically different, market value.

The economic role of land-use laws in general, and historic designation in particular, is to protect the context within which the individual property is situated. No one pays a premium for a heritage house for the privilege of having to ask permission from some governmental body to put new shingles on the roof. Rather a homeowner will pay a premium for the assurance that the neighbor across the street will not be allowed to make inappropriate changes to his house that will have an adverse visual and value effect on the one's own house.

A sampling of studies demonstrates how this pattern manifests itself in the market place. A recent longitudinal study conducted in Philadelphia, Pennsylvania, United States, looked at property value changes over an extended period, 1980–2008 (Econsult Corporation 2010). Over this nearly 30-year timeframe, properties in both local historic districts and National Register historic districts saw rates of appreciation that outpaced the Philadelphia market in general, as shown in figure 5.1. Further, the study found that "homes in local historic districts enjoy an immediate 2 percent increase in values relative to the city average, once local designation has taken place; and thereafter, they appreciate at an annual rate that is 1 percent higher than the city average."

In Philadelphia, the value premium attached to the local historic districts is 8 percent greater than for the National Register districts. In Louisville, Kentucky, United States, researchers at the University of Louisville found that, over the period 2000 to 2007, properties in local historic districts commanded a premium of between US$59,000 and US$67,000 and that properties in those districts saw rates of appreciation 21 percent greater than in the Louisville market as a whole (Gilderbloom et al. 2009).

FIGURE 5.1

Historic District Premiums in Philadelphia, Pennsylvania, 1980–2008

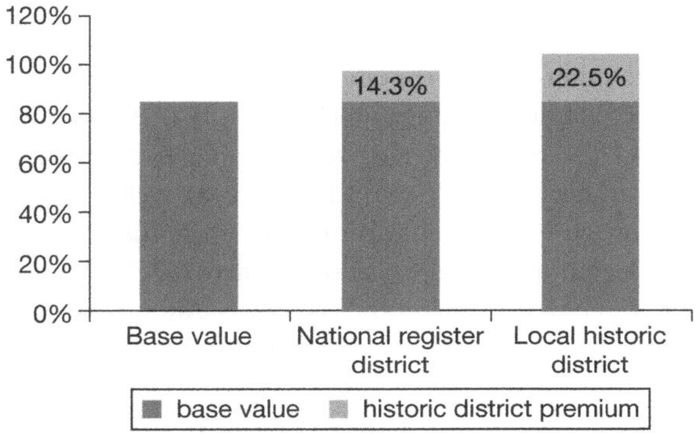

Source: Econsult Corporation 2010.

What is particularly notable is not just the difference in appreciation rates between historic houses and houses in the rest of the market, but the difference seen in local historic districts as compared to National Register historic districts. Unlike in many countries, listing on the National Register puts no limitations on what a private owner can do with the property. Even a National Historic Landmark—the highest designation a property can have—could be torn down at any time by its owner.[4] The only limitations on what can be done with the property arises from local legislation; that is, being listed in a local historic district.

In one of the most complex property value analyses in Europe, researchers from VU University in Amsterdam looked at both individual landmarking and location within a heritage district to determine the impact of those variables on property value (Lazrak et al. 2010). They found these gains:

- Premium paid for monuments (that is, individually landmarked properties): 26.9 percent;
- Premium paid for location within 165 feet of a monument: 0.28 percent; and
- Premium paid for location within a heritage district: 26.4 percent.

These findings are consistent with a similar hedonic pricing analysis that looked at the historic American city of Savannah, Georgia, United States. There the researchers found a premium of 1.7 percent for an individually landmarked structure, and a 21–22 percent premium for being located within a local historic district (Cebula 2009).

The four studies discussed above are included in this chapter mainly because: (1) they are recent, (2) they are representative of the findings of most heritage property value studies, and (3) they were conducted using a sophisticated methodology. But those research findings are not unusual. One American research project reviewed more than a dozen studies of cities around the country over different time periods and saw consistently higher property values in historic districts compared to other neighborhoods. The findings are summarized in figure 5.2 (Department of Urban Planning and Design, City of Tucson, Arizona 2007).

While much of the property value research has been done in the United States, revealing findings come from elsewhere as well. A recent Canadian study looked at property sales data from 32 heritage districts in the province of Ontario (Architectural Conservancy of Ontario 2009). The researchers presented their data somewhat differently than the studies described above. They looked at whether houses in historic districts sold for more, less, or the same as similar nearby houses not in historic districts. As can be seen in figure 5.3, nearly 80 percent of all sales were either for the same price or greater than proximate non-designated housing.

As such property values research continues to be conducted, different analysts have begun looking at more nuanced issues. Recent studies include the following:

• An Australian study found that historic houses in heritage districts commanded an average premium of 12 percent, but that the most historically significant houses garnered a 47 percent premium over the least significant historic houses (Deodhar 2004).

• An analysis of historic districts in Memphis, Tennessee, found that while houses in historic districts were worth 14–23 percent more than comparable

FIGURE 5.2
Property Value Premiums for Historic Districts in U.S. Cities

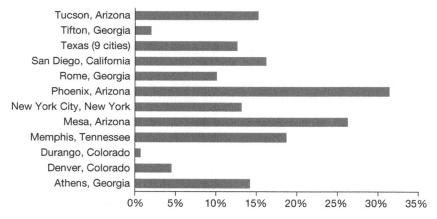

Source: City of Tucson 2007.

FIGURE 5.3

Property Sales in 32 Historic Districts in Ontario, Canada

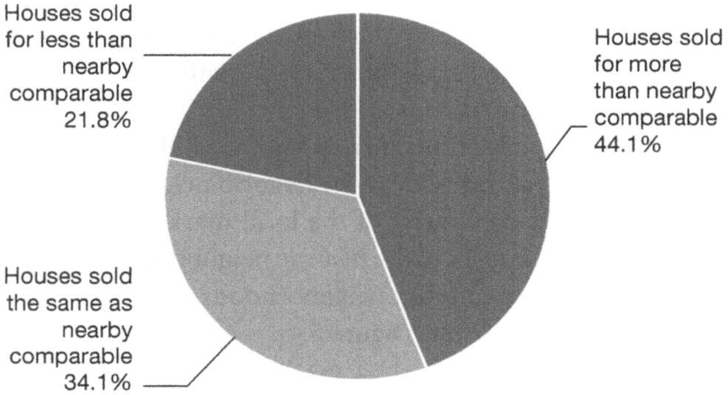

Houses sold
for less than
nearby
comparable
21.8%

Houses sold
for more
than nearby
comparable
44.1%

Houses sold
the same as
nearby
comparable
34.1%

Source: Architectural Conservancy of Ontario 2009.

housing, that premium also benefited new infill houses in the historic districts (Coulson and Lahr 2005).

• Designated historic districts tend to have higher rates of participation in neighborhood associations and improvement projects, which relates to residents' desire to protect shared public spaces from decline (Department of Urban Planning and Design, City of Tucson, Arizona 2007).

While there may be a temptation to assume that historic housing is occupied mainly by the wealthiest households (particularly in countries with advanced economies), that does not prove to be the case in both developed and developing countries. In the town of Aurora, Illinois, United States, 82 percent of the houses that were sold in historic districts were also in low-income census tracts, but still managed to command a value increment of 6–7 percent over the rest of the local market (Coffin 1989).

A doctoral dissertation considered the impact of historic district designation on property values in three fast-growth American cities—Dallas, Texas; Atlanta, Georgia; and Phoenix, Arizona—and three slow-growth cities—Pittsburgh, Pennsylvania; Cleveland, Ohio; and Cincinnati, Ohio. The study found that "the positive appreciation effects of local historic designation in slow-growth central cities were higher than in fast-growth central cities by 7.7 percent, suggesting that historic designation has a role to play in urban revitalization for areas striving to improve property values despite slow population growth" (Ijla 2008).

Nonetheless, much of this real estate data were taken from periods of real estate appreciation, when increases in value are not surprising. What about in times of economic downturns? Less research has been conducted about such conditions, but, again, a pattern emerges from what has been learned. Looking at property values in historic districts in Washington, DC, the researcher concluded: "In short, it may be that historic districts are more likely to experience a certain indemnification from extremely modulating property values, perhaps because of a higher degree of investor confidence in these officially recognized and protected areas" (Gale 1991).

After the real estate market downturn in the late 1990s, Canadian researchers looked at patterns of value decline in 24 Ontario neighborhoods, comparing historic district properties to the rest of the local market (Shipley 2000). They found that almost half the houses in the historic neighborhoods (47 percent) had less value decline than those in other neighborhoods, while another 32 percent retained their value at the same rate (figure 5.4).

With the collapse of the real estate markets in 2007, first in the United States and then quickly spreading around much of the world, real estate prices experienced the greatest decline in two generations. The real estate crisis quickly became a crisis for financial institutions and the construction industry. As a consequence of falling values and increasing unemployment, many properties went into foreclosure. A recent study looked at foreclosure rates in six local historic districts in Philadelphia, as compared to ten comparable, nearby neighborhoods that are not historic districts (Broadbent 2011). The findings, shown in figure 5.5, were significant. The likelihood of a property being in foreclosure was twice as great in a comparable neighborhood as in a historic district. This suggests not that the historic district residents were more financially prudent, but rather that, with a less steep value decline,

FIGURE 5.4

Property Value Declines in 24 Ontario Communities During Economic Downturns, 1976–97

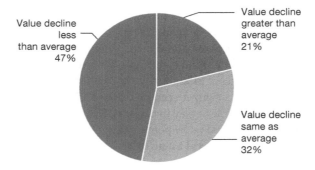

Value decline less than average 47%

Value decline greater than average 21%

Value decline same as average 32%

Source: Shipley 2000.

FIGURE 5.5

Foreclosures per 1,000 Housing Units in Philadelphia, Pennsylvania, October 2008–September 2009

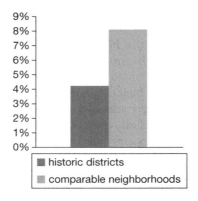

Source: Broadbent 2011.

properties could more easily be sold by a family with financial difficulties before the foreclosure process had taken place.

So the data regarding the relationship between historic designation and property values are largely consistent and positive. There is a caveat to these studies, however. Virtually all of them limit their analysis to residential properties and properties in heritage districts (rather than individually landmarked buildings not within a district). It is likely that, were analyses conducted on commercial properties and on individually landmarked buildings, the results would be less dramatic. As was noted above, a major reason for the value enhancement of properties within a historic district is that actors in the real estate market have confidence that the context within which the property exists will be appropriately maintained. For an individually landmarked building that is subject to limitations and restrictions, but where the nearby properties are not, there will be greater uncertainly that the quality of the context of the neighborhood will be maintained.

For commercial property, whether a historic designation helps or hurts the value will depend on two variables: (1) is it located in a commercial district that is growing and therefore facing development pressures? and (2) is there a significant difference between what is permitted in a commercial district under the zoning law (regarding scale, density, and nature of development) for non-heritage buildings and for heritage buildings that may be subject to additional restrictions? If, for example, a two-story historic building is situated in a rapidly developing commercial district where the zoning would allow a ten-story building, it would not be surprising to find that the land if vacant would be worth more than the land and the building combined. Further, if the historic building cannot be razed, but an adjacent non-designated building can be demolished and replaced with a larger building, it is probable that the adjacent building would command a higher price based on that speculative premium.

That is not to suggest that there should not be individual landmarking, or that commercial buildings should not also receive historic designation and protection. It does suggest, however, that higher real estate values and faster rates of appreciation are unlikely to be the strongest arguments for designation.

But while this chapter has focused mainly on the positive effects of heritage designation on property values, buildings and sites having heritage character can play a role in enhancing property values in other ways. That is when there is a comprehensive strategy that includes conservation of the built heritage as a tool for promoting area regeneration, especially in historic city centers. Such a strategy may certainly include the listing and protection of heritage buildings, but that will be just one of the contributors to property value enhancement.

Over the last two decades there have been numerous successful heritage-based urban regeneration efforts. Excellent examples are Aleppo, Syria; Salvador de Bahia, Brazil; Edinburgh, Scotland; Ghent, Belgium; Verona, Italy; Quito, Ecuador; St. Petersburg, Russia; and Elmina, Ghana.

As different as these cities are, in most instances their regeneration strategy contained similar principles, actions, and components:

- There was a comprehensive, multiyear development strategy;
- The limits of the protected heritage area were clearly defined and designated as a preferred location for private investment;
- Fiscal incentives were provided to attract and leverage private capital;
- The public sector made significant early investment in improving infrastructure and providing public services;
- Restoration and conservation work for iconic heritage buildings was undertaken by the public authorities, often with technical and resource assistance provided by the nonprofit sector—such as by international and national nongovernmental organizations (NGOs)—and by private and public foundations;
- Assistance programs were established to attract and retain businesses, particularly small businesses, in the project area;
- There was overall planning and management for the effort, including a systematic monitoring and tracking of the changes taking place; and
- A regulatory protection layer was placed on the area and duly enforced, accompanied with design and building operations guidelines.

Because each of these operational concepts was a part of a comprehensive strategy, it would be difficult to disaggregate the relative impact of each component. However, the overall outcome of these heritage-based strategies is clearly positive. (See box 5.2.)

BOX 5.2

Comprehensive Urban Revitalization Strategies Help Conserve Jordan's Historic Cities

Jordan Cultural Heritage, Tourism, and Urban Development Project
(Project number 081823)
Total Project Cost: US$71.1 million
Total Loan Amount: US$56 million
Approved: January 2007 – Ongoing

The objectives of the project are to support tourism development in five historically and culturally important cities—Jerash, Karak, Madaba, Salt, and Aljoun—and contribute to local economic development. For each of the cities, a comprehensive, multiyear strategy of investments is underway. The components of the strategy include (1) improvements to street networks and allied public spaces; (2) rehabilitation and cleaning of building facades; (3) renovation and preservation of selected heritage buildings through adaptive reuse; (4) rehabilitation and upgrading of pivotal urban spaces; (5) support traffic and parking management plans; and (6) detailed design guidance and supervision.

Source: Jordan Cultural Heritage, Tourism and Urban Development Project Appraisal Document.

For instance, in the historic city center of Quito, Ecuador, the value of old non-rehabilitated structures and deteriorated space increased ten-fold within a decade, due to the spillover effect of the capital improvement program, as seen in figure 5.6 (Jaramillo 2010).

The historic city core of Salvador de Bahia, Brazil, was inscribed on the World Heritage List in 1985. The historic city core is also on the national heritage list and for two decades has been under the protection of a local heritage ordinance. Within the historic center of Salvador are four neighborhoods, one of which—Pelourinho—has been the focus of a concentrated strategy of heritage-based regeneration for 20 years. This effort, which has included significant publicly funded infrastructure renewal and building restoration, has paid off in rising property values. In 2010, an analysis was made of property values in Pelourinho as compared to two other districts within the historic city core, to the historic city core as a whole, and to a comparable commercial neighborhood not within the center. As seen in figure 5.7, property values in Pelourinho topped all others (Mendes Zancheti and Gabriel 2010).

FIGURE 5.6
Effects of Capital Improvement Program on Property Values in Historic Center of Quito, Ecuador

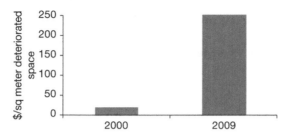

Source: Jaramillo 2010.

FIGURE 5.7
Property Values in Salvador de Bahia, Brazil, 2010

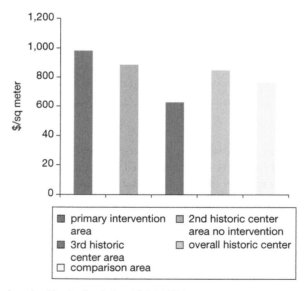

Source: Author, based on Mendes Zancheti and Gabriel 2010.

Oaxaca de Juarez, Mexico, provides another example of a city that has used the rich architectural heritage of its historic city core as the vehicle for regeneration. Unlike in many other cities in the developing world, the city center of Oaxaca de Juarez was never abandoned, and always retained an important regional commercial and political role. To capitalize on the strengths of the center, the city's redevelopment strategy contained five major elements (Quatersan and Romis 2010):

- Keeping institutional functions in the center, including the seat of public administration and the institutions devoted to education, religion, commerce, and healthcare;
- Maintaining a mix of low, middle, and upper income residents living in the city core;
- Promoting cultural tourism based on the abundant heritage resources;
- Attracting private capital from both investors and consumers; and
- Attracting participation of the public and private sectors and of civil society early in the heritage conservation efforts.

This strategy has resulted in substantial increases in property values. In 2010, unrenovated property in the historic city core was selling for US$1,200 per square meter. This is double what the property brought (at US$600 per square meter) a decade earlier. By contrast, unrenovated property just outside the city center could be purchased in 2010 for about US$430 per square meter.

Why Is the Marketplace Willing to Pay a Premium for Heritage Properties?

The best hedonic pricing models will tell us that buyers in the marketplace are willing to pay extra to buy a house in a protected heritage district. What it does not tell us is why. There are clearly a number of reasons, and the motivation no doubt varies from one buyer to another. But in general it is reasonable to assume the value premium is driven by four categories of explanations: heritage, neighborhood characteristics, proximity, and public policy. (See box 5.3.)

The category of heritage includes the quality of heritage buildings that is often not found in newer construction; the aesthetic appeal and workmanship of heritage structures; the prestige that is sometimes associated with living in a historic district; and, for some people at least, a basic cultural commitment to preserving the built heritage by living in it.

Neighborhood characteristics are almost always independent of the inventory of housing and instead generate a monetary reward for features such as pedestrian accessibility to services and amenities, mixed use, and urban character—all three of which are generally absent from most newer neighborhoods.

Proximity characteristics reflect that concept of "location, location, location" discussed earlier, but especially location near specific amenities. Because most cities throughout the world have grown outward from their core, historic residential neighborhoods tend to be near historic city centers. When that center is

---

BOX 5.3

Urban Upgrading Increases Property Values in the Historic Medina of Tunis

Tunisia Third Urban Development Project (Project number 005652)
Total Project Cost: US$25 million
Total Loan Amount: US$25 million
Approved: December 1982 – Closed: June 1993

The Tunisian authorities, with assistance from the World Bank, prepared a project to help provide better shelter and improve urban services for low-income families. The Hafsia Quarter in the historic medina of Tunis was chosen due to its seriously deteriorated neighborhoods and its high incidence of poverty. The project supported conservation of the medina's heritage by (1) establishing design guidelines for all new construction and renovations, (2) upgrading basic infrastructure and urban services, (3) constructing residential and commercial buildings on vacant land, (4) selling serviced land to private developers, and (5) using the municipality's returns from sales to fund the renovation of about 47,000 square meters of low-income housing.

From the start of the project in 1982 to its completion in 1993, property values rose by 12 percent in the medina versus an increase of 8 percent for property on the urban fringe. The increase in value is seen as largely due to location and employment factors. Forty-three percent of new residents in the medina work in the adjacent central business district, and 24 percent work in the medina itself (62 percent of residents walk to work). Other factors that contributed to the rise of property values include the neighborhood's distinctive character and the government's visible commitment to improving the area.

Source: Graduate School of Design, Harvard University and Association Sauvegarde la Médina Tunis. Case Study: Tunis, Tunisia Rehabilitation of the Hafsia Quarter 1998.

---

healthy or experiencing a revival, there is, at least among segments of the market, an expressed preference to be close to some of the amenities and services offered. Also, however, as was demonstrated in some of the studies discussed earlier, there seems to also be a nominal premium attached to being near an individual landmark—such as the mosque and/or the suk (marketplace).

Finally there are public policy reasons. A city begins making a commitment to a historic area by adopting a comprehensive heritage-based regeneration strategy. That strategy may include elements such as offering incentives to developers, investing in public infrastructure, restoring iconic buildings, and improving the provision and quality of public services. The enhanced physical environment is intended to enhance the economic environment, and when that happens private investments ensue, generating positive externalities in the form of improved quality of life. Hence, property values generally tend to rise.

However, one of the most important public policy actions is first identifying and then protecting a city's heritage resources. When there is public confidence that the quality and character of a heritage district will be protected, a sizable subset of the property market will display that confidence by paying a premium to own property there. (See box 5.4.)

BOX 5.4

A Wide-Ranging Set of Project Components Supports Development in Georgia

Georgia Regional Development Project (Project number 126033)
Total Project Cost: US$70 million
Total Loan Amount: US$60 million
Approved: March 2012 – Ongoing

The government of Georgia aims to develop the local economy in the Kakheti region, which was a key juncture on the Silk Road and has long been at the heart of the country's ancient culture, history, and economy. Through an integrated approach the project focuses on (1) upgrading the urban infrastructure in the historic city cores of Telavi and Kvareli and the heritage village of Dartlo, which will include rehabilitating all public utilities and space (including parks); (2) restoration of the facades of 150 publicly and privately owned buildings with historic architecture; (3) management and development of 11 cultural heritage sites (including public parking, toilets, souvenir shops, and information kiosks); (4) provision of incentives to the private sector to invest in tourism in Kakheti (including free public infrastructure and streamlined business start-up procedures); and (5) improved management of tourist destinations and the development of two leisure travel clusters (cultural heritage/ wine tasting and adventure/ecotourism). The ultimate goal is to attract private investments, promote public-private partnerships, and revitalize local business activity.

Source: Georgia Regional Development Project Appraisal Document.

It has been seen that the heritage designation has the greatest positive impact on real estate values when:

- There is a broad community understanding and appreciation of the historic significance of the heritage structures;
- There is consistent enforcement of the regulations to safeguard heritage;
- The "sticks" of regulation are paired with the "carrots" of incentives; and
- There are clear, illustrated guidelines on what is expected of owners of historic properties written in layman's language.

How Does a Premium for Heritage Properties Affect Low-Income Households?

However, acknowledging the generally positive impact of heritage designation on property values raises another fundamental issue that must be addressed: What is the impact of heritage designation on the low-income households? This question is vital because: (1) in most of the world, the city (or town) center holds the greatest concentration of heritage assets; and (2) particularly in much of the developing world, city centers have become primarily and sometimes entirely the habitat of the low-income households. So how does heritage designation, and any subsequent rise in property value, affect such households? This is a major concern for institutions such as the World Bank, whose explicit corporate mission is to reduce poverty in the world. It is legitimate, therefore, to ask: Will a heritage-based economic development or center-city revitalization program have an adverse impact on the very people the institution is trying to assist? A particular concern is the socioeconomic demographic change called "gentrification," which is defined as "the process of renewal and rebuilding accompanying the influx of middle-class or affluent people into deteriorating areas that often displaces poorer residents."[5]

It is useful to consider the typical pattern of decline that has affected many city centers and older residential neighborhoods.

- First, there is a gradual departure of middle-class households and of stable businesses that cater to them. The reasons for this departure are varied but could include a family's desire for more space or public amenities; a preference for "new" space; changing of household patterns; or increased household income that allows for car ownership, enabling the family to move to a suburban or outlying area with more space and access to nature.
- As this pattern of departure accelerates, public services in the city center begin to deteriorate and levels of maintenance of public spaces and buildings decline.

- Private owners begin to mirror the public sector and invest less in property maintenance; little new investment takes place.
- Lower levels of maintenance and reinvestment in center-city property lead to higher vacancy rates, lower rents, and ultimately lower values.
- By this point, social issues such as public safety concerns arise, hastening the departure of once-stable businesses and many of the remaining middle-class families.
- Regardless of local systems of taxation—real estate taxes, sales (value added) taxes, business license fees, building permit fees, and income taxes—revenues to the public sector decline, leaving even fewer resources to devote to the area.
- At this stage of the process, there is a shift from owner occupancy (whether as resident or business operator) to tenant occupancy. This is often accompanied by a pattern of absentee owners who are usually less accountable for basic property maintenance.
- At a point when value declines are sufficiently deep, some property owners will simply walk away from the property or go into default. Land title and ownership rights become increasingly unclear and the number of non-paying, often illegal, occupants increases.
- As a result, the neighborhood or the former commercial district has become almost exclusively home to lower-income households or informal businesses.

Rarely does the decline cycle automatically reverse itself. In fact it is often exacerbated by public policies that may include reduced allocation of resources for housing, transportation, education, healthcare, recreation, taxation, infrastructure investment, or other needs. Such policies actually encourage effective abandonment of the center city and older residential neighborhoods. While many of the underlying causes of this cycle of decline may be social, the most visible economic effect of the decline is on real estate.

Social and real estate–related economic conditions are at the core of a public policy decision to use the built heritage areas as the focus for downtown regeneration. This represents a sea change from earlier generations' approach to heritage conservation, in which the protection of historic buildings was an end in itself—saving one or more iconic buildings for their own sake. Increasingly, cities are adopting a strategic approach that employs preservation management and heritage conservation not as ends in themselves but as the means for broader development outcomes, specifically for attracting the return of middle-class families and businesses to downtown areas. In this approach, heritage designation is pursued as just one part of the effort to renew and rebuild an area. Research findings suggest that heritage designation is often a key element underpinning the innovative urban renewal schemes, helping to promote increased rents and property values. However, as has been noted in this chapter, the historic centers have become almost exclusively the habitat of low-income households. Therefore such a renewal strategy could have the adverse effect of pricing the poor out of that market—gentrification.

For the proponents of inclusive urban development strategies, too often even the use of the phrase "gentrification" generates both anger and angst, when what is necessary is to step back and consider the process more objectively. In any urban strategy operation there are both positive and negative outcomes; however, the consequences of so-called gentrification should be weighed when initiating a heritage-based strategy.

Gentrification: Assessing the Positives

On the positive side, frequent outcomes include the following:

- *Potentials for reinvestment.* When a heritage area has been selected to receive public investment in capital improvements of major buildings and in infrastructure, the confidence of individual private-sector investors is increased, leading them to acquire and redevelop existing properties. Using public investment as leverage to encourage private investment is always part of the renewal strategy of center city efforts in general and of heritage-based strategies in particular.
- *Increased property ownership.* As was noted above, the cycle of decline is often accompanied by a shift from owner occupants to tenant occupants in both residential and commercial properties. Heritage-based regeneration efforts often spur a reversal of that pattern by attracting the return of owner occupants, particularly in the residential sector.
- *Improved public services.* Commonly the level and quality of basic public services—garbage collection, street cleaning, maintenance of public squares, and public safety—improves significantly in heritage-based efforts. In part this is because the local government commits to improve services in the targeted area as a means to build public confidence and attract private investment.
- *Improved businesses climate.* As the economic makeup of the area improves, new businesses are started and existing businesses relocate to the neighborhood. This pattern is the result of two parallel factors: (1) as there is more investment and a greater number of households with spendable income, there is simply a greater opportunity for business start-up and relocation; and (2) particularly early in the cycle of regeneration, the rent levels are still relatively low as compared to other areas of the city. Since the cost of occupancy is a major consideration, particularly for small businesses, this rent competitiveness adds to the area's appeal.
- *More renovation of vacant properties.* Often the first properties to be acquired and rehabilitated are those that have been vacant. These are favored targets

both because the acquisition price will likely be lower and also the complication of having to deal with existing tenants is lessened.[6] It is important to note that proximity to an empty or abandoned building has one of the greatest adverse impacts on the value of other properties. So when a formerly vacant building is rehabilitated and put back into use, there will often be a value enhancement of nearby buildings.

- *More adaptive reuse projects.* Apart from general cycles of decline, one of the major reasons why heritage buildings too often sit vacant is that they have, or are perceived to have, lost their utility—known in real estate terms as functional obsolescence. Perhaps the use for which the building was constructed no longer exists, or the use is met in a decidedly different physical configuration. Buildings can also suffer from functional obsolescence due to antiquated or inefficient building installation systems—heating, plumbing, electricity, and so on—or from a spatial configuration that is seen as unsuitable for corporate and private users. Functional obsolescence is one of the most common justifications for the demolition of a heritage building. Adaptive reuse is the reinsertion of a new utility into an existing building.
- *Expanding tax revenues.* With reinvestment, in-migration of middle-class families and stable businesses, reduction of vacancy, and increases in property values, there comes a corresponding increase in local tax revenues. In fact, it is not uncommon that the biggest economic beneficiary of a heritage-based regeneration program will be the local government.
- *Creation of new jobs.* As people and businesses move back into a neighborhood, almost automatically new jobs are created. Those households will bring with them disposable income that will be used to purchase goods and services. The new businesses will need to hire employees. Building renovation is a labor-intensive activity, so a wide range of workers (from common laborers to skilled craftsmen) will be needed to rehabilitate the heritage buildings.
- *Property appreciation.* As will be seen in the research cited below, one of the most consistent patterns of heritage-based regeneration programs and historic designation of neighborhoods is that property values will not only go up, but will likely go up at rates greater than in the market as a whole.

It may be stating the obvious, but rents and values have to go up if private capital will be attracted on a sustained basis to a targeted area. Without increasing rents and values there will not be sufficient financial resources to pay for adequate maintenance, let alone the major capital investment that heritage buildings often require. The exception to this is if the public sector gives deep and ongoing subsidies to the private sector. While some governments are willing to provide significant subsidies as a catalyst investment in the early stages of a revitalization effort, few governments today are either willing or able to provide subsidies on a permanent basis.

So the positive outcomes of "gentrification" read like the outcomes of any successful economic development initiative—new investment, new businesses, new jobs, increased tax revenues, higher levels of owner occupancy, and reduction of vacancy. But while these results are positive, they can still have a negative social impact, namely on the poor households that have been the primary occupants of the targeted heritage area.

Gentrification: The Negative Aspects

The following are the negative consequences of "gentrification":

- *Rising rents.* As noted above, rising rents are a strong indicator of an improving economic environment, and are a necessary precursor to sustained private investment. But for the payers of those rents, this is obviously a negative aspect, particularly when there is little or no opportunity for increased income to offset the increased rent. In older city centers in much of the developing world, it is not unusual to have many tenants occupying space for which no rent is being paid. Any rent at all is, therefore, an increase, and may be beyond the occupants' financial capacity to pay.
- *Rising taxes.* In many parts of the world a major source of revenue is property taxes. Usually property tax is an ad valorum tax, which is a levy based on the market value of the property. If a consequence of gentrification is increased property values (and it usually is), then that means an increase in the property taxes on the appreciating asset. While new owners and investors have likely built rising taxes into their purchase assumptions, existing owners, particularly those of modest means, probably have not. While rising rents are a problem for low-income tenants, rising property taxes are a problem for low-income owners.
- *Potential change of community character.* Neighborhoods and city centers are not just defined by their buildings; more importantly they are defined by the people who live there. As new groups move in, and particularly when the in-migration of one group is accompanied by an out-migration of another group, the community character of the area may change. This change will most certainly be seen in differences in economic status of the new residents and probably in their educational and occupational status as well. In some instances the incoming group may also be from a different ethnic group, religion, race, or even language group. (See box 5.5.)
- *Loss of power and sense of ownership by the local resident groups.* In an area inhabited almost exclusively by low-income households, there might not be much actual power or ownership, but there may be a sense of power and ownership. Long-term residents may share a sense of community, bonded by

---

BOX 5.5

Urban Upgrading and Keeping Residents in Place Conserves Historic Neighborhoods in Shaoxing, China

China, Zhejiang Urban Environment Project (Project number 066955)
Total Project Cost: US$334.3 million
Total Loan Amount: US$133 million
Approved: January 2004 – Closed: June 2011

Under the Zhejiang Project, the city of Shaoxing has repaired and upgraded modest Ming and Qing dynasty housing in the canal-side neighborhoods of its historic but deteriorating city core. To conserve streetscapes and housing patterns, it was necessary (as it is in many cities) to decrease the extreme residential densities that had evolved over time. However, the goal of Shaoxing's housing program was to create a healthier living environment while keeping as many of the neighborhood residents as possible in place. This was important to conserve the existing social fabric and networks that support daily life, especially for the poor. In the end, about 8,000 low-income households remained in place and benefited from upgraded housing and services, and around 700 households were resettled to modern apartments outside the historic city core. Today, the historic neighborhoods and their traditional waterside lifestyle continue as they have for many decades. Shaoxing's leaders see the neighborhoods as an important tourism asset, with tourists' spending providing a source of income for the neighborhoods' low-income residents.

Source: Ebbe, K., G. Licciardi, and A. Baeumler. 2011.

---

their common experiences and social ties. As the neighborhood renewal process evolves, increasingly attracting new residents with a different (and likely higher) level of income, as well as political and social influence, long-term residents may feel a loss of power and ownership that can have an adverse effect on community ties and structures.

• *Potential conflicts between new and long-term residents.* The shift in the sense of power and ownership can spark conflicts between new and long-term residents. Lifestyles may also be decidedly different, and what one group considers the norm another group might find offensive.

Thus even an economically successful heritage-based regeneration program may result in unanticipated and negative social and political consequences. But the potential consequence that will have the most direct relationship to the economic changes in real estate is the phenomenon known as social displacement. The simplistic description of displacement is this: property values and rents go up; newcomers who can afford it move in; long-term poorer residents who cannot afford to stay are pressured by the economic and social changes to move out. For the World Bank the issue of relocation (or, as it is termed, triggering an involuntary resettlement) is always a consideration when evaluating a potential project and its effects. Usually relocation is recognized when a government action forces people to move so that a highway can be built, for example, or a dam constructed. But increased rents and rising property values can also cause involuntary resettlement, not through direct action of the government but through the indirect (often gradual) transactions of the marketplace.

But like gentrification in general, the issue of displacement, or involuntary resettlement, should not be oversimplified. First, not all departure is characterized as forced displacement. People, businesses, and households move for a variety of reasons in addition to not being able to afford the increased rent. Second, there will always be some economic displacement, regardless of which neighborhood it is and whether it is targeted for heritage-based regeneration. If the rent is due and the renter can't afford to pay, more often than not this default causes the renter to move. This principle is enshrined in all rental contracts, for neighborhoods housing wealthier and lower-income households alike. Third, some departures can represent an economic gain, when owners take the opportunity to sell their property for more than they expected to fetch—hardly a negative outcome. Fourth, when the involuntary resettlement of households is properly conducted and households are moved into structures that are vacant and adequate, they haven't really been displaced.

There is at least some evidence that in a gentrification processes, many businesses and households will make an effort to remain in the neighborhood, even if it means further stretching their very limited budgets. After all, infrastructure and public services have been upgraded, creating a better physical environment and improved public safety. There are more and better stores in the area, as well as other new businesses. New jobs may be available.

On reflection, the positive outcomes of a heritage-based revitalization strategy far outweigh the negative ones. Further, it is important to recognize a simple fact: barring massive and ongoing public subsidies, neighborhoods that are mainly poor will not have the financial resources to maintain existing buildings and to secure a minimum of public safety, let alone generate sufficient funds to properly care for heritage buildings. The goal should be economic integration, which includes the low-income communities but also the rehabitation of heritage areas by households and businesses with the financial resources to make the necessary investments.

Mitigation Strategies

Despite the fact that the positive outcomes of gentrification outweigh the negative ones, this does not relieve public officials from the political and social responsibility of addressing the needs of the local residents who make up the low-income community and who have been long-term residents of the area.

The combination of seemingly disparate stakeholders, and the variety of instruments available—including local laws, entrepreneurial skills in the public and NGO sectors, financial resources, and political will—can affect what strategies will be used, but there are eight common responses to mitigate the residential displacement problem:

- *Public housing for resettlement.* It is not unusual for the public sector to own heritage buildings at the beginning of the regeneration process that are not needed for government services. Around the world there are numerous examples of heritage buildings being converted into housing for low-income residents. Local governments could integrate the existing low-income households into the heritage revitalization process by making available a range of housing alternatives in rehabilitated heritage buildings.
- *NGO-initiated housing.* NGOs have been effective in addressing a range of social issues, including assisting low-income communities with their housing needs. Helping NGOs to acquire, redevelop, and manage housing aimed at low-income households can be a way of strengthening that sector, building capacity in development and management, and at the same time providing needed housing of this strata of population.
- *Inclusionary housing policies.* During the early implementation of a neighborhood regeneration effort, as the higher-income households begin to move into a formerly derelict heritage area, private-sector actors will identify heritage buildings that are appropriate for adaptive reuse as residential units. With the "stick" of regulation, the "carrot" of incentives, or some combination of the two, the private sector may be stimulated to include in their redevelopment plans units that make provision for low-income residents who are currently living in the district. This mixed-income development pattern seems to work best when between 10 and 25 percent of the units are targeted for lower-income households.
- *Local hiring mandates.* Especially in the early stages of a heritage regeneration effort, there are likely to be public incentives for the private sector to act. These might be in the form of low-interest loans, grants, tax abatements, technical assistance, fee waivers, additional development rights, building code flexibility, or other types of incentives. Providing what are essentially public benefits to a private investor gives the public sector some leverage with the recipient.

That leverage can be used to encourage or mandate requirements to hire from the available labor pool found in the low-income community.

- *Low-income housing ownership programs.* One of the most effective means of integrating long-term tenants into a secure and lasting habitation of a neighborhood is to assist them in becoming homeowners. This is a strategy that is necessarily limited to the working citizenry, in that any homeownership program will require proof of employment and regular payments for the mortgage, insurance, taxes, and utilities. However, transforming renters into owners accomplishes two things: (1) households are no longer at risk of being displaced because of rising rents, and (2) households may experience financial benefit from the long-term appreciation of the neighborhood.[7]

- *Long-term rental subsidies.* Another way to keep low-income tenants in a gentrifying neighborhood is to subsidize rents in private-sector housing developments. While this requires a long-term commitment to funding from the public sector, it is possible that the enhanced tax revenues from the district could be used as a cross-subsidy to support the rent expenditures of the lower-income households.

- *New construction of affordable housing.* In most heritage areas that have deteriorated—both residential and commercial—there is vacant land. These empty parcels might have resulted from the demolition of a structure deemed no longer safe, from land clearance for a speculative development project that was never built, or from fire or other disaster. Often these vacant parcels end up in public hands or can be cost-effectively acquired by the public sector. As part of a comprehensive strategy, these parcels can be allocated for redevelopment for low-income or mixed-income housing. However, it should be a prerequisite that there be design guidelines to assure that any new construction on these parcels is compatible with the historic character of the district.

- *Job training programs.* Ultimately individuals and families get out of poverty because they have secured productive employment. Within commercial and residential heritage neighborhoods that are experiencing revitalization, there will be job opportunities. Some of these openings will be for highly skilled artisans for the restoration of heritage buildings; others will be for maintenance jobs for buildings and public spaces. Additionally, new businesses established in the area will seek to hire employees. All of these represent opportunities to provide job training for existing residents so that they become direct and long-term beneficiaries of the regeneration process.

All of the above strategies aim to keep existing residents in the heritage area rather than simply creating new housing projects for them elsewhere. (See box 5.6.)

BOX 5.6

Lebanon Project Is Mitigating the Impact of Urban Upgrading on Housing for Poor Households

Lebanon Cultural Heritage and Urban Development Project
(Project number 050529)
Total Project Cost: US$61.9 million
Total Loan Amount: US$31.5 million
Approved: April 2003 – Ongoing

The government of Lebanon benefitted from co-financing from the World Bank and the governments of France and Italy to undertake an extensive project aiming at improving conservation and management of the country's built heritage, increasing local economic development, and enhancing the quality of life in the five historic city cores of Baalbeck, Byblos, Saida, Tripoli, and Tyre. Two additional loans from the World Bank (US$27 million) and from the French government (€21.5 million) have been approved in 2012, bringing the overall project cost to approximately US$117 million.

Among its interventions, the project supports the rehabilitation of historic housing stock in city cores. Since these areas provide the main residential opportunities to the poorest segment of the urban population, measures have been put in place to maintain the inhabitants in the immediate vicinity of their original housing. An illustration of this is the three apartment buildings constructed to resettle about 70 families who were previously living in slum-like conditions in the ancient complex of Khan Al Askar (Tripoli), which was successfully rehabilitated through the project. It is also expected that the rehabilitated Khan Al Askar will provide job opportunities for the local residents.

Source: Lebanon Cultural Heritage and Urban Development Project Appraisal Document.

It should be noted that not just residents may be displaced as a consequence of the regeneration process; businesses, particularly small businesses, can be affected as well. Many of the above strategies can be applied to small businesses as well as households. A heritage building could be redeveloped by the public or NGO sector to house small businesses that are in danger of being priced out of their existing space. Low-interest loans could be provided to small businesses so that they can acquire their business premises. The business equivalent of job training can be provided: capacity building and management assistance to businesses so that they are prepared to capitalize on the nature of the new market.

An exemplary case of a way to address the needs of small businesses is found in Quito, Ecuador. There, street vendors had become so ubiquitous that public safety and pedestrian and vehicular circulation were compromised. It was felt that the problem had to be addressed before a heritage-based center city revitalization program could be successful. Other cities had simply forcibly removed street vendors without consideration of how or if those businesses would survive. Quito officials decided to take a different path. After extensive consultations with street vendors and other stakeholders it was decided that the city would build an enclosed shopping venue within the heritage district to which the vendors could relocate. The rents would be kept low so that these micro-businesses could continue to exist. As a result these small entrepreneurs remained within the heritage district, are off the streets, and are sharing in the prosperity that has been realized in the historic center city of Quito.

So there are a variety of approaches to address the potentially negative effects on low-income residents when a heritage-based regeneration strategy is undertaken. Whatever mitigation measures are used, they are most effective when:

- An urban strategy, including resettlement planning, is formulated in consultation with key stakeholders and agreed upon before implementation of the regeneration process.
- There is active, meaningful outreach to and systematic planning exercises with local organizations and residents.
- There are educational programs for the community broadly, and for the existing low-income residents particularly, regarding the significance and importance of the heritage resources.
- A share of the enhanced revenues resulting from the regeneration is channeled to the local government and earmarked for reinvestment for the benefit of existing low-income residents, funding such activities as building and conservation skills training, management capacity building, and assistance to community-led micro-business initiatives.
- The strategy is comprehensive, addressing not just providing housing but also healthcare, job training, transportation, recreation, and education.

Conclusion

Heritage buildings are real estate. As properties, these are bought, sold, and rented in the marketplace. While heritage buildings have aesthetic, cultural, social, educational, and environmental value, they can also have significant economic value.

Using tools and techniques from traditional real estate valuation approaches as well as methodologies from environmental economics, analysts around the world have begun to evaluate the impact of heritage designation and its accompanying regulations and restrictions on real estate values. Approaches vary from answering a relatively simple query—"What is the value per square foot of properties within historic districts as compared to values within the same city not within a district?"—to more complex hedonic pricing approaches, such as using linear regression to isolate the contributory value of heritage listing after all other variables have been accounted for.

A growing body of research findings, based on studies of international examples, consistently demonstrates that heritage conservation pays. And the most straightforward evidence that heritage pays is the willingness of buyers not just to pay for heritage properties, but to pay extra for them.

This commonly found economic premium has a multitude of public policy implications. Rising property values will often mean increased revenues for local governments, a greater willingness of financial institutions to make loans, a greater likelihood of private-sector investment, and fewer heritage buildings lost to demolition by inaction and neglect.

At the same time, rapidly rising property values often mean higher prices for vacant land, resulting (when there is no, or not enough, protection for heritage buildings) in demolition of smaller historic buildings to make room to erect larger new structures. The other consequence of rising property values is the potential adverse effect on low-income households, particularly renters, who may suffer displacement due to the economic as well as social changes. It is important, therefore, to identify early on strategies to mitigate the threats both to existing buildings and to long-term residents.

Heritage monuments and historic districts need periodic and often substantial reinvestment in infrastructure upgrades, preservation management, and conservation works so that these places may contribute to regenerating the economic, cultural, and social life of city centers. Furthermore, heritage buildings—which form the core of historic city centers—incorporate aesthetic, cultural, social, environmental, and educational values that must be passed on to future generations. These buildings are a unique endowment, but also a steadily diminishing resource—in some cases even at risk of disappearing. To counter the possible irreversible loss of heritage buildings and the non-economic values they hold, heritage buildings need to have economic value today.

Along with robust commitments of public and/or third-sector[8] funds for the care and continuance of heritage places, investments are also going to have to come from the private sector. The private sector is far more likely to make an investment in an area with rising property values than one with stagnant or declining values. Further, as property values increase, the amount of public resources required as subsidies or incentives decreases.

The sustainable preservation management of historic urban fabric starts when heritage buildings are first identified and then protected, when there is a comprehensive approach in public policy toward safeguarding of heritage assets along with strategic investments made to upgrade public infrastructure, and when private-sector investment in those buildings is captured. Where these elements are in place, the economic value of heritage places is being demonstrated around the world, confirmed by a robust and growing body of research.

Notes

1. As was noted earlier, the total economic value of a heritage building is its use value plus its non-use value(s). This chapter only deals with the direct use value.
2. A relatively low-cost approach to track building condition is to simply take digital photographs of the exteriors of every heritage building on a regular basis—every 6–12 months. While not a precisely measureable indicator, at least it is relatively easy to determine if general physical conditions are getting better or worse. If building conditions are improving, that inherently implies that someone is making an investment in the buildings, and investment itself is both a cause and an effect of enhanced property values.
3. Using this approach it is important to identify any capital improvements that may have been made to the property between the two selling dates, as that, rather than simple appreciation, may be the cause of the higher selling price.
4. The exception is if the owner of the property is the federal government itself, or if federal government funds are being used as part of the project. Even this exception doesn't guarantee that the property will not be razed, but it does mean there will be a rather extensive review process and a consideration of alternatives before the demolition can be taken.
5. http://www.merriam-webster.com.
6. There is an exception to this general principle: when a "vacant" building is actually occupied by those who have no established legal right to be there and may be paying no rent. In some situations the political, regulatory, or social processes of emptying the building so that redevelopment can take place can be both expensive and burdensome.
7. Rising property taxes can be a difficulty for low-income housing owners. But this is a cash flow problem, not a wealth problem; their underlying asset is appreciating in value. Therefore a relatively simple solution can be implemented by allowing the property taxes to simply accrue until the property is ultimately sold or transferred to younger family members, at which point the deferred taxes can be collected.
8. The third sector is usually defined as including nongovernmental organizations as well as philanthropic and voluntary activities.

References

Architectural Conservancy of Ontario. 2009. *Heritage Districts Work!* http://www.arconserv.ca/news_events/show.cfm?id=184

Broadbent, K. 2011. "Assessing the Impact of Local Historic District Designation on Mortgage Foreclosure Rates: The Case of Philadelphia." Master's thesis, University of Pennsylvania.

Cebula, R. J. 2009. "The Hedonic Pricing Model Applied to the Housing Market of the City of Savannah and Its Savannah Historic Landmark District." *The Review of Regional Studies* 39 (1).

Cherry, M. 2001. "Listing as an Instrument in Managing Change to Historic Buildings." In *Historic Cities and Sacred Sites: Cultural Roots for Urban Futures,* ed. I. Serageldin, E. Shluger, and J. Martin-Brown, 247–257. Washington, DC: World Bank.

Coffin, D. A. 1989. "The Impact of Historic Districts on Residential Property Values." *Eastern Economic Journal* 9 (3). http://www.jstor.org/pss/40325269

Coulson, N. E., and M. L. Lahr. 2005. "Gracing the Land of Elvis and Beale Street: Historic Designation and Property Values." *Real Estate Economics* 33 (3). http://onlinelibrary.wiley.com/doi/10.1111/j.1540-6229.2005.00127.x/abstract

Deodhar, V. 2004. *Does the Housing Market Value Heritage? Some Empirical Evidence.* Sydney, Australia: Macquarie University. http://www.heritage.wa.gov.au/assets/files/LG_publications/SyndeyResearchHousingMarket.pdf

Department of Urban Planning and Design, City of Tucson, Arizona. 2007. *Benefits of Residential Historic District Designation for Property Owners.*

Econsult Corporation. 2010. *The Economic Impact of Historic Preservation in Philadelphia.* http://www.preservephiladelphia.org/wp-content/uploads/Econ_Report_Final.pdf

Gale, D. E. 1991. *The Impact of Historic District Designation in Washington, DC.* Occasional Paper No. 6, Center for Washington Area Studies, George Washington University, Washington, DC. http://www.gwu.edu/~gwipp/The%20Impact%20of%20Historic%20District%20Designation.pdf

Gilderbloom, J. I., M. J. Hanka, and J. D. Ambrosius. 2009. "Historic Preservation's Impact on Job Creation, Property Values, and Environmental Sustainability." *Journal of Urbanism* 2 (2). http://pdfserve.informaworld.com/486835__913321085.pdf

Ijla, A. 2008. *The Impact of Local Historic District Designation on Residential Property Values: An Analysis of Three Slow-Growth and Three Fast-Growth Central Cities in the United States.* Cleveland State University. http://etd.ohiolink.edu/view.cgi/Ijla%20Akram.pdf?csu1206539169

Jaramillo, P. 2010. *The Sustainability of Urban Heritage Preservation: The Case of Quito.* Inter-American Development Bank. http://idbdocs.iadb.org/wsdocs/getdocument.aspx?docnum=35334775

Lazrak, F., P. Nijkamp, P. Rietveld, and J. Rouwendal. 2010. *The Market Value of Listed Heritage: An Urban Economic Application of Spatial Hedonic Pricing.* Amsterdam: VU University.

Mendes Zancheti, S., and J. Gabriel. 2010. *The Sustainability of Urban Heritage Preservation: The Case of Salvador de Bahia.* Inter-American Development Bank. http://idbdocs.iadb.org/wsdocs/getdocument.aspx?docnum=35343131

Narwold, A., J. Sandy, and C. Tu. 2008. "Historic Designation and Residential Property Values." *International Real Estate Review* 11 (1): 83–95.

Quatersan, A., and M. Romis. 2010. *The Sustainability of Urban Heritage Preservation: The Case of Oaxaca de Juarez.* Inter-American Development Bank. http://idbdocs .iadb.org/wsdocs/getdocument.aspx?docnum=35303038

Shipley, R. 2000. "Heritage Designation and Property Values: Is There an Effect?" *International Journal of Heritage Studies* 6 (1). http://www.heritageoshawa.ca/docs/ readingroom/heritage-planning/heritage-designation-and-property-values.pdf

Stipe, R. 1983. "Why Preserve Historic Resources." In *Readings in Historic Preservation.* New Brunswick, NJ: Rutgers University, Center for Urban Policy Research.

Taddei Neto, P. 2001. "Policies of Historic and Cultural Heritage Preservation in Brazil." In *Historic Cities and Sacred Sites: Cultural Roots for Urban Futures,* ed. I. Serageldin, E. Shluger, and J. Martin-Brown, 41–45. Washington, DC: World Bank.

6

Governance in Historic City Core Regeneration Projects

Eduardo Rojas
Lecturer in Historic Preservation, University of Pennsylvania (U.S.)
Former Principal Urban Development Specialist, Inter-American Development Bank

The focus of this chapter is on the governance issues raised by historic city core regeneration projects. Further, it explores processes through which the heritage values of historic city cores lead different stakeholders to support, finance, and implement conservation activities. The proposed analytical framework is tested in four Latin American cities: Oaxaca, Quito, Salvador de Bahia, and Valparaiso. These mid-size cities, with very high urban growth rates, feature important historic city cores that are included on the United Nations Educational, Scientific and Cultural Organization (UNESCO) World Heritage List and are the subject of active conservation efforts. From the governance perspective, the conservation strategies that managed to engage the interest of a wider group of actors are those of Oaxaca and Quito. In both cities, the conservation process was able to adapt and create new uses for urban heritage assets that also have economic use and non-use values. The chapter concludes that the sustainability of the conservation process is attributed, in part, to the greater diversification and mix of uses and users of the historic city core, and, in part, to the financing scheme which does not depend on the fortunes of only one activity or the budget allocation of a sole institution. In addition, expansion of the residential land uses brings stability to the process and generates demand for local commerce.

Introduction

This chapter discusses the contribution that the governance arrangements can make to attain the sustainable conservation of historic city cores, as a means to enhance the livability and economic vibrancy of cities. It uses the broad definition of governance proposed by Bell: "The use of institutions, structures of authority and even collaboration to allocate resources and coordinate or control activity in society or the economy" (Bell 2002). Consequently, the analysis focuses on a wide array of issues including laws, regulations, procedures for decision making, public institutions of command and control, institutional arrangements for promoting inter-sector and public-private coordination, and the institutional as well as expert capacity of the personnel devoted to the task.

The discussion centers on the governance issues posed by the conservation of one type of urban heritage, historic city cores, and how the governance process affects the sustainability of the conservation effort. The discussion uses an operational definition of sustainability, adapted to this specific area of concern: the conservation of a historic city core is considered sustainable when: (1) the area is attractive to a wide variety of users that demand space for developing residential, commercial, service, cultural, and recreational activities; (2) private investment is available, supplying the demand for space for these activities and maintaining the historic characteristic of private buildings; and (3) public resources are used mostly for the provision of public goods. The normal operation of the markets only rarely leads to such outcomes in historic city cores; thus, some form of government intervention is almost always required. Furthermore, the needs and preferences of modern society call for historic city cores to be rehabilitated and adaptively reused without losing their historic character.

Governance: Values, Actors, and Processes in the Conservation of Urban Heritage

An urban heritage area—including the network of streets and public spaces, the built structures, and the land-use pattern—comprises material assets that carry different values for different actors. Consequently, their valuation must take into consideration a broad range of interested actors—henceforth termed stakeholders—and the wide variety of reasons why they consider these assets valuable. The decision-making process leading to the regeneration of historic city cores must include a broad spectrum of stakeholders to balance their distinct competing interests. Reaching a workable agreement to support regeneration of historic city cores is the main challenge for the governance of urban heritage.

Values of Urban Heritage

The discussion of the values of the urban heritage, below, follows Throsby's schema to assess the multiple values of heritage in which a tangible heritage property is understood both as fixed capital that could be income-producing, generating a flow of economic benefits, and as cultural capital generating a flow of noneconomic benefits for society, generically called socio-cultural benefits (Throsby 2000). Figure 6.1 presents the schema used in the discussion that follows.

The most widely recognized values are linked to the noneconomic benefits that the urban heritage generates for a community—those that satisfy peoples' social or spiritual needs. This category of socio-cultural values refers to some that are hard to define and quantify, including aesthetic, spiritual, social, historic, and symbolic values. Aesthetic values refer to the benefits community members may derive from being in the presence of an object that is considered aesthetically beautiful. Spiritual values involve the identification by individuals and communities of buildings or places with their religious practices or traditions such as honoring their ancestors. Social values arise when the heritage assets lead to interpersonal relationships valued by the community—for instance, places for gathering, discussion, or social interaction where events held within are enhanced because of those places' nature as heritage sites. Places that are linked to events of local, national, or world history are considered to have historic value, and when the heritage reflects community-shared values it is said to have symbolic value. (See box 6.1.)

The use values refer to those assigned to urban heritage by individuals or social groups that appropriate its utility and/or the economic return it produces. These can be direct use values, as in the case of a heritage property used for offices that

FIGURE 6.1
The Values of Urban Heritage

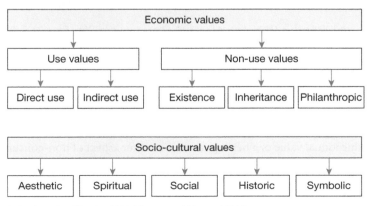

Source: Author based on Throsby 2002; Mourato and Massanti 2002.

BOX 6.1

Adaptive Reuse Preserves a Symbol of Identity and Distinctiveness for the City of Chongqing in China

China, Chongqing Urban Environment Project (Project number 049436)
Total Project Cost: US$535.9 million
Total Loan Amount: US$200 million
Approved: June 2000 – Closed: March 2009

The main objective of this project was the development of large-scale urban infrastructure—including water supply and waste-water management—in the municipality of Chongqing. At the city's request the project also supported the conservation and adaptive reuse of a 10,000 square meter site comprising several merchants' guild halls built during the Qing Dynasty (1644–1911). These halls represent an array of cultural values including Chongqing's history as a flourishing trading port on the Yangtze River; the high quality of architecture and craftsmanship attained during the Qing period; and the rise of organized associations, which eventually became modern chambers of commerce. These buildings were restored and adapted as venues for a cultural center with theater, exhibit hall, and museum. The project component has enhanced economic development in the city center by: (1) providing a focal point for the municipality's civic events; (2) creating a new tourism site; and (3) stimulating small-business start-ups in the adjacent neighborhoods. The social benefits of the restoration include: (1) conserving evidence of Chongqing's built heritage and artistic achievements for future generations; (2) strengthening the community's identification with their history as a city of river-based traders; and (3) providing a pleasant and educational place to experience local cultural heritage.

Source: K. Ebbe et. al. *Urban Heritage Strategies: Chongqing, China.* World Bank, 2005.

---

yields higher rents than other similar buildings by virtue of its heritage status. There are also indirect use values, such as the value gained by non-heritage properties that benefit from their location in proximity to heritage properties. These values are linked to the public good characteristics of the urban heritage. The educational value of a heritage asset is another aspect of non-consumption use that falls into this category.

Non-use values capture the less-tangible economic benefits that the urban heritage affords. The existence value captures the benefits that certain people derive from the fact that a specific heritage asset simply exists, even though they may have no intention of visiting or using these assets directly. The existence value includes the option value, which captures the interest of individuals or groups in keeping open the possibility that they might make future use of the heritage site's facilities. Other non-use values are the inheritance values that reflect individuals' or groups' interest in bequeathing the heritage asset to future generations, and the philanthropic value of the asset, which includes the public relations or branding image value to those who invest in it without using it.

Improvements in methods to attach a monetary worth to the range of values allow insights into the preferences of individuals or community groups but do not directly lead to the adoption of conservation policies. If values of heritage assets are to be reflected in actions toward their conservation, recognition of these multiple values must be incorporated into social processes through which public and private resources are devoted to multiple and competing uses.

Actors in the Conservation of the Urban Heritage

Actors involved in the regeneration of historic city cores—the stakeholders—vary widely. Recent experience shows that the broad spectrum of stakeholders may include the following: conservationists; individuals and organizations of the civil society interested in the different manifestations of the culture of a society, who traditionally advocate heritage conservation: different levels of government responsible for financing rehabilitation efforts; representatives of the local community; property owners; real estate investors; households; and the business community (Rojas and Lanzafame 2011). This chapter argues that it is critical for all mentioned groups of stakeholders to be involved in the implementation of a conservation process aimed at the adaptive regeneration and development of urban heritage areas.

The different stakeholders have different motivations and incentives for engaging in the conservation of the urban heritage. Much of the generous financing of urban heritage conservation activities and projects is supported by organizations linked to the cultural groups (foundations, trusts, cultural associations, and clubs) that channel resources (funds, time, and talent) of individuals and groups to the conservation of heritage assets, including historic city cores. The British National Trust, English Heritage, and similar trusts established in the United Kingdom, the United States, Australia, Italy, Jamaica, and other countries are good examples of such organizations. (See box 6.2.) Visitors touring cities may also become interested parties and actors in the conservation process (and so, capturing their views can have an impact on decisions concerning the allocation of resources) (Carson et al. 2002).

Government bodies at the national and local levels are formally entrusted with setting the parameters and norms of stewardship and contributing to

---

BOX 6.2

The Bali Heritage Trust Supports Tangible and Intangible Cultural Assets

Indonesia, Bali Urban Infrastructure Project (Project number 036047)
Total Project Cost: US$278 million
Total Loan Amount: US$110 million
Approved: May 1997 – Closed: September 2004

The Provincial Administration of Bali, with the assistance of a World Bank loan, launched a project to improve basic infrastructure—including roads, water, and drainage systems—covering historic city cores of the island. The aim was to address the challenges of increasing rates of urbanization. Due to the importance of cultural tourism activities to the island's economy, the project also included investments for the protection of heritage. One key achievement supported by the project was the establishment of the Bali Heritage Trust (BHT), a semi-government body partly financed by the provincial government and the private sector, to provide systematic management and conservation of Bali's cultural assets. Since its inception in 2003, BHT has supported educational programs, public discussions, and training sessions to enhance local residents' awareness of cultural heritage, and drafted the Bali Cultural Heritage Conservation Act. In addition, BHT built an inventory of Bali's heritage that was forward looking at the time, due to its inclusion of both tangible and intangible cultural heritage.

Source: Bali Urban Infrastructure Project Appraisal Document and Implementation Completion Report.

---

the long-term conservation process. Key government institutions include the national or regional heritage boards or commissions that are responsible for the normative and technical tasks; this includes making decisions about which urban areas and buildings to list as heritage assets worthy of protection, and adopting policies and regulations to safeguard them. The local government is the principal agent or stakeholder, due to its role as the leading body oversee-ing urban heritage areas, often empowered to make a long-term commitment to maintaining their integrity. Thus, local government plays an essential role in initiating and sustaining the conservation process of historic city cores.

Government decisions have vast consequences for the use and development of these listed assets, affecting landlords, real estate developers and other potential business investors, residents, and others. Conservation regulations often limit the freedom of landlords to dispose of their properties and may constrain business owners who set up shop in heritage areas. Governments and concessionaries of public utilities may find it more costly to provide services in these areas due to the conservation regulations. Households may either derive benefit or be negatively affected by urban heritage conservation restrictions—possibly valuing living in a historic city core, possibly being priced out of the market by the process known as gentrification. The process through which the values held by each of the stakeholders enters into the decision-making process, and the ways in which their contributions are incorporated in the financing of the conservation and development process, are critical components of the governance process for historic city cores.

Spheres of Action for Valuing and Allocating Resources

The valuation of historic city cores involves actions that occur in several spheres of social interaction. For instance, the research on the historic or aesthetic value of a place or building occurs in the realm of the social sciences' scientific inquiry. Other actions take place in the political arena, such as the enactment of urban land-use and building regulations to preserve an urban heritage area, and the allocation of public resources to the conservation effort. Some forms of social interactions are essentially private, such as the decision of a household to acquire a home in a heritage area. Other actions that are essentially private are still strongly influenced by public regulations. An example would be the philanthropic donation of private resources to conservation efforts that is encouraged by and also bounded by tax exemptions granted by the government. Table 6.1 lists some of the most significant activities involved in the valuation of urban heritage areas taking place in different spheres of social interaction.

Two intertwined processes deserve a more detailed analysis: first, the institutional process of listing and regulating heritage assets, allocating resources for their protection, and leading the urban heritage conservation process; and, second, the market processes through which for-profit private actors get involved.

The listing process for urban areas—those containing important or significant heritage assets—commonly pertains to a public-private realm and involves proponents who are usually members of cultural groups, as well as the national heritage boards that are mostly made up of specialists, academics, and scientists who often are also members of the same socio-cultural strata. Often this is the case when the heritage designation process does not include the affected communities. International treaties and the organizations charged with their implementation—the World Heritage Convention managed by UNESCO and other nongovernmental organizations (NGOs) such as the International Council on Monuments and Sites (ICOMOS)—play significant roles in advocating for and promoting the recognition and conservation of listed heritage. Their

TABLE 6.1

Activities Involved in the Valuation of Historic City Cores

Spheres of social interaction	Activity
Scientific	• Historic research • Ethnographic studies • Archaeological research • Aesthetic studies • Cultural analysis • Anthropological research • Education and training
Cultural groups	• Assessment of the public relations value of urban heritage • Negotiations with owners • Getting incentives from the government • Securing partners for the operation and maintenance of the assets
Grassroots	• Community involvement in support of preservation • Participation of nongovernmental organizations and civil society in the decision-making process • Mass media dissemination of the values and benefits of urban heritage preservation • Community stewardship and safeguarding of cultural landscapes and monuments
Market transactions	• Purchases of properties for preservation and development • Sales and purchases or preserved and developed space • Rental of commercial and residential property
Institutional	• Setting up a national heritage institution • Enacting regulation and safeguard policies • Listing of urban heritage sites • Managing land-use and building regulations • Offering fiscal incentives • Providing public-sector leadership • Coordination, sequencing, and determining the scale of interventions • Developing systems of incentives and penalties that apply to stakeholders

Source: Author.

decision-making processes are akin to the institutional processes leading to the enactment of conservation legislation in the countries, involving a mixture of technical and political considerations. (See box 6.3.)

The allocation of public resources and funds targeted for urban heritage conservation is subject to more public scrutiny than listing procedures, if only because of the many competing demands on the scarce resources and funds of local, state, or national governments. However, the scope of actors involved is mostly confined to those who are involved in the budgeting process. Typically

---

BOX 6.3

Multiple Enhancement Activities Resulted in World Heritage Listing in Four Cities of Mauritania

Mauritania Cultural Heritage Project (Project number 064570)
Total Project Cost: US$5.5 million
Total Loan Amount: US$5 million
Approved: June 2000 – Closed: March 2005

The government of Mauritania, assisted by a World Bank loan and in collaboration with UNESCO, prepared a project implemented in four historic city cores in Mauritania; namely, Ouadane, Chinguetti, Tichit, and Ouallata. Upon project completion, these four cities were then nominated to and inscribed on the World Heritage List (WHL). The WHL listing provided these cities with key planning and management instruments and activities leading to positive valorization and economic development. Chief among these interventions are: (1) conservation and development plans; (2) preparation of practical maintenance and rehabilitation manuals; (3) approval of regulatory texts; and (4) onsite learning centers for capacity building in selected sites. Other project achievements included establishment of the Ministry of Culture, empowered to prepare regulations and conduct capacity building for human resources development and lead in the institutional reform.

Source: Mauritania Cultural Heritage Project Appraisal Document and Implementation and Completion Report.

---

the members of cultural groups raise public awareness of the importance of the conservation of the urban heritage through public forums and the media. These activities contribute to create the conditions for local elected officials to rally central government agencies to provide resources and funds for local heritage assets.

Key activities executed by the local government include identifying and designating cultural heritage assets and other places of historic significance, supervising and conducting routine maintenance and conservation works for public spaces, making improvements to infrastructure and public spaces located within the heritage area, regulating the conservation actions of private stakeholders, and, above all, ensuring that the public and private interventions are effectively coordinated, executed in the proper sequence, and are robust in scale (Rojas 2004).

The other area of action to consider closely is the market process. Private investors interested in bidding for properties in historic city cores—real estate developers, families buying houses, and businesses seeking central locations—may face several constraints to taking action in heritage conservation. The most significant is the real (or perceived) commercial risk that they confront in deteriorated, abandoned, or overused historic city cores. Private investors and property owners may not have sufficient incentives or the capacity to address the complex problem of reversing deterioration or halting a downward trend.[1] In addition, property owners and developers have traditionally opposed the listing of urban properties and areas as historic because of concerns about restrictions on property development such listing can bring. Often at the time of listing, there is little clarity on the long-term urban development consequences of enforcement of listing requirements; in particular, property owners may worry about how such restrictions might affect their ability to develop their properties (OMA 2010).

As discussed above, the local authority, as the only actor with a long-term commitment is, in principle, capable of launching a regeneration process by investing in the rehabilitation of infrastructure and public spaces, and in the conservation and development of heritage buildings. In fact, it should be noted that correcting market failures that lead to the undersupply of conserved space for multiple uses in historic city cores and preservation of the public goods supplied by urban heritage areas are becoming central concerns of local governments. Public agencies are usually rallied to take this on by constituencies interested in the conservation of their urban heritage. Alas, not many local administrations have the capacity to undertake these types of activities.

Progress in Urban Heritage Conservation in Latin America

In Latin America, historians, artists, intellectuals, and some architects practicing within the principles of the modern movement were the first to call attention to the threats to buildings of historic or artistic interest in the rapidly growing cities of the region. For instance, in Brazil and Mexico, as early as the 1930s, such citizens were pressing for the conservation of urban colonial and eclectic buildings and archaeological and historic sites threatened by urban renewal schemes or looting. They lobbied politicians for the passage of heritage conservation legislation and led the establishment of government institutions devoted to the protection of the heritage, such as the National Institute of Historic and Artistic Heritage of Brazil (IPHAN) and the National Institute of Anthropology and History of Mexico (INAH). To date, most Latin American countries have at least some legislation protecting the urban heritage as well as institutions implementing this legislation; a few countries have also initiated public actions geared to supporting the long-term conservation of this heritage.

The long road to sustainable urban heritage conservation is marked by several development stages. As mentioned before, the first stage of the conservation movement starts with cultural groups. Most countries in Latin America are still in their first phase in the movement toward preserving and developing urban heritage (Rojas and Moura Castro 1999). This phase includes isolated actions to preserve specific buildings. Funding for such actions comes from philanthropy or sporadic allocations from the central, state, or local governments. In this phase—which for most countries started in the late 1950s and is still continuing—socio-cultural values are the dominant drivers of action, and the only economic value of heritage places acknowledged in some instances is the direct consumption use by tourists. Underpinning the official public policy regarding which cultural patrimony is to be preserved and promoted is a political choice fundamentally aimed at protecting elements of a national or regional identity. The narrow set of values put into play—the result of the involvement of few actors and mostly through activities undertaken within the scientific and elite transactions spheres of social interaction—leads to narrowly defined and executed interventions. Table 6.2 shows the limited variety of actors and spheres of social interaction involved in this type of intervention.

The conservation decision-making process focuses mostly on the physical qualities of the buildings and less on the uses and the potential partners that may contribute to sustaining the preserved heritage asset. Figure 6.2 presents the typical steps of the traditional conservation decision-making sequence that focuses mostly on the socio-cultural value of the assets and the authenticity of the conservation interventions. Consequently the buildings are mostly devoted to public uses and are often underutilized.

In this phase of concern for the conservation of the historic city cores, the uses for the conserved assets rank low in the decision-making chain, thus having little influence on the allocation of funds and resources. This outcome is the result of a misalignment, or asymmetry, in the relations among the actors involved in the process. At this point, most of the funding for conservation activities is provided by private philanthropists or by the taxpayers' contributions to the central government. These actors, in turn, are not the main beneficiaries of the conservation efforts; rather conservation may help just the local communities, tour operators, or other specific groups, depending on the particular case. This approach leads to inconsistent interventions, cannot mobilize all possible funding, and does not guarantee the long-term sustainability of the conserved assets.

A more developed stage in urban heritage conservation is marked by involvement of the governments and public institutions in the process. Confronted with the limitations of the initial approach, cognizant of the wider set of values assigned to urban heritage by the communities that use these areas, and responding to commitments made to international organizations, several

TABLE 6.2
Actors and Spheres of Social Interaction Involved in the Conservation and Development of Historic City Cores

	A: When only historic values act as motivators				
	Spheres of social interaction				
Stakeholders	Scientific inquiry	Transactions of the elite	Grassroots	Market transactions	Political processes
National government					X
Regional government					
Local government					
Real estate investors					
Entrepreneurs					
Consumers					
Households					
Scholars	X				
Cultural groups					X
Philanthropy		X			
Organizations of the civil society					
NGOs		X			X
Community organizations					

	B: With multiple values at play				
	Spheres of social interaction				
Stakeholders	Scientific inquiry	Transactions of the elite	Grassroots	Market transactions	Political processes
National government					X
Regional government					X
Local government		X	X		X
Real estate investors				X	
Entrepreneurs				X	
Consumers				X	
Households			X	X	
Scholars	X				
Cultural groups		X			X
Philanthropy		X			
Organizations of the civil society					
NGOs		X	X		X
Community organizations			X		X

Source: Author.

FIGURE 6.2

Traditional Conservation Decision-Making Sequence

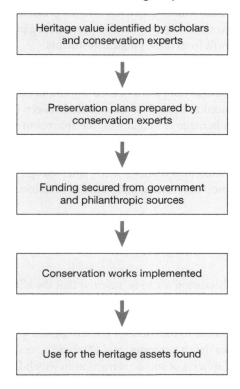

Heritage value identified by scholars
and conservation experts

↓

Preservation plans prepared by
conservation experts

↓

Funding secured from government
and philanthropic sources

↓

Conservation works implemented

↓

Use for the heritage assets found

Source: Author.

Latin American countries moved to what can be called a second phase in the conservation of urban heritage (Rojas and Moura Castro 1999). Brazil and Mexico pioneered this phase and at the closing of the 20th century were joined by countries such as Colombia, Peru, and Ecuador, and soon after by Chile.

In this phase, the economic values assigned to urban heritage go beyond the economic non-use values (including the existence and inheritance values) and expands to a broader range of values such as historic and aesthetic values and the direct-use value related to tourism. Cultural groups are joined by organizations of the civil society, nongovernmental organizations, and community organizations—thus enlarging the scope of the cultural heritage assets considered for conservation, and promoting greater public-sector involvement in the conservation of urban heritage. National, regional, and local governments start budgeting funds for the conservation of urban heritage (albeit at limited levels and with significant annual variations). Competing for resources with many pressing social and infrastructure needs, and often executed by understaffed institutions with little experience, these efforts are not usually effective. As in the previous phase, the national taxpayers are not directly involved in the decision-making process, nor are those who will directly benefit from these public investments.

These problems are at the core of the difficulties experienced by most communities in mobilizing financial, institutional, and human resources toward sustained conservation and development of their important historic city cores. The difficulties can be traced to the lack of direct links between the spheres of social interaction in which heritage is valued with the spheres in which financial and institutional resources are allocated for the conservation of listed heritage. In this stage, the results still fall short of the desired mark: the outcomes are usually sporadic and uncoordinated interventions with rather meager involvement of the local communities, property owners, and potential investors.

Adaptive Reuse: A Sustainable Approach to Urban Heritage Conservation

From the previous discussion it can be inferred that the allocation of resources (in terms of volume and stability of the flow of funds) devoted to urban heritage conservation would increase with: (1) the engagement of a diverse range of actors (stakeholders) committed to the cause of conserving the urban heritage due to the diversity of values that it possesses, and (2) these actors' active involvement in a wider variety of spheres of social interaction in which financial and human resources are allocated to the task. Possible strategies for promoting the diversification of stakeholders include documenting and disseminating information about the historic, artistic, symbolic, spiritual, and social values embedded in a given urban heritage area. This could attract the interest of a wide variety of social actors who could be willing to contribute resources and provide political support to the conservation effort.

An alternative strategy is the promotion of the historic city core area as a desirable place to live and work; hence, enticing the interest of real estate investors to refit and preserve space for new uses in the area, and attracting new residents and businesses. The potential economic and financial benefits associated with the use values of the heritage area can mobilize new actors to join in the process—households, businesses, real estate investors—adding diversity to the set of supporters and financers of the process. These new actors can add creativity and ingenuity that will complement the public administration's efforts to conserve the heritage due to its existence and inheritance values, the most common drivers for public intervention. Table 6.3B indicates how the array of actors involved in the process grows when the variety of values brought into play expands. Also the conservation of the historic city core is transacted in a wider variety of spheres of socioeconomic interaction, mainly involving real estate markets. This is in sharp contrast to the limited set of stakeholders and spheres of social interaction involved when only the historic values of a heritage area are the drivers of the preservation management and conservation process.

Essential to establishing a long-term sustainable urban heritage conservation and development process is a better alignment of the contributions of the expanded set of actors so as to ensure that those who promote urban heritage conservation coincide to the greatest extent possible with those who pay for the required interventions and with those who directly benefit from the results. The expanded set of actors with varied interests leads to a diversification of the spheres of social interactions in which the values of the urban heritage are acknowledged and acted upon. The governance consequence of such a strategy is that activities and decisions taking place in the scientific, political, and community involvement spheres shall be coordinated with those occurring in the philanthropy arena and the real estate markets.

Challenges of the Adaptive Reuse Approach to Urban Heritage Conservation

Implementation of the proposed approach to conservation poses a significant governance challenge, as it requires realigning the interests of the key stakeholders in the conservation of the urban heritage so that they may work toward a common goal.

Responding to the multiple values of heritage requires a change in perspective for the interventions. Urban heritage conservation and development activities are best served when integrated into a larger urban rehabilitation process that tackles not only the physical decay of the heritage areas but also the larger context of social, economic, and cultural issues of turning these areas into fully functional and developed portions of the city. This approach will allow for the direct-use values to be realized through expanded appreciation and consumption of heritage assets for residential, commercial, and recreational uses. (See box 6.4.)

Sustainable urban heritage conservation requires the design of institutional mechanisms that can pool the funds and resources of the various actors and channel them into activities for which each has the greatest comparative advantage. Moreover, it should also assign the risks inherent to urban heritage conservation to the actors who are best suited and have the most interest in taking them on in view of the potential benefits; for example, profits accrued in the case of real

---

BOX 6.4

Historic Moon Lake Is a Valuable Asset for Greater Ningbo in China

China, Zhejiang Multicities Development Project (Project number 003473)
Total Project Cost: US$231 million
Total Loan Amount: US$110 million
Approved: March 1993 – Closed: May 2003

In planning for an infrastructure upgrading project in the historic city core of Ningbo, a policy discussion with city officials raised their awareness and increased their commitment to conserving the historic city core, especially its centerpiece: the Moon Lake. The lake and its surrounding public space—with shaded walkways, benches, and playgrounds—is a valuable urban oasis in an extremely dense city. Originally, the city's plans for the lake's development were to sweep away all existing buildings and landscaping on its east bank and replace them with high-rise apartment blocks. However, over the course of project preparation, Ningbo's planners began emphasizing conservation and recreational use of the lake. Today, the historic lakefront is a focal point for relaxation for Ningbo's residents, contributing to maintaining the relevance and attractiveness of the historic core for the city at large. The lake acts as a physical link between the city core, historic neighborhoods, and commercial areas, thereby connecting all the elements of a high-quality urban lifestyle for residents and providing an attractive destination for tourists.

Source: Ebbe, K., and D. Hankey. *Ningbo China: Cultural Heritage Conservation in Urban Upgrading.* Washington, DC: World Bank, 1999.

---

estate investments, or improvement in relations with the communities in the case of private philanthropies. In principle, financing mechanisms must be capable of generating a mix of resources that will enable all those involved to contribute in proportion to the benefits received and according to their particular interests. For instance, financing might combine a special fund from tax contributions to cover the costs of conserving cultural heritage assets and public spaces, and resources from real estate investors to finance profit-making investments.

These mechanisms may also allow private philanthropies to find investment niches that satisfy their charitable and public relations objectives; usually this involves restoring buildings and public spaces valued by the communities, such as historic and iconic monuments, museums, heritage housing, or traditional places of social interaction. A well-implemented conservation program usually increases the market value of the properties, and part of that gain may be captured by the public administration to finance its expenses. Of course, determining how to estimate the expected risks and benefits and then allocating them with equity is a daunting management challenge if such a framework for funding is to be created.

The decision-making process leading to investments in the conservation of the urban heritage assets will certainly need to change. The identification of uses with social or market demand that are compatible with the carrying capacity of the assets must be brought up at the outset of a decision-making process, not at the end as it usually is. Figure 6.3 shows the sequence of decisions that places sustainability through adaptation at the center of the concern, in contrast to the traditional process indicated in figure 6.1.

FIGURE 6.3
Sustainable Conservation Decision-Making Sequence: Adaptive Reuse

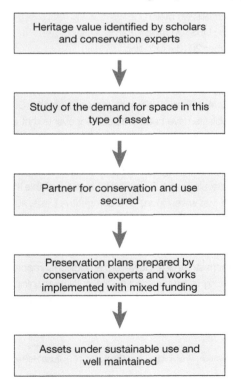

Source: Author.

The approach to heritage conservation can only flourish if conceived as promoting the adaptive rehabilitation and development of the heritage assets; it may require a more flexible approach to conservation than currently in use. When adaptive rehabilitation is intended, conservationists, planners, and developers must have some freedom to adapt the buildings and public spaces to contemporary uses that meet current social or market-based demand. (See box 6.5.) The extent to which a particular building can be altered varies with each case, depending on the historic, aesthetic, symbolic, and social values

---

BOX 6.5

Private Sector Investment Is Used as a Criterion for Sub-Project Selection in Russia

Russian Federation Preservation and Promotion of Cultural Heritage Project (Project number 120219)
Total Project Cost: US$250 million
Total Loan Amount: US$100 million
Approved: December 2010 – Ongoing

To spur economic and social development, the Russian government aims to promote heritage conservation in four oblasts (territorial divisions)—Leningrad, Pskov, Novgorod, and Tver—which are located between St. Petersburg and Moscow. These oblasts have been the scene of events that are seminal to the creation of Russian national identity, and they house monuments that have universal significance. Main project components will support the rehabilitation and improvement of cultural heritage sites and institutions, and also capacity building for integrated site development. Funds will be made available through a demand-driven mechanism that will support, on a competitive basis, sub-project proposals made by oblasts and cultural institutions. Selection will be based on such criteria as: (1) being in compliance with federal and regional legislation on cultural heritage and environmental protection, and (2) compatibility with municipal and regional development strategies. However, an additional important criterion is the degree of cofinancing to be provided by the oblasts, municipalities, and especially the private sector. Moreover, one of the project's key indicators of overall success will be the share of stakeholders' cofinancing to support the cultural heritage project investments.

Source: Russian Federation: Preservation and Promotion of Cultural Heritage Project Appraisal Document.

and attributes held by the asset. Some buildings (such as the more iconic and emblematic ones) will require full conservation, while others may only need typological conservation, so they may be changed to be adapted to new uses without losing their basic characteristics. The conservation and development of other buildings having mostly a contextual value in the historic city cores should be granted greater flexibility.

As an example, the historic conservation plan of Cartagena de Indias in Colombia includes this approach (Rojas 1999). Decisions leading to the scrutiny, identification, and classification of historic structures are complex and will benefit from contributions from key stakeholders, including scholars, conservationists, planners, developers, organizations of the civil society, and the community. The broader the scope of participants involved in these decisions, the stronger the social support for the effects of the conservation effort on the urban heritage.

Coalescing such varied interests does not occur spontaneously and requires political will and leadership. Exercising this role requires significant political capital by elected officials, as most of the heritage values (including existence, bequest, aesthetic, spiritual, social, historic, and symbolic values) are of interest to the whole community and, after made explicit through research, are given priority through activities taking place in the political realm of social interaction. Furthermore, these values can only be protected by agencies that represent the community. In a democratic context, these interests are well represented by elected government bodies. Moreover, the public sector is responsible for the adequate provision of public goods and urban services not supplied by the private sector. The public administration is also the only agency capable of coordinating the different actors operating in deteriorated urban heritage areas, and of mitigating the bias of individual actors toward certain values to the detriment of others. The local agency's leading role is key to establishing a sustainable urban heritage conservation vision and a process that is consistent with the community's objectives.

Values in Action: Decision Making in the Conservation of Historic City Cores

The frame of reference presented in the previous sections has many operational implications for the design and implementation of heritage conservation and development programs. This section will present the most salient implications using concrete experiences of conservation processes underway in the historic cores of four cities of Latin America—Oaxaca in Mexico, Quito in Ecuador, Salvador de Bahia in Brazil, and Valparaiso in Chile—which are all inscribed on the World Heritage List. The local governments of these cities operate in different institutional contexts: highly decentralized in the case of Brazil, fairly decentralized in Ecuador and Mexico, and highly centralized in Chile. In addition, they adopted different approaches and institutional structures for the conservation of their historic city cores, allowing comparisons about the key aspects of the frame of reference presented in this chapter: actors involved, the decision-making process for conservation activities, and financing arrangements. The choice was made to present contrasting experiences in each aspect and bring the other cases into the discussion to enrich the presentation of the issues (Rojas and Lanzafame 2011).

The Tale of Four Cities: Oaxaca, Quito, Salvador de Bahia, and Valparaiso

The historic city cores considered in this analysis are the foundational areas of cities established by the Spanish and Portuguese navigators in the 16th century. Until the mid-20th century, these cities functioned as important commercial and later manufacturing centers, retaining significant cultural heritage assets in their central areas. The cities are endowed with a rich and diverse array of public buildings and spaces considered of importance for their historic, aesthetic, social, and spiritual significance.

In the historic city cores of Latin America, outstanding pre-Columbian monuments and structures are interspersed with government buildings, churches, convents, hospitals, military installations, and defensive walls built during the colonial period; many offer refined examples of baroque or neoclassical architecture and of the military engineering of the period. Salvador da Bahia was established by the Portuguese as the first capital city of colonial Brazil and functioned as an important port city. Salvador's historic city core is dotted with baroque churches, some of which date from the 17th century, and monumental public administrative structures. In all four cities, the ensemble of urban heritage has been enhanced with the addition of public buildings, residences, and various types of industrial architecture typical of the late 19th and early 20th centuries, which are increasingly praised by the communities. In the four cases discussed here, the historic core concentrates and offers the best serviced areas of the cities.

In the second part of the 20th century, the historic cores of these cities underwent a gradual loss of their economic base, followed by significant demographic shifts of resident population and business to new developments built in the periphery. This process was particularly acute in Salvador and less so in Valparaiso and in Quito, which retained the seat of government and financial activities. The case of Oaxaca stands out because its historic core never lost its vibrancy, retaining key urban economic activities and a diverse mix of social strata. However, all these cities lost population and suffered a significant change in land uses and users. At the end of the 20th century these historic city cores also had larger concentrations of low-income households and of elderly populations than the rest of the city. Low-income residents and low-productivity informal economic activities have increasingly occupied these areas' public and private urban spaces. Most of these uses overtax the carrying capacity of cultural heritage assets, furthering the deterioration processes. A vicious cycle of abandonment and physical deterioration ensued. Figure 6.4 shows the loss of population of the historic city cores in the 1990–2000 period while the cities continued growing.

Concern for the heritage assets at risk located in the historic city cores usually emerges soon after the onset of the deterioration process, but it takes a long time for this concern to lead to concrete actions. In the case of Quito, it took about 50 years from the initial statement of intention to conserve the historic city cores in the 1940s to the establishment of the rescue fund for monuments—Fondo de Salvamento (FONSAL), which devotes public funds and resources to the conservation of the outstanding monuments. (Figure 6.5A indicates the timeline and process of establishing FONSAL.) The fund was established after the 1978 earthquake that damaged the historic city core, and it became a milestone accomplishment for the Ecuadorian conservation movement. It demonstrates the preeminence of the public sector in initiating and leading the conservation process, with the relatively late arrival of the private-sector actors.

FIGURE 6.4

Oaxaca, Quito, Salvador de Bahia, and Valparaiso: Population Dynamics of the Historic City Cores (World Heritage Sites) versus the Metropolitan Area, 1990–2000

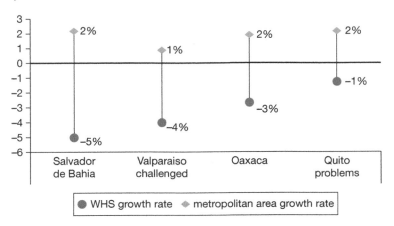

Source: Author.

FIGURE 6.5

Quito and Oaxaca: Timelines and Actors Involved in the Interventions for the Preservation of the Historic City Core

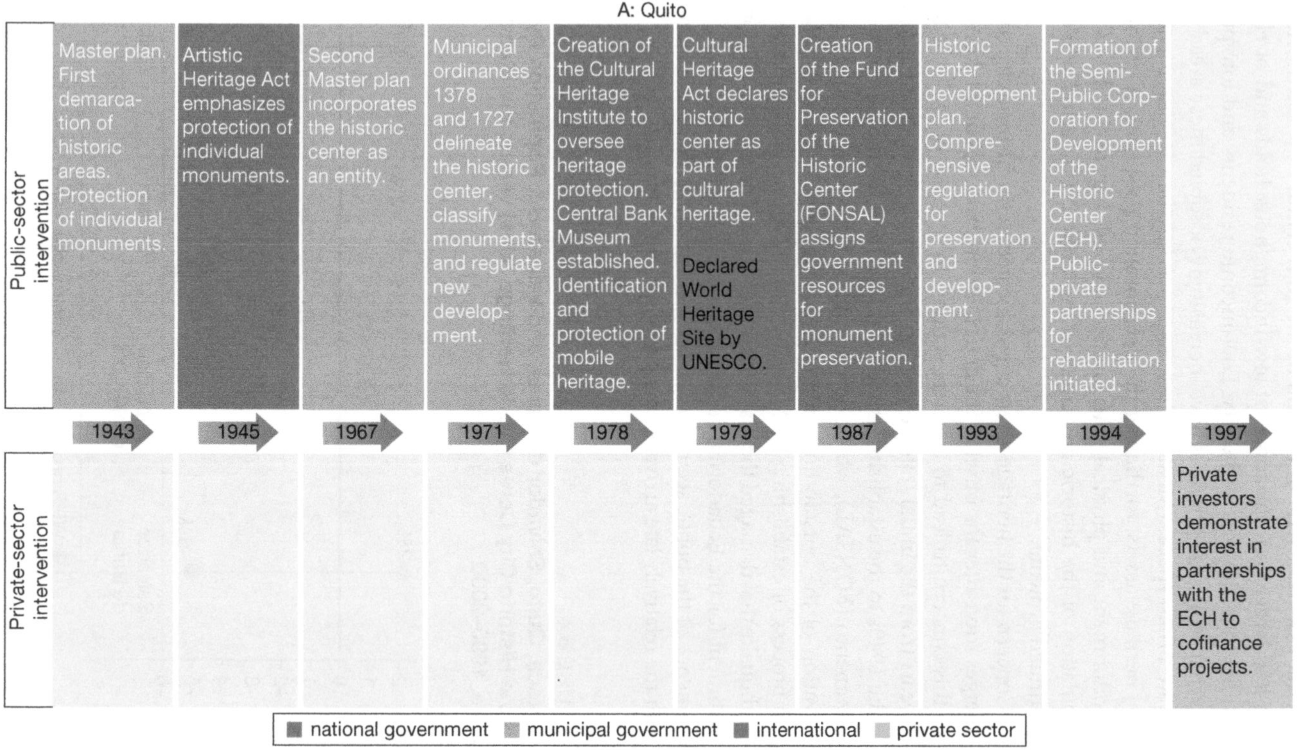

A: Quito

	1943	1945	1967	1971	1978	1979	1987	1993	1994	1997
Public-sector intervention	Master plan. First demarcation of historic areas. Protection of individual monuments	Artistic Heritage Act emphasizes protection of individual monuments.	Second Master plan incorporates the historic center as an entity.	Municipal ordinances 1378 and 1727 delineate the historic center, classify monuments, and regulate new development.	Creation of the Cultural Heritage Institute to oversee heritage protection. Central Bank Museum established. Identification and protection of mobile heritage.	Cultural Heritage Act declares historic center as part of cultural heritage. Declared World Heritage Site by UNESCO.	Creation of the Fund for Preservation of the Historic Center (FONSAL) assigns government resources for monument preservation.	Historic center development plan. Comprehensive regulation for preservation and development.	Formation of the Semi-Public Corporation for Development of the Historic Center (ECH). Public-private partnerships for rehabilitation initiated.	
Private-sector intervention										Private investors demonstrate interest in partnerships with the ECH to cofinance projects.

■ national government ■ municipal government ■ international ■ private sector

Source: Rojas 1999.

B: Oaxaca

Event	Designation as Historic Patrimonial Area.	Inscription in the UNESCO WHL.	Preparation of a first heritage buildings catalogue.	The Alfredo Harp Helú foundation was created and started rehabilitation of buildings in the historic center.	Restoration of the Santo Domingo church and monastery complex and reconversion in cultural center.	Special plan for the historic center.	Habitat program combining federal, state, and city government resources.	The NGO Casa de la Ciudad was created.	The state government started the repaving program.	A specific management plan for the historic center was developed.	A second catalogue of heritage buildings was created.
Year	1976 ⇧	1987 ⇧	1987 ⇧	1990 ⇧	1994 ⇧	1998 ⇧	2003 ⇧	2004 ⇧	2005 ⇧	2007 ⇧	2007 ⇧
Public sector	In March 1976 the federal government designated Oaxaca as a Historic Patrimonial Area.	Oaxaca achieved the inscription in the WHL within the first Mexican sites as early as 1987 – "Historic Centre of Oaxaca and Archaeological Site of Monte Albán".	The Compilation of this first catalogue started right after the inscription in the Unesco WHL.		This restoration acted as catalyst for the mobilization of resources. Local painter and civil society leader Francisco Toledo and the banker Alfredo Harp supported the construction of the cultural center. Starting from this moment, public, private, and civil society sectors have invested considerably in Oaxaca's historic center.	This plan (Plan Parcial de Conservación del Centro Histórico de la Ciudad de Oaxaca) analyzed specific problems and suggested concrete solutions for this complex area.	The Habitat Program (2003–2009) is a program of SEDESOL to help reduce urban poverty and improve the quality of life of marginalized urban dwellers by combining the goals of social policy with those of urban development and land-use policies implemented by the federal government.		The program started in 2005 and is still in process of implementation. By 2009 the repaving was completed in the core of the historic center.	The idea of creating this plan (Plan de Manejo para el Centro Histórico de la Ciudad de Oaxaca) came from the need to meet UNESCO guidelines and answer specific problems related to the historic center. INAH granted the city government an award for the plan.	In 2007, the city government in collaboration with INAH developed a new catalogue of heritage buildings, including colonial buildings as well as those built at the beginning of the 20th century.
Private and civil society sector				The Alfredo Harp Helú foundation was created and started rehabilitation of buildings in the historic center.	Restoration of the Santo Domingo church and monastery complex and reconversion in cultural center.			The NGO Casa de la Ciudad was created.			

Legend: ▦ International ▦ mixed public funds ▦ federal government ▦ state government ▦ city government ▦ private sector and civil society

Source: Quartessan and Romis 2011.

The decay of the historic city cores occurred amid other developments: the rapid expansion of the peripheries that led to the loss of economic activities and importance of the historic city cores of Salvador and Quito; the deterioration of the economic base in Valparaiso, highly dependent on port and industrial assemblage activities during the import substitution period of the economic development of the country; and social unrest in Oaxaca (figure 6.5B) that hurt the tourism industry. In turning the deterioration process around, Quito counted on the role of its historic city core as the seat of the national government, and Oaxaca on the strong local identity shared by its inhabitants. Salvador and Valparaiso were not lucky enough to have such advantages, and weak performance of the local institutions worsened their plight.

The case studies show that the initial concern expressed about the deterioration of the historic city cores emerged among members of cultural groups, and their urging prompted public authorities to organize the listing and protection of the urban heritage areas. However, cultural groups acted only sporadically to preserve outstanding buildings at risk, with these efforts mainly funded by philanthropic institutions. As discussed earlier, this level of activity did not lead nor contribute to the establishment of a sustainable conservation and development process. As it can be observed in all the reviewed cases (table 6.3), the justification for conservation was concerned with the historic and aesthetic values of the heritage areas—the main concerns articulated then by cultural groups.

An in-depth analysis of the actors that have participated in the conservation process and its actions indicates that the process in Salvador and Valparaiso corresponds quite closely to the pattern of a process driven mostly by the historic and aesthetic socio-cultural values of the heritage (table 6.3A). In Quito and Oaxaca, the combination of actors and actions corresponds to patterns that are closer to the processes driven by a more diversified set of values attached to the heritage (table 6.3B). The differences are in the number of actors involved, limited in the former case, more diverse in the latter ones. The other major difference is the diversity of spheres of social interaction in which values are put into play: mostly political and linked to transactions within the elite in Salvador and Valparaiso, but also including the market and grassroot spheres in the cases of Oaxaca and Quito (Rojas 2012).

The more diverse set of actors operating in the cases of Oaxaca and Quito, and their engagement in preserving assets holding a wider variety of values, led to enlarging the scope of conservation activities. These included attracting funds and resources from a more varied set of actors—thus providing a stronger basis for more sustainable conservation processes. However, this kind of process poses a more complex governance challenge: the coordination and correct sequencing of the interventions of all the stakeholders. A closer look at the institutional arrangements used in the conservation efforts under

TABLE 6.3

Oaxaca, Quito, Salvador de Bahia, and Valparaiso: Year of Inclusion and Justification for Inclusion on the World Heritage List

City	Year	Justification for the Listing
Oaxaca	1987	The historic city core contains a total of 1,200 historic monuments, spared by the evolution of the city, and has been inventoried and listed. The major religious monuments (cathedral, Santo Domingo, San Francisco, San Agustín, San Filipo Neri, Soledad, etc.), the superb patrician townhouses (including the home of Cortés), and whole streets lined with other dwellings combine to create a harmonious cityscape, and reconstitute the image of a former colonial city whose monumental aspect has been kept intact. Fine architectural quality also characterizes the 19th-century buildings in this city that was the birthplace of Benito Juarez and which, in 1872, adopted the name of Oaxaca de Juarez. The city is also endowed with an important ensemble of pre-Columbian architecture, the Zapotec necropolis of Monte Alban.
Quito	1978	The historic city core is a harmonious ensemble where the manmade and the natural elements are brought together to create a unique and transcendental city. With its historic core and heritage buildings, the city is an outstanding example of the baroque school of Quito, a fusion of European and indigenous art and urban architecture.
Salvador de Bahia	1985	Established as the first capital of Brazil, from 1549 to 1763, Salvador de Bahia witnessed the blending of European, African, and Amerindian cultures. From 1558 it was also the first slave market in the New World, with slaves arriving to work on the sugar cane plantations. The city has managed to preserve many outstanding colonial, baroque, and renaissance buildings. Special features of the historic city core include the brightly colored houses, often decorated with fine stuccowork.
Valparaiso	2003	The city participated in an early phase of globalization in the late 19th century when it became the leading mercantile port for the shipping routes on the Pacific coast of South America. The historic city core and its layout, infrastructure, and architecture characterize the seaport city, which has a unique geographical and topographical environment. The geographical conditions of Valparaiso are so severe that the adaptation of the streets, public spaces, and buildings to the natural landscape gave rise to an entirely original urban structure.

Source: UNESCO World Heritage List: http://whc.unesco.org/en/list.

discussion allows an analysis of how feasible it is to expand the set of actors and values supporting the process. Given that the institutional arrangements are closely connected to the mode of financing of the conservation process, these topics will be discussed first to provide background for the institutional analysis.

Financing

Central administrations are more committed to the conservation of historic city cores when they succeed in elevating the visibility of the patrimony to the category of international significance by placing it on the World Heritage List (UNESCO 1972). This often leads to attracting funding for the planning and implementation of conservation programs from national and international institutions. However, often there is a mismatch between the volume of funds allocated by government institutions and the amount of funds and resources actually needed to accomplish the required interventions. The overwhelming presence of the public actors in the financing and implementation of the rehabilitation projects in historic city cores may crowd out other stakeholders.

This is the case in Valparaiso, where all the financing is provided by the central government. In Salvador as well, all the funding is provided by the upper-tier institution, the government of the state of Bahia, which is the second-tier institution in the federal structure of Brazil. In both cases, the local authority was sidelined and did not contribute to the effort, while private investors have concentrated in the most profitable areas in Valparaiso and have not participated at all in Salvador. The conservation program of the historic city core of Oaxaca received support from both the federal and the state institutions, but the local government has made significant investments as well, while Quito had some funding from resources collected by the provincial administration but most of the funding was provided by the municipality.[2] Quito and Oaxaca managed to attract more private investment than Valparaiso and Salvador.

The seemingly intractable scale of the problem of restoring and revitalizing historic city cores, coupled with the stream of private benefits that this can generate, makes full public funding impractical, inefficient, and unequal. It is impractical for the simple reason that it is not possible to raise the amount of funds required from all levels of public administration to bear the costs of the conservation effort; it is inefficient because public investment may crowd out private investments when applied to assets that have use value through demand in the real estate market; it is unequal when public funds benefiting private-sector owners and users are not returned to the public treasury.

Quito and Oaxaca managed to partially avoid the pitfalls of full public financing of the conservation effort. In Quito, the institution in charge of the conservation and development of the historic city core—Empresa del Centro Histórico de Quito, (ECHQ)—managed to attract private investment to some of the conservation projects that could meet a demand in the local real estate market. Oaxaca, on its part, has had private investment involved in the conservation process almost from the beginning, a tribute to the strong commitment of the local stakeholders and entrepreneurs to their historic city core.

Figure 6.6 contrasts the sources and uses of funds in the conservation efforts of Valparaiso and Quito: while in the former the central government bears the burden of financing all the interventions, in the latter several sources of funding contribute to the effort. In Quito, public and private sources of funding are used in combination for tackling the most vexing issues affecting the historic city core. For instance, private investors were initially reluctant to expand the supply of rehabilitated space for formal upscale commercial activities, arguing that there was no proven demand for this type of space given that all upscale commerce has migrated to shopping centers located in the periphery.

FIGURE 6.6

Quito and Valparaiso: Sources of Funding for the Preservation Programs

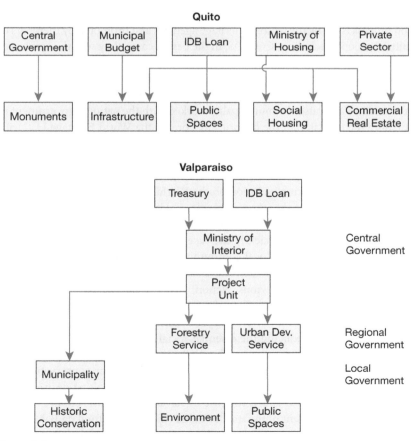

Source: Author.

The ECHQ shared risks with landowners and investors and proved the feasibility of selling or renting commercial space to new businesses willing to establish themselves in the historic city core. In Valparaiso public and private actors have operated independently, resulting in most private investment concentrating in two sectors of the real estate market: second homes for weekend use and spaces for commercial activities linked to service tourism. Furthermore, private investments have been concentrated mostly in two sections of the historic city core, the Cerro Alegre and Concepción neighborhoods, which cover less than one-fourth of the area included in the World Heritage Site. These contrasting outcomes can be partly explained by the institutional arrangements used to implement the conservation process.

Nominating important heritage properties for inclusion on UNESCO's World Heritage List is a prerogative of the national authorities—under the condition of a Member State and signatory of the World Heritage Convention. The nomination process is led by the national heritage agencies and promoted by members of cultural groups, including ICOMOS. In the best of cases, they seek the opinion of local groups but rarely of the resident community. In Salvador, the resident community had negligible involvement in the process. In Quito, organizations of the civil society were active supporters of the municipality in promoting the nomination, and in Valparaiso the municipality worked with the national government in pursuing the inclusion of the historic city core on the World Heritage List, with sporadic involvement of local stakeholders within the community. In Oaxaca the nomination was promoted by local organizations of the civil society, but the community had scarce input in the process.

The process of seeking inclusion on the World Heritage List is often pursued with little clarity about the purpose besides a desire for the pride, prestige, and international attention that listing may bring, and with that the expected positive impact on tourism. This is clearly the case in Salvador, and, predictably, a few years after the nomination local communities still saw little advantages arising from the listing (Mendes Zancheti and Gabriel 2011).

As discussed in the previous section, institutional arrangements used to implement the conservation effort affect its outcomes and sustainability. The dominance of one institution on the process tends to crowd out other interested parties, hence reducing the essential social support base that could bring vitality, creativity, innovative approaches to the project concept design, and additional funds to the project. This leaves the sustainability of the conservation process subject to the vagaries of having a single institution making decisions and finding funding sources. This is the case in Salvador, where the culture institute linked to the government of the state of Bahia (Instituto Cultural da Bahia, ICB) was charged with the responsibility as the executing agency of the rehabilitation and conservation of the historic city core.

Over a period of 15 years, the ICB invested nearly US$46 million in the physical rehabilitation of 35 city blocks containing almost 600 properties (see table 6.4). The ICB selected the blocks based on the criteria of level of decay, available resources, and location in the historic city core. Occupants, mostly low-income households, were induced to seek accommodations elsewhere in the city with monetary compensations, or were temporarily relocated if they were not willing to leave. The ICB developed the projects following the traditional process described in figure 6.1 and undertook all the rehabilitation work on the private properties and public spaces. The renovated buildings were returned to the owners with the obligation that they repay part of the cost either in cash or by letting the ICB rent out part of the properties for an agreed period of time.

The top-down approach adopted in Salvador had several consequences:

- Led to a uniform approach to rehabilitation that is often contested as inaccurate by conservationists outside the ICB;
- Promoted the historic city core as a place for tourism and recreation to the detriment of all other residential and community functions;
- Did not make space available for privately financed projects;
- Alienated the municipal government, leaving the ICB with the responsibility of maintaining all public spaces and policing the area; and
- Displaced original residents who could not return to the area due to the higher rents.

The amount of funds invested per year varied widely, in tune with the capacity of the ICB to secure transfers from the state government, jeopardizing project

TABLE 6.4

Salvador State Government Investments in the Preservation Management of the Historic City Core

Stages	Implementation period	Number of city blocks	Number of properties	Investment contracted amounts (in US$)
Stage 1	1992–93	4	89	11,221,701
Stage 2	1992–93	2	47	2,805,811
Stage 3	1992–94	3	58	3,010,136
Stage 4	1992–94	8	183	12,512,766
Stage 5	1996	2	48	10,245,607
Stage 6	1997–2006	6*	83	7,103,112
Stage 7	1999–Ongoing	10	88	8,624,614
Total		35	596	55,523,750

Source: Mendes Zancheti and Gabriel 2011.

* Number of city blocks partially rehabilitated.

sustainability, which, to this day, is dependent on these allocations. Salvador's failed experience is by no means an exception to the many other places that have also opted to fix their decayed stock of buildings and: (1) did not engage local communities; and (2) did not attempt to expand the range of actors involved in the process; and (3) managed to develop only one economic value of the heritage, the use value for tourism and recreation.

Other urban uses—such as fostering diversified local commerce and services, and strengthening the educational, sports, and cultural activities and government institutions—were largely absent. Also missing were community-oriented programs to improve local workers' capacity in a range of conservation skills, or efforts to provide affordable housing. Further, the institutional structure was unable to tackle the central governance issue of coordinating the involvement of all meaningful stakeholders; the state government was left acting alone. The conservation program of Valparaiso may end up falling into a similar predicament, as the executing unit set up by the central government has not managed to engage local stakeholders nor to raise more funds and resources from the municipality or pair up its resources with the private sector.

Quito tried from the outset of the conservation process to mobilize a range of other sources of funding and set up a mixed-capital corporation capable of undertaking all the functions of a real estate developer as well as executing public works under contract from the municipality. The municipality approved in 1992 the Master Plan for the Integrated Rehabilitation of the Historic Areas of Quito that defined the objectives, norms, and rules for the conservation of the World Heritage Site. The regeneration of the historic city core proceeded through the coordinated interventions of the planning office, the municipal district administration for the historic city core, and the corporation. The main objective of the municipality was to turn the heritage area into a well-served, accessible, and diversified commercial center capable of competing with suburban malls, with the added attraction of its heritage values (Rojas 1999).[3] In addition to improving the public infrastructure, public spaces, and accessibility to the historic city core, the corporation entered into partnerships with land owners and investors to develop several pioneering projects:

- Built new retail and commercial space for upscale and middle-income customers;
- Rehabilitated office space for private business and public institutions;
- Built new cultural facilities in refitted iconic buildings, such as the city museum and a public library;
- Upgraded existing historic structures for commercial uses—boutique hotels, restaurants, art galleries, and craft shops catering to tourists and citizens alike;

- Erected theaters and cultural facilities; and
- Provided affordable housing to retain part of the local population and attract new residents.

The project attracted private investors who undertook their own projects triggered by the substantial investments in public infrastructure, public safety, and heritage preservation undertaken by the ECHQ. Table 6.5 shows the mix of investments that took place in the historic city core of Quito. These results indicate that Quito has succeeded in tackling the governance challenge of coordinating the actions among an array of stakeholders, as well as raising private-sector funding for the commercial components of the project. Through the activities of the public-private corporation, the municipality managed to greatly expand the scope of economic values put into play in the conservation of the historic city core, putting heritage assets to a wide variety of uses.

Results

Although it is not possible using a retroactive assessment of project experience to establish direct causality between the governance issues in the four cities' conservation efforts and some of the results of those efforts, a handful of observations are worth mentioning. From the governance perspective, the conservation strategies that managed to mobilize and engage the interest of a wider group of actors are those of Oaxaca and Quito. In both cities, the conservation process could adapt and create new uses for urban heritage assets that, on top of having retained their historic, aesthetic, spiritual, and social values, also have economic use and non-use values. These assets are occupied and maintained by a variety of enterprises, households, consumers, and public and private institutions, contributing to the sustainability of the conservation. The greater range and mix of social and economic activities found in the historic city core are seen in the presence of residential, commercial, and institutional land uses. As it can be observed in figure 6.7, Oaxaca and Quito have more institutional (public and private) and residential land uses than Salvador and Valparaiso.

The sustainability of the conservation process is attributed, in part, to the greater diversification and mix of uses and users of the historic city core, and, in part, to the financing scheme, which does not depend on the fortunes of only one activity or the budget allocation of a sole institution. The expansion of the residential land uses also brings stability to the process, generating demand for local commerce and other services catering to the resident community. In contrast, the number of residents decreased in Valparaiso and Salvador, which further depressed the demand for local commerce and services.

TABLE 6.5
Quito Investments in the 2000–05 Period

Type	Contributions from	2000	2001	2002	2003	2004	2005	Subtotal
					Projects by type			
Housing	Municipal	34	97	169	16	20	44	380
	Private	19	20	51	16	20	44	170
Office	Municipal	6	4	5	–	19	28	62
	Private	6	3	5	–	19	28	61
Commerce	Municipal	13	1,195	29	–	416	28	1,681
	Private	12	5	19	–	27	28	91
Parking	Municipal	3	27	81	11	13	17	152
	Private	3	21	9	11	13	17	74
				Number of projects				
Project proposals	Municipal	13	35	22	19	19	24	132
	Private	10	29	20	17	17	24	117
Building permits	Municipal	11	17	12	9	13	13	75
	Private	8	11	10	7	11	13	60
Surface sq. meters	Municipal	11,445	19,679	21,615	13,384	14,779	7,871	88,773
	Private	2,228	4,962	8,000	5,612	8,608	7,871	37,312
				Investment				
Investment US$	Municipal	735,024	848,163	938,221	1,165,866	1,110,631	–	4,797,905
	Private	146,328	393,042	890,151	587,200	1,404,395	1,446,770	4,867,886

Source: Jaramillo 2011.

FIGURE 6.7

Oaxaca, Quito, Salvador de Bahia, and Valparaiso: Land Uses, 2010

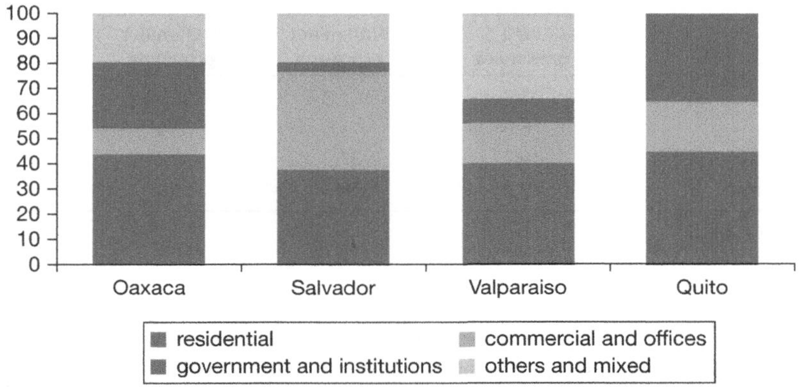

Source: Author.

The fact that the historic city core of Oaxaca retained its main functions and is still the administrative, commercial, and service center of the metropolitan area clearly contributed to the preserved condition of its building stock. Table 6.6 indicates that less than 2 percent of the buildings of the historic city core are in ruins or very poor condition. This is the level expected in any dynamic area of a city where the private sector provides and/or maintains residential, commercial, and service space, and the government cares for public spaces and the provision of basic urban services. Therefore, at least in this respect it can be said that the historic city core of Oaxaca has attained a capacity level of conservation that fits the concept of sustainability as defined in this chapter. It is also worth noting that the retention of the central functions in Oaxaca is in part due to the willingness of the population and businesses to be housed in older buildings that are not equipped with modern amenities.

However, not all actors agree with such decisions: the state administration moved its offices to a suburban location allegedly to decongest the historic city core, but also to gain more space in new buildings. It is to be hoped that the inhabitants of Oaxaca will not find the trade-off of comfort for heritage value too taxing in the future. By comparison, more than 12 percent of the buildings in Quito, Salvador, and Valparaiso are in ruins or very poor condition. The large size of the historic city core of Quito—encompassing more than 300 hectares—may explain the fact that, in spite of 15 years of well-executed public and private investments, there is still a significant number of buildings in a poor state of

TABLE 6.6

Oaxaca, Quito, Salvador de Bahia, Valparaiso: Condition of the Building Stock of the Historic City Cores, circa 2010

City	Well preserved	With minor problems	With major problems	In ruins
Oaxaca	97.6	1.0	0.9	0.5
Quito	75.9	11.5	12.6	
Salvador de Bahia	49.7	37.9	6.2	6.2
Valparaiso	79.0	8.3	8.0	4.7

Source: Author.

conservation. For Salvador and Valparaiso, this may be attributed to the short-comings in the choice of the conservation strategies, particularly the inability to engage the resources and resourcefulness of actors other than the state or central government.

Despite the impressive results obtained in Quito, due to the initial strategy that incorporated the diversity of projects implemented and the variety of stakeholders involved, conservation efforts are still fragile and subject to much uncertainty. New issues are challenging the sustainability of the conservation process and need to be addressed. One of the problems observed is that prices for the properties located in the historic city core increased rapidly over the last five years, discouraging investors. Owners are keeping rents very high even for properties in ruins or very poor condition. This is a governance problem that is, at the same time, a sign of success (since price increases signal that the real estate market is capturing the growing demand) and a curse (as it stalls private investment and makes commercial space and housing less affordable).[4]

A second problem reported is that in recent years most investments in the historic city core are flowing mainly to tourism and entertainment businesses, tending to overspecialize the area in these sectors (Jaramillo 2011). As some of these businesses generate negative externalities over other land uses—for instance, the noise and late hours of bars and clubs are nuisances for the local residents and housing markets—the negative trend reinforces itself. This also applies to the case of Salvador, where the historic city core is overspecialized in tourism and recreation activities to the detriment of a more diversified neighborhood economy that can provide stable demand for preserved space (Mendes Zancheti and Gabriel 2011). Residents in Valparaiso also complain of the loss of local commerce displaced by tourism activities (Trivelli and Nikimura 2011). Land-use regulations and the granting of business permits can counter this trend but at high political and public relations costs for the conservation programs. Retaining and encouraging the development of a combination of residential, commercial, service, administrative, recreation, and tourism activities requires a great deal of consensus among the population and business community, particularly because needed measures may go against the workings of the market.

In 2007, the municipality of Quito introduced important changes in the governance structure operating the conservation of the historic city core. Taking into account the success attained by the ECHQ in the conservation management of the historic city core, the mayor transformed this institution into a metropolitan urban development corporation charged with responsibilities that include the implementation of settlement upgrading and projects for low-cost housing, public transportation, and new parks throughout the city. The management structure of the new corporation was put in charge of many pressing and complex tasks, including addressing a backlog of activities in the historic city core.

However, the loss of focus on the historic city core halted public investment in conservation, as well as public-private partnerships, and further discouraged private investment already affected by the rise in land prices. Expediency moved the mayor to tap the best management team available for addressing pressing citywide projects, to the detriment of the historic city core. Figure 6.8 shows the dramatic fall in investment in the historic city core that started in 2008. This outcome indicates the fragility of the governance mechanisms that must balance the interests of many actors to ensure the long-term sustainability of an urban heritage conservation process based on the adaptive rehabilitation of heritage assets. It also highlights the need to establish and support specialized institutions to manage these programs, as they require a territorial focus and a complex skill mix to undertake many interrelated actions that call for close collaboration of the public and private sectors.

FIGURE 6.8

Quito: Investment Volumes in US$ Millions, 1996–2007

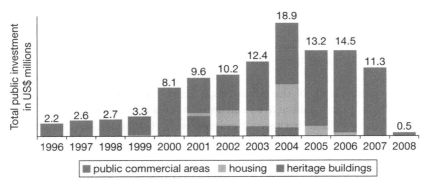

Source: Jaramillo 2011.

Conclusion

The far-reaching governance of a heritage conservation process based on the adaptive rehabilitation of historic city cores calls for striking a balance between conserving the values of the heritage and promoting the best uses of the available heritage assets. To meet such an overarching objective, agreement must be reached among the stakeholders concerning the relative weight of the different values and the trade-offs between conservation, adaptation, and development rights. This is usually attained through transactions taking place in several spheres of social and economic interaction in which the values of heritage are assessed and established based on the rules set up by governments and sanctioned by the markets.

These rules have their origin in the multiple heritage preservation laws and systems of incentives embedded in the tax codes and land-use regulations. In the initial stages of the heritage preservation effort, the legal and regulatory structures for conservation focus on identifying and listing heritage assets and applying laws to protect them, but the bulk of responsibility for maintaining this heritage is left mostly to the private owners.

The observed outcome is that little conservation takes place.[5] In the most advanced stages of the process, the government, in addition to placing urban heritage areas under protection, also leads the conservation process, bringing into the task a wide variety of stakeholders with their financial resources and management capabilities (Dalmau 1998). A more advanced stage in heritage preservation is the adaptive rehabilitation of heritage assets for uses with sustained social or market demand.

The lessons from several international experiences indicate that, to effectively implement urban heritage conservation programs using the adaptive rehabilitation approach, the institutional mechanisms to manage the process are as crucial as the financial resources (Rojas 2012). The effective use of the financial resources to accomplish the expected results depends on the efficient operation of institutional mechanisms to coalesce and mobilize contributions according to stakeholders' capacity to bear the risks and capture the returns of the conservation process. Furthermore, the process must ensure the effective coordination of key actors (Rojas 2004).

The sustainability of the conservation process is enhanced when a given urban heritage area is attractive to an array of users interested in a range of values associated with the heritage. Conservation efforts must strive to promote the economic values of the heritage as a complement and support for the conservation of the socio-cultural values that have motivated action. A flexible approach to preservation management and conservation is needed, to allow public and private partners to adapt heritage assets for new uses that are in line with social or market demand.

However, this will align the conservation of the urban heritage with the well-documented urban development principle that change is the essence of cities and that the cities and their neighborhoods are constantly in transformation (see box 6.6). Freezing the physical characteristics and uses of the assets of an urban heritage area does not contribute to adaptation and change, nor does it support these assets' sustainable preservation. Trying to "freeze time" can easily change the transformation process from one having a positive impact of sustained adaptive rehabilitation and conservation of values to one having a negative impact leading to abandonment and physical decay. The analysis of the conservation processes in the four mentioned cities indicates that avoiding the latter always require accomplishing the former.

BOX 6.6

Balancing Conservation with the Demands for Access and Mobility in a Major Metropolitan Area in China

China, Xian Sustainable Urban Transport Project (Project number 092631)
Total Project Cost: US$414.3 million
Total Loan Amount: US$150 million
Approved: June 2008 – Ongoing

The key challenge for the city of Xian is balancing the conservation of the city's traditional character with the demands of a municipality with an urban population of 5 million, high-tech industry, and world-class universities. Consequently, the city is making improvements in transport infrastructure and mobility management that will create a more livable environment within the historic city core (i.e., the Ming Walled City). Rather than widening roads to accommodate increasing traffic in the walled city, the project aims to reduce congestion by diverting traffic around and outside the city walls. The noise, pollution, and parking needs within the walled city are to be further reduced by developing bicycle paths that connect all the major sites and promoting bicycle touring. In addition, the project is supporting streetscape improvements, safer conditions for walking and cycling, and traffic-calming measures. These positive changes will improve the daily lives of residents.

Source: Ebbe, K., G. Licciardi, and A. Baeumler. 2011.

Notes

1. It can be safely argued that the conservation and development of urban heritage areas is but a special case of the wider problem of rehabilitation of urban areas and faces financial and institutional challenges similar to those confronted by brownfield development discussed by Francesca Medda in this book.
2. Note that resources were added from the rescue fund for monuments (FONSAL).
3. The CCHQ undertook a wide variety of investments to attain this objective.
4. This challenge may affect the governance mechanism of the conservation process. Public administration has very few instruments to counter this trend. It can either increase taxes on properties over a certain price or acquire them by eminent domain if a public need can be demonstrated. Both alternatives are difficult to traverse. The government can also expand the public-partnership efforts of the past and try to lure owners to contribute properties into projects by offering expedient approval processes and risk capital for their development.
5. Often, owners neglect or even abandon their listed heritage in the hope that physical decay will force local authorities to order the property's demolition and free owners from their obligations to preserve it. Worse yet, once the heritage property is ruined, this may free the owners from any legal impediment to develop the land and allow them to sell the valuable parcel of land where the heritage structure stood before.

References

Bell, S., ed. 2002. *Economic Governance and Institutional Dynamics*. Melbourne: Oxford University Press.

Carson, R., R. C. Mitchell, and M. Conaway. 2002. "Economic Benefits to Foreigners Visiting Morocco Accruing from the Rehabilitation of the Fez Medina." In *Valuing Cultural Heritage*, S. Navrud and R. Ready, eds. Cheltenham: Elgar.

Dalmau, J. A. 1998. "Renovación del Centro Histórico de Barcelona." In *La Ciudad del Siglo XXI. Experiencias Existosas de Gestión del Desarrollo Urbano en América Latina*, ed. E. Rojas and R. Daughters. Washington, DC: Inter-American Development Bank.

De la Torre, M., ed. 2002. *Assessing the Values of Cultural Heritage*. Los Angeles: Getty Conservation Institute Research Report.

Getty Conservation Institute. 2000. *The Values and Heritage Conservation*. Los Angeles: Research Report.

Jaramillo, P. 2011. "Quito." In *City Development: The Experiences of Ten World Heritage Sites*, ed. E. Rojas and F. Lanzafame. Washington, DC: Inter-American Development Bank.

Klamer, A., and W. Zuidhof. 1988. "The Values of Cultural Heritage: Merging Economic and Cultural Appraisals." In *Economics and Heritage Conservation*. Los Angeles: Getty Conservation Institute.

Mendes Zancheti, S., and J. Gabriel. 2011. "Salvador de Bahia." In *City Development: The Experiences of Ten World Heritage Sites*, ed. E. Rojas and F. Lanzafame. Washington, DC: Inter-American Development Bank.

Mourato, S., and M. Mazzanti. 2002. "Economic Valuation of Cultural Heritage: Evidence and Prospects." In *Assessing the Values of Cultural Heritage*, ed. M. De la Torre et al., 51–76. Los Angeles: Getty Conservation Institute Research Report.

OMA. 2010. "Cronocaos." Office of Metropolitan Architecture and Rem Koolhaas Exhibit at the Venice Biennial.

Peacok, A., and I. Rizzo. 2008. *The Heritage Game: Economics, Policy and Practice.* Oxford: Oxford University Press.

Quartessan, A., and M. Romis. 2011. "Oaxaca." In *City Development: The Experiences of Ten World Heritage Sites*, ed. E. Rojas and F. Lanzafame. Washington, DC: Inter-American Development Bank.

Rojas, E. 1999. *Old Cities New Assets: Preserving Latin America's Urban Heritage.* Baltimore: The Johns Hopkins University Press.

Rojas, E. 2004. *Volver al Centro. La Recuperación de Areas Urbanas Centrales.* Washington, DC: Inter-American Development Bank.

Rojas, E. 2012. "Government Interventions in Latin American World Heritage Sites." PhD thesis, Department of Architecture, Urbanism and Arts of the Universida de Lusofona de Humanidades e Teconolgias, Lisboa.

Rojas, E., and R. Daughters, eds. 1998. *La Ciudad del Siglo XXI. Experiencias Existosas de Gestión del Desarrollo Urbano en América Latina.* Washington, DC: Inter-American Development Bank.

Rojas, E., and F. Lanzafame, eds. 2011. *City Development: The Experiences of Ten World Heritage Sites.* Washington, DC: Inter-American Development Bank.

Rojas, E., and C. Moura Castro. 1999. "Lending for Urban Heritage Conservation: Issues and Opportunities". Sustainable Development Department, Technical Papers (SOC-105), Washington, DC: Inter-American Development Bank.

Throsby, D. 2002. "Cultural Capital and Sustainability Concepts in the Economics of Cultural Heritage." In *Assessing the Values of Cultural Heritage*, ed. M. De la Torre et al., 101–117. Los Angeles: Getty Conservation Institute Research Report.

Trivelli, P., and Y. Nikimura. 2011. "Valparaiso." In *City Development: The Experiences of Ten World Heritage Sites*, ed. E. Rojas and F. Lanzafame. Washington, DC: Inter-American Development Bank.

United Nations Educational, Scientific and Cultural Organization (UNESCO). 1972. *Convention Concerning the Protection of the World Cultural and Natural Heritage.* Paris: UNESCO.

7

UNESCO World Heritage List, Tourism, and Economic Growth

Rabah Arezki
Economist, International Monetary Fund,
with Reda Cherif, and John Piotrowski

This chapter investigates whether tourism specialization is a viable strategy for development. The authors estimate standard growth equations augmented with a variable measuring tourism specialization using instrumental variables techniques for a large cross-section of countries for the period 1980–2002. To identify a causal relationship between specialization in tourism activities and economic development, the authors introduce a novel instrument for tourism based on the United Nations Educational, Scientific and Cultural Organization (UNESCO) World Heritage List, finding that there is a positive relationship between the extent of tourism specialization and economic growth. This instrument proves to be a strong one, in that the presence of World Heritage sites significantly fosters tourism activities. The study indicates that an increase of one standard deviation in the share of tourism in exports leads to about 0.5 percentage point in additional annual growth, everything else being constant. The result holds against a large array of robustness checks. The chapter concludes by stating that one advantage of tourism development as opposed to a manufacturing, export-oriented strategy is that it requires less capital, infrastructure, and skilled labor. However by nature, the tourism industry relies on a limited set of services produced with little room for expansion and labor reallocation, thus it needs to be part of a comprehensive strategy of economic diversification in order to be sustainable and inclusive.

Introduction

In the last few years, international tourism has emerged as one of the fastest-growing sectors of the world economy. The average growth of international tourism arrivals over the period 2003–07 has reached 7 percent (ITB World Travel Trends Report 2009), and the tourism market is likely to continue to grow in the decades to come. Many countries have tried to seize the opportunity by embarking on tourism-oriented policies and programs. Indeed, inspired by a number of success stories attributed to tourism specialization, more and more developing countries are contemplating such a strategy in order to emerge from the development trap.

Tourism, by virtue of being a labor-intensive activity, could allow the large pool of unemployed and under-unemployed individuals in developing countries to get a decent job and in turn create the conditions for a sustained and broad-based growth. Figure 7.1 suggests that there exists a positive relationship between the extent of specialization in tourism and long-term GDP growth.[1] In other words, this positive correlation suggests that countries that have specialized in tourism have experienced higher economic growth that countries that did not, with all other factors being equal. This chapter tackles a fundamental question in assessing the impact of tourism specialization on economic development.

FIGURE 7.1
Economic Growth and Tourism Specialization

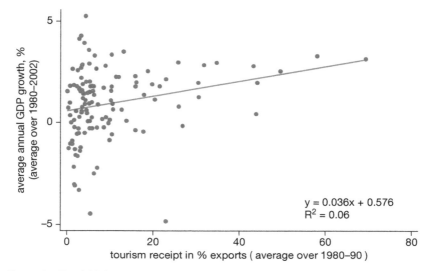

$$y = 0.036x + 0.576$$
$$R^2 = 0.06$$

Source: Arezki et al. 2012.

It quantifies the apparent positive relationship that is shown in figure 7.1 and corrects for bias arising from potential endogenous aspects in a growth regression that includes tourism specialization.

One can think of many channels through which international tourism may affect growth. The foreign direct investment (FDI) associated with tourism can bring managerial skills and technology with potential spillover benefits to other sectors (Aitken, Hanson, and Harrison 1997; Blomstrom and Kokko 1997; and Borensztein, De Gregorio, and Lee 1998). Policies designed to foster tourism—by improving security, stability, and openness—can also enhance growth in other sectors. Tourist expenditures undoubtedly feature income elasticity above one. This puts tourism in contrast to many other goods that poor countries tend to specialize in; expenditure shares for agricultural goods decline with income, reducing the scope for growth. The latter fact has often been highlighted as problematic in development economics (Prebish 1950 and Singer 1950).

On the other hand, an expansion of the tourism sector may increase the relative price of non-traded goods, crowding out the factors of production at the expense of the traded goods sector, a phenomenon known as "Dutch disease" (Copeland 1991; Chao et al. 2006). More generally, earlier literature on service activities and economic growth suggests that increased services specialization may diminish productivity growth, as resources shift toward this technologically stagnant sector (Baumol 1967). Some authors have argued that many services are essential intermediate goods, producing positive spillovers and facilitating economic growth (Oulton 2001). Recent work by Acemoglu and Guerrieri (2008) builds on the non-balanced growth literature. They propose a two-sector model in which the more capitalistic sector grows faster than the rest of the economy, but because the relative prices move against this sector, its price-weighted value grows slower than the rest of the economy.

Empirical studies that investigate the impact of tourism on growth generally find a positive correlation between tourism receipts and the growth rate, especially for poor countries (Sequeira and Macas Nunes 2008). Most of these studies exploit the time-series variation. We choose to focus instead on the long-term growth of a large cross-section of countries.[2] Furthermore, to our knowledge, no study provides a valid instrument to correct the potential endogenous aspect of the level of tourism specialization in growth regressions. We argue that not addressing this issue could bias the estimation of the coefficient associated with tourism in growth regressions. Unobservable variables such as managerial skills, which are crucial inputs in tourism activities, could directly explain both high economic growth and a high level of tourism. This would lead to an upward bias in the estimation of the impact of tourism specialization on economic growth.

Moreover, security and health issues—such as political instability, criminality, and malaria—are detrimental to both tourism and growth. While associated proxy variables could be controlled, limited data availability for a large cross-section and significant measurements errors (especially in the measurement of institutional quality) could lead to even more bias. This chapter fills the gap in the existing literature by providing an instrument to address potential endogeneity issues associated with tourism specialization.

To do so, we estimate standard growth models augmented with the extent of specialization in tourism using instrumental variables techniques for a cross-section of up to 127 countries over the period 1980 to 2002. The instrument is based on the number of sites on the UNESCO World Heritage List (WHL) per country.[3] This list is an outcome of an international treaty called the World Heritage Convention adopted by UNESCO in 1972. It embodies the goal of encouraging the identification, protection, and preservation of cultural and natural heritage around the world considered to be of outstanding value to humanity.

Since 1978, the World Heritage Committee meets once a year to decide which sites will be added to the WHL. The inscription of many sites on the list is a testimony to their universal recognition as important sources of tourism affluence—as is the case of the pyramids of Egypt, the Grand Canyon in the United States, and the old city of Sanaa in Yemen. Inclusion on this list is also a powerful boost to attracting tourism to an area.[4] We argue that this instrument satisfies the exclusion restriction; namely, that it affects growth only through tourism, because the presence of exceptional natural sites or cultural vestiges created centuries or millennia ago should not directly affect modern growth performance. Recent literature has shown some evidence of the persistence of institutions, cultural capital, and social capital in explaining income per capita, even when taking a very long term-perspective (Acemoglu et al. 2001; Guiso, Sapienza, and Zingales 2008; Tabellini 2007). The focus of this chapter is on the impact of specialization in international tourism, a relatively recent phenomenon, on economic growth—instead of the level of income per capita.

Results suggest that there is a robust positive relationship between tourism receipts (as a share of exports) and growth. An increase of one standard deviation in tourism specialization leads to an increase of around 0.5 percent in annual growth, everything else being constant. A direct application of our estimation is to assess whether tourism-oriented strategies could realistically yield the sustained growth experienced by the so-called "Asian tigers," whose strategies relied instead on the export of manufactured goods. In other words we will assess the extent to which the causal relationship between tourism and economic growth is not only statistically significant but also economically significant that is strong enough to ignite economic development. The chapter continues with a discussion of the validity of the instrument in use;

a description of the data, estimation strategy, and results; our robustness checks; and our conclusion. (See box 7.1.)

UNESCO World Heritage List as an Instrument for Tourism Specialization

As discussed above, the instrument for tourism is based on the number of sites on the UNESCO World Heritage List (WHL) per country. We argue that the presence of cultural or natural sites that are valued by tourists is likely to affect growth only through tourism activity. However, biases in the process of selection of the WHL could lead to a violation of the exclusion restriction. In the following, we describe our instrument further and discuss its validity in terms of coverage, political clout over the selection process, and the inclusion of natural sites as opposed to only cultural sites.

BOX 7.1

Tourism Is an Important Part of the Development Strategy for Sub-Saharan Africa

In 2010, the World Bank's Finance and Private Sector Development group for Sub-Saharan Africa (SSA) announced a tourism strategy employing wide client country consultation and based on evidence that tourism is well suited to energize SSA economies. Thanks to the appeal of Africa's historic cities, natural landscapes and wildlife, and rich cultural heritage, tourism has grown steadily over the past 20 years at a rate of over 5 percent. In 2008, there were more than 29 million tourist visits to Africa. Tourism contributed about 8 percent to GDP for the region and generated more than 10 million direct and indirect jobs and US$42 billion in export revenues. This translated into a significant 12.6 percent of total exports. The strategy cited several key reasons for the emphasis on the sector, including tourism's ability to (1) encourage pro-business policies and reforms that help small and medium enterprise development, (2) stimulate foreign investment, (3) help diversify exports, (4) trigger infrastructure improvements, (5) benefit women (women manage more than 50 percent of hospitality businesses in SSA), and (6) generate income for biodiversity and cultural heritage conservation.

Source: Africa Tourism Strategy: Transformation through Tourism. World Bank. 2010.

Coverage

Countries submit nomination proposals for properties within their territory to be considered for inclusion in UNESCO's World Heritage List. As of 2006, 181 state parties around the world have signed the convention. The proposed list of sites is first nominated and then independently reviewed by two advisory bodies. The final decision is then made by the World Heritage Committee (UNESCO 2008). On average, 30 new sites have been added annually between 1978 and 2008. The World Heritage sites are global in geographic coverage, as shown in figure 7.2. This is important as it ensures that results based on this instrument are not conditional on belonging to a certain region.

This study constructed a dataset recording the year each cultural site was built.[5] Table 7.1 summarizes our dataset, divided into regions, and a historical timeline corresponding to major civilizations. It indicates that there are relatively few sites built in the 20th century (less than 3 percent of the total) and that the majority of the sites (65 percent) were built more than five centuries ago.

Furthermore, table 7.1 indicates that Western, and in particular European, civilizations have the greatest number of sites compared to other periods and civilizations. This is not a source of violation of the exclusion restriction per se, as the existence of sites should only affect growth through the tourism channel. However, there is a potential for our instrument to be correlated with the intensity of social, cultural, and political life in the last two to five centuries. In turn, it could lead to a correlation between the level of income, as well as the

FIGURE 7.2
UNESCO World Heritage Sites

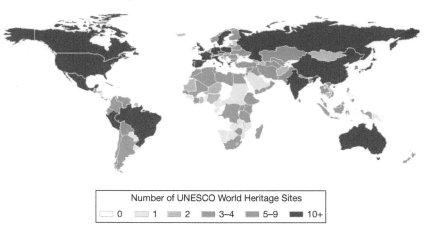

Number of UNESCO World Heritage Sites

☐ 0 ▨ 1 ▨ 2 ▨ 3–4 ▨ 5–9 ▮ 10+

Source: Authors.

TABLE 7.1

Regional and Historical Distribution of World Heritage Sites (2002)ᵃ

Region	Cultural				Naturalᵇ	Total
	10th B.C.-14th A.D.	15th-17th	18th-19th	20th		
Africa	13 (Early man, Islamic)	9 (Zimbabwe)	3 (Colonial)	0	38	63
Asia	68 (Buddhist, Hindu)	19 (Ming, Mughal)	6 (Qing)	2	57	152
Middle East	47 (Mesopotamia, Egypt, Islamic)	2 (Ottoman)	1 (North Africa)	0	5	55
Europe	219 (Greece, Rome, Middle Ages)ᶜ	53 (Renaissance)	42 (Enlightenment, Industrial Rev.)	12	74	400
Latin America	24 (Aztec, Inca, Maya)	38 (Spanish, Portuguese)	8 (Independence)	2	42	114
Total	371	121	60	16	216	784

Source: Authors based on UNESCO data.

a Following UNESCO classification, North America is part of the European region.

b Includes "mixed" sites, i.e., those sites classified under both natural and cultural criteria.

c The Middle Ages account for 143 of the 219 European sites during this timeframe.

quality of institutions, in the modern period, and the proposed instrument. Recent studies provide evidence that formal institutions, cultural capital, and social capital, respectively, are persistent over time and could have long-lasting effects on income per capita (Acemoglu et al. 2001; Guiso, Sapienza, and Zingales 2008; Tabellini 2007). We address this concern by controlling for the initial level of income as well as for the quality of institution and trade openness.[6] We also use the dataset we constructed to verify the robustness of our results to the sequential exclusion of recently built sites (20th century, 19th to 20th centuries, and so on up to fifth century BC) from the WHL.

Finally, world political developments have affected the composition of the WHL. The breakup of the Soviet Union resulted in a number of newly created Central Asian countries receiving sites in the early 1990s. So a test was conducted of the robustness of our results to the impact of those political developments on our UNESCO-based instrument by using versions of the WHL from different years. (See box 7.2.)

Political Clout

If there is a relationship between alliances of various natures (such as economic, strategic, or other) and site inscription, then our proposed instrument may not

---

BOX 7.2

The World Bank Has Supported Investments at Many UNESCO World Heritage Sites

Of all World Bank projects with cultural or natural heritage components, 120 have focused on World Heritage sites. These projects have supported investments in conservation and rehabilitation; infrastructure improvements; legal, institutional, and policy frameworks; site management plans; and technical assistance for 188 individual sites, of which 112 are cultural sites, 71 are natural sites, and 5 are mixed (cultural and natural) sites. Within the World Bank–defined regions, areas with the most projects are Sub-Saharan Africa, Latin America/ Caribbean, and Middle-East/North Africa with 52, 50, and 48 projects respectively. The Europe/Central Asia and East Asia/Pacific Regions have championed 21 and 14 projects respectively, and the South Asia Region has supported 3 projects at World Heritage sites.

Source: Anthony Bigio and Rana Amirtahmasebi. World Bank and World Heritage Sites, Portfolio Review, 2011.

be valid in the sense that it would violate the exclusion restriction. Indeed, the instrument would be correlated with unobserved assistance from rich countries to poor countries in the form of development assistance, FDI, technology transfers, and military and security cooperation. In turn, such assistance is potentially associated with faster growth. To verify whether political clout influences World Heritage designations, we calculated the correlations between each country's number of World Heritage sites and its voting coincidence with the G7 countries at the UN Security Council.[7] Table 7.2 presents the results. The correlation between sites and voting coincidence with all G7 countries ranges between 0.17 and 0.28. The upper-bound correlation is driven by Western countries, especially by the European ones.

However, this chapter primarily focuses on a potential systematic bias in the selection of World Heritage sites in developing countries, which could then benefit from different forms of assistance. Therefore, we recalculated the correlation between sites and voting coincidence, excluding OECD countries. In this case, the correlation between sites and voting coincidence with all G7 countries

TABLE 7.2

Correlation between Total UNESCO World Heritage Sites and Average UN Voting Coincidence, 1980–2000

	Barro & Lee (2005)	Kegley & Hook (1991)	Thacker (1999)
Correlation coefficients for all countries (except G7) with:			
Canada	0.29	0.26	0.19
France	0.30	0.28	0.19
Germany	0.28	0.25	0.19
Italy	0.29	0.26	0.20
Japan	0.30	0.24	0.20
United Kingdom	0.28	0.26	0.17
United States	0.24	0.20	0.56
G7	0.28	0.26	0.17
Correlation coefficients for non-OECD countries with:			
Canada	0.08	0.10	−0.09
France	0.10	0.11	−0.09
Germany	0.08	0.10	−0.08
Italy	0.08	0.10	−0.09
Japan	0.10	0.12	−0.08
United Kingdom	0.07	0.08	−0.11
United States	0.01	−0.02	−0.18
G7	0.07	0.09	−0.10

Source: Authors.

decreases to between –0.10 and 0.07. Those correlation coefficients suggest that coincidence of voting between a given country with G7 countries (as a whole or taken individually) is at best not influencing the number of sites added to the WHL for that country. Thus, we find little evidence of political clout of the kind that would invalidate our instrument.[8]

Table 7.1 indicates that the bulk of the World Heritage sites are cultural sites, although the number of natural sites has been rising recently. An important aspect in the selection of natural sites is the way governments protect them. Thus, the existence of natural sites on the WHL could be linked to governments' environment protection efforts, which in turn could signal improved governance. (See box 7.3.) Creating protected areas and biodiversity conservation zones could also have direct consequences on the economy.[9] In addition, natural sites could be capturing natural capital that could have a direct effect on economic growth not running necessarily through tourism. This could potentially violate the exclusion

---

BOX 7.3

Environmental Protection Projects Help Sustain World Heritage Sites

Bangladesh Forest Resources Management Project (Project number 009470)
Total Project Cost: US$58.7 million
Total Loan Amount: US$49.6 million
Approved: June 1992 – Closed: December 2001

This project's objective was to protect Bangladesh's environment while establishing management systems responsive to the country's economic, environmental, and social goals. One of the target areas for this work, the Sundarbans, was declared a World Heritage site during project implementation. While World Bank records do not show that project work was specifically directed toward enlisting the site, efforts to conserve the Sundarbans benefited from project investments that developed detailed natural resource and biological surveys and conservation management plans. Working in tandem with the government, the project improved management and protection in the Sundarbans, ensured fauna and flora conservation, and established mangrove plantations that have assisted with land accretion and fishery habitat conservation.

Source: Bangladesh Forest Resources Management Project Project Appraisal Document and Implementation and Completion Report.

restriction and invalidate our instrument. Thus, we further verify the robustness of our results by excluding natural sites from the list.

Empirical Investigation

Data and Specification

To quantify the effect of tourism specialization on long-term economic growth, we estimate standard growth models augmented with a proxy that captures the extent of specialization in tourism (in terms of exports of goods and services). Appendix I contains a description of the variables and their sources (table 7.4) as well as the list of the countries included in the sample (table 7.5). The dependent variable is the growth of GDP per capita over the period 1980–2002 in Purchasing Power Parity (PPP) constant international U.S. dollars, denoted *Growth*. Tourism specialization, hereafter denoted *Tourism*, is measured by the average of tourism receipts as a share of exports of goods and services for the period 1980–1990.[10,11]

The study adds other controls to the specification that are standard in the growth literature.[12] Initial income, denoted *Income*, is the logarithm of GDP per capita in constant international U.S. dollar in 1980. Average education, denoted *Education*, is the logarithm of the share of population with primary education in 1980 (Barro and Lee 2005). The study also uses distance to the equator, denoted *Distance*, as a proxy for geography. It controls for malaria prevalence that could have direct impact on growth, as suggested by Sachs (2003), but also for the distance to countries that are sources of tourists. The price of capital goods relative to consumption goods, denoted *Kprice*, is taken from Heston, Summers, and Aten (Klenow and Hsieh 2007). Real trade openness, denoted *Trade*, is proxied by the sum of exports plus imports of goods and services in current dollars divided by GDP in PPP constant international U.S. dollars as suggested by Alcala and Ciconne (2004).[13] The quality of institutions, hereafter denoted *Institution*, is measured by the average law and order index over the period 1980–2002 taken from Political Risk Services (2009).

The instrument for *Tourism* is the number of World Heritage sites per 100,000 inhabitants in the year 2002.[14] We also use kilometers of coastal zone, hereafter denoted *Coastal*, and related interactions as additional instruments for *Tourism*. The instrument for *Trade* is the logarithm of trade predicted by a gravity-based equation, denoted *lnfrinstex*, as suggested by Frankel and Romer (1999). The instrument for *Institution* is the fraction of individuals speaking English as a primary language (Hall and Jones 1999). We alternatively use the fraction of individuals speaking a European language as a primary language, also from Hall and Jones (1999), and the logarithm of settlers' mortality, hereafter *Insetmort*, suggested by Acemoglu, Johnson, and Robinson (2001).

Results

Growth regressions are estimated using instrumental variables techniques (IV).The first and the second stage of the various IV regressions performed are shown in table 7.3. Standard errors for the second stage and first stage are corrected for the statistical pitfalls stemming from sub-populations having different variabilities than others, using standard White correction. Regressions (1) through (3) are growth regressions augmented with *Tourism* but excluding other endogenous variables. Regressions (4) and (5) control for *Trade* and *Institution*, respectively, using their associated instruments. Regression (6) includes both *Trade* and *Institution*.

Results of the second stage regressions, shown in the lower panel of table 7.3, point to a remarkably robust coefficient associated with *Tourism*. The coefficient ranges from 0.012 to 0.017 and is always significant across all specifications. Overall, the signs and magnitudes of the coefficients of the common regressors for economic growth are consistent with standard growth regressions. The sign associated with *Income* is always negative, supporting the convergence hypothesis, albeit not always significant. The regressions also provide evidence of the positive impact of *Education*, the negative effect of *Kprice*, and a positive impact of *Institution* on economic growth, as expected. *Trade* has the expected positive sign but is not significant in most regressions. This result could be explained partly by the inclusion of *Distance* in our benchmark specification.

Equation (2) constitutes our benchmark specification. Our results suggest that, with all other factors being equal, an increase in tourism by one sample standard deviation, that is 8 percentage points (where *Tourism* is measured in percentage), implies an increase in growth per capita by 10.4 percent. Such an increase over a 22-year period corresponds to an annualized additional growth of about 0.5 percentage points per year. This is a significant number but should be put in perspective with the required expansion in tourism receipts.

The upper panel in table 7.3 shows the results of the first stage IV regressions. *UNESCO* is significant in all the first stage regressions of *Tourism*. The *p*-value associated with the *F-test* indicates that the instrument used for *Tourism* is not weak in all the first stage regressions. Excluding regression (1), its coefficient ranges from 29 to 32. In addition, *Engfrac,* corresponding to the fraction of the population speaking English, has a positive coefficient in the first stage regression of *Institution* but the *F-test* indicates that the instrument tends to be weak, as shown in equation (5) and (6). In contrast, the coefficient associated with *Infrinstex* in the first stage regression for *Trade* has the right sign and is

TABLE 7.3
Benchmark Regressions

First Stage Variables	(1) Tourism	(2) Tourism	(3) Tourism	(4) Tourism	(4) Trade	(5) Tourism	(5) Institution	(6) Tourism	(6) Trade	(6) Institution
UNESCO	13.768*** [2.851]	29.982*** [6.751]	29.408*** [7.066]	27.939*** [6.863]	-3.814 [23.662]	32.055*** [7.066]	-0.133 [0.400]	29.289*** [7.464]	7.963 [22.756]	-0.042 [0.443]
Income		-1.042* [0.551]	-1.494* [0.772]	-1.375* [0.605]	8.072** [3.725]	-0.679 [0.620]	0.551*** [0.130]	-1.539 [0.988]	10.810** [4.533]	0.554*** [0.132]
Education		1.096 [1.224]	1.549 [1.383]	1.318 [1.206]	3.715 [3.803]	0.574 [1.301]	-0.100 [0.157]	1.435 [1.445]	-2.563 [3.725]	-0.126 [0.162]
Distance		0.028 [0.038]	0.036 [0.039]	0.027 [0.042]	-0.031 [0.248]	0.004 [0.035]	0.038*** [0.008]	0.004 [0.040]	-0.125 [0.262]	0.040*** [0.007]
Kprice			1.304 [2.376]					1.592 [2.328]	-2.549 [8.539]	-0.382 [0.285]
Infrinstex_dk				1.421* [0.834]	24.110*** [5.786]			1.694 [1.059]	26.157*** [7.126]	0.115 [0.161]
Engfrac_dk						1.495 [3.842]	0.446 [0.306]	3.541 [4.175]	8.815 [9.332]	0.628* [0.336]
Constant	8.162*** [1.028]	10.827** [5.053]	7.415 [9.414]	17.327*** [6.304]	36.735* [20.294]	9.613* [5.206]	-1.677* [0.860]	12.305 [10.729]	51.242 [37.186]	0.232 [1.606]
F test	23.32	19.72	17.32	10.62	14.97	10.53	1.25	6.54	10.39	1.18
p value	0.000	0.000	0.0001	0.0001	0.000	0.0001	0.2906	0.0005	0.000	0.3236
Observations	127	96	93	94	94	88	88	84	84	84
R-squared	0.180	0.194	0.216	0.208	0.411	0.223	0.685	0.278	0.490	0.719

Second Stage Variables	(1) Growth	(2) Growth	(3) Growth	(4) Growth	(5) Growth	(6) Growth
Tourism	0.015*** [0.005]	0.013** [0.006]	0.017** [0.007]	0.012** [0.006]	0.015*** [0.006]	0.013* [0.008]
Income		-0.082 [0.069]	-0.008 [0.074]	-0.139** [0.069]	-0.258* [0.143]	-0.337** [0.140]
Education		0.158** [0.066]	0.112* [0.060]	0.163** [0.071]	0.205*** [0.075]	0.214** [0.087]

(continued next page)

TABLE 7.3 *continued*

First Stage Variables	(1) Tourism	(2) Tourism	(3) Tourism	(4) Tourism	(4) Trade	(5) Tourism	(5) Institution	(6) Tourism	(6) Trade	(6) Institution
Distance	0.100 [0.067]	0.013*** [0.004]	0.012*** [0.004]	0.015*** [0.004]		0.002 [0.008]			-0.002 [0.008]	
Kprice		-0.255** [0.118]							-0.163 [0.144]	
Trade				0.003 [0.003]					0.004 [0.003]	
Institution						0.295 [0.203]			0.388** [0.186]	
Constant		-0.027 [0.433]	0.572 [0.497]	0.245 [0.423]		0.481 [0.609]			1.400* [0.754]	
Kleibergen-Paap rk Wald F statistic	23.316	19.724	17.32	4.745		1.19			0.971	
Stock-Yogo weak ID test critical values (10 percent maximal IV size)	16.38	16.38	16.38	7.03		7.03				
Stock-Yogo weak ID test critical values (15 percent maximal IV size) 8.96	8.96	8.96	8.96	4.58		4.58		⋮		⋮
Stock-Yogo weak ID test critical values (20 percent maximal IV size) 6.66	6.66	6.66	6.66	3.95		3.95				
Observations	127	96	93	94		88			84	
R-squared	0.056	0.212	0.256	0.266		0.334			0.157	
Robust standard errors in brackets										

Source: Authors.

Robust standard errors in brackets.

*** *p*<0.01, ** *p*<0.05, * *p*<0.1

significant—shown in equations (4) and (6). The *F-test* for the instrument used for *Trade* indicates that the instrument is not weak. Overall, Kleibergen-Paap statistics shown in the lower panel of table 7.3 are greater than the Stock and Yogo 10 or 15 percent critical values for most of the regressions except for equation (5) and (6). That result indicates that the introduction of the instruments used for *Institution* weakens the identification. The main result related to *Tourism* holds when we use *Eurfrac*, corresponding the fraction of the population speaking one of the major languages of Western Europe: English, French, German, Portuguese, or Spanish, and *Lnsetmort* individually and/or in combination with *Engfrac* as instruments for *Institution*.[15] We now turn to testing the robustness of our main results.

Robustness[16]

The study first conducted a number of robustness checks on the instrument. We used various versions of the WHL in the IV regressions, as shown in table 7.6 in Appendix II. Results are virtually unchanged whether we use the list from 1997 or 1992. The coefficients associated with *Tourism* in the second stage regressions range between 0.013 and 0.015.

The study then used exclusively the number of cultural sites as an instrument for *Tourism* in the IV growth regressions. As discussed previously, the process of selection of natural sites is a potential source of statistical bias in our estimation results stemming from the fact that both the selection of natural sites and economic growth could be explained by a variable we have omitted to include in our regression analysis. Once again our results are virtually unchanged. Indeed, the coefficient associated with *Tourism* in equation (2) of appendix table 7.7 when using only cultural sites equals 0.015 (compared to 0.013 in our benchmark regression). Further, appendix table 7.8 shows results of the regressions (1)–(8) where sites built in the 20th century, 19th to 20th centuries, and up to 5th century BC were respectively subtracted. The sign, magnitude (ranging from 0.013 to 0.016), and significance of the coefficients associated with *Tourism* are all in line with our main result.

The study also used, in addition to the UNESCO World Heritage sites, kilometers of coastal zone, the square of the latter variable, and its interaction with the distance to the equator. Indeed, coastal area is likely to exogenously drive tourism activity. Controlling for *Trade*, this provides a valid instrument in the sense that it satisfies the exclusion restriction. Once again, our results hold. The coefficient associated with *Tourism* ranges from 0.013 in our benchmark regressions to 0.016, as shown in appendix table 7.9. The Hansen-J test indicates that the over-identifying restrictions are valid. The Kleibergen-Paap statistics indicate that the instruments are not weak, albeit at the 10 percent level.

The study checked the robustness of the results using different definitions and data sources for the dependent variable; namely, economic growth. Computation of GDP data in PPP differs between the World Bank (2008) and Heston and et al. (2006) datasets (Johnson et al. 2009). Also, using per capita GDP versus per worker is likely to alter our results given the large size of the unemployed population in many countries. Appendix table 7.10 shows the results using various PPP GDP data from Penn World Table 7.2 (PWT). Results are qualitatively unchanged, but the coefficients associated with *Tourism* now range from 0.013 to 0.024. The method of computation of PPP used in PWT and the use of GDP per worker instead of per capita increase the marginal effect of *Tourism* on growth.

We also tested the robustness of our results to the presence of outliers. Our main results hold when excluding observations with a relatively high leverage (Besley, Kuh, and Welsch 1980; Davidson and Mac Kinnon 1993, 32–9).[17] We also suspect that the size of a country matters, as indicated in figure 7.1 which shows that small tourism-oriented islands (most of the points in the upper-right corner) have grown faster than the average. Yet control variables such as education are not available for most of these countries, and hence they are excluded from the regression sample—the smallest country we have in our benchmark regression, equation (2) in table 7.3, is Iceland which corresponds to the bottom 15th percentile. Thus, the result obtained is not driven by this group, and we might expect a bigger effect of tourism on growth if we could include them. Further, we find that excluding the biggest countries in terms of population yields a greater coefficient of tourism on growth.[18] Therefore, big countries in the sample seem to decrease the size of the effect.[19] Big countries are "over-represented" in the sample because of data availability.[20] To check, we removed countries belonging to the top 15th percentile. The results are similar in magnitude and significance.

Finally, we re-estimated our model using first-differences, using 10-year and 5-year spans to estimate the impact of the *change* in tourism on the *change* in growth, as in Dollar and Kraay (2003). Naturally, this method increases the sample size and exploits mainly the time-series variation. Our results are two-fold. First, we find that the change in tourism has no statistically significant impact on the change in growth when using both ordinary least square and IV. Second, the various instruments used in the IV regressions appear to be weak when exploiting the within variation. The lack of consistency of these results with our cross-sectional approach can be explained by the fact that the within country variation of *Tourism* is about three times smaller than the between variation. This justifies the cross-sectional approach adopted in the present chapter. Moreover, the tests performed indicate that the various instruments used, including the number of sites added to the WHL between two periods, are weak, as seen in the first-stage regressions.[21]

Conclusion

The aim of this study is to quantify the relationship between tourism specialization and growth while correcting for endogenous aspects. We suggest an instrument to correct for the endogeneity of variables measuring tourism specialization in growth regressions based on the UNESCO WHL. The authors estimate growth equations augmented with the share of tourism receipts in total exports using instrumental variables techniques for a large cross-section of countries. The study indicates that the gain from tourism specialization can be significant, and that this result holds against a large array of robustness checks.

An increase of one standard deviation in tourism activity would lead to an annualized additional growth of about 0.5 percentage point per year, all other factors being equal. Additional annual growth of this magnitude is not to be ignored. However, one has to think about the opportunity cost of a solely tourism-based strategy given other paths for development, most noticeably the "Asian miracles." On one hand, it is likely that developing tourism requires less capital, infrastructure, and skilled labor when compared to a manufacturing, export-oriented strategy. On the other hand, it seems to rule out the type of growth record in the Asian miracles (on the order of 6 percent per year over 20 years). To illustrate this point, let us consider the "typical" developing country in the sample. It would have about 1 percent expected annual growth and an 8 percent tourism share of exports of goods and services. To reach growth of 6 percent per year, it would need to increase tourism receipts as a share of exports by more than 70 percent, or 10 times the standard deviation. It is, to say the least, very unlikely for most countries to achieve such a target.

In theory, the authors can explain why a solely tourism-based strategy cannot "make a miracle." The sustained high growth stems from a country's ability to constantly enter new technologies and quickly reallocate labor in the production of these new goods, as the productivity gains from learning-by-doing are highest in the first stages of production (Lucas 1993). By nature, the tourism industry presents different features. It relies on a limited set of services produced with little room for expansion and labor reallocation; thus, it needs to be part of a comprehensive strategy of economic diversification in order to be sustainable and inclusive. (See box 7.4.)

BOX 7.4

Tourism Is Coupled with Development of Other Sectors for Economic Diversification

Zambia Support for Economic Expansion and Diversification Project
(Project number 071407)
Total Project Cost: US$28.15 million
Total Loan Amount: US$28.15 million
Approved: July 2004 – Closed: November 2011

In partnership with the government of Zambia, this project aimed to reduce the vulnerability of the country's economy to shocks by supporting the diversification of its sources of growth. To counteract Zambia's dependence on the export of copper (over 70 percent of foreign exchange earnings) the project focused on developing tourism, gemstone production, and agribusiness. The country boasts Victoria Falls (a World Heritage site), rich biodiversity and wildlife areas, more than 42 million hectares of arable land and ample renewable water resources, and the second largest deposit of high-quality emeralds in the world. The project supported improvements in policy and regulatory frameworks, public investments to stimulate private sector activity, and government capacity building to support a diversified and export-oriented economy.

Source: Zambia Support for Economic Expansion and Diversification Project Appraisal Document.

Appendix I: Data Description and Sources

TABLE 7.4
Data Description

Database	Units	Descriptor	Code
Growth variables			
World Bank (2008)[a]	PPP constant international U.S. dollars	GDP per capita growth between 1980 to 2002 (natural logarithm difference)	Growth
World Bank (2004)[b]	Percentage of total exports of goods and services	Average annual tourism receipts	Tourism
World Bank (2008)	Logarithim of GDP per capita in PPP constant international U.S. dollars in 1980	Initial income	Income

(continued next page)

TABLE 7.4 *continued*

Database	Units	Descriptor	Code
Barro and Lee (2000)	Logarithim of fraction of population in 1980	Initial primary school attainment	Education
Dollar & Kraay (2003)	Latitude of capital city	Distance to the equator	Distance
Heston (2006)	Ratio of price indices	Price of capital goods relative to consumption goods	Kprice
World Bank (2008)	Nominal imports plus exports divided by GDP in PPP constant international U.S. dollars	Real openness, as described by Alcala & Ciccone (2004)	Trade
ICRG (2009)	Index value	Average annual law and order index	Institution
Instruments			
UNESCO (2009) & World Bank (2008)	Number of sites per 100,000 inhabitants[c]	UNESCO World Heritage Sites	Unesco
Dollar & Kraay (2003)	Logarithm of predicted trade share of GDP	Predicted trade, based on a gravity model using population and geography, as described by Frankel & Romer (1999)	Infrinstex
Dollar & Kraay (2003)	Fraction of total population	Fraction of a country's population speaking a European language as a mother tongue, as described by Hall & Jones (1999)	eurfrac
Dollar & Kraay (2003)	Fraction of total population	Fraction of a country's population speaking a English as a mother tongue, as described by Hall & Jones (1999)	engfrac
Dollar & Kraay (2003)	Logarithm of mortality rate	Colonial settler mortality, as described by Acemoglu, Johnson, & Robinson (2001)	Insetmort
CIA (2009)	Kilometers	Coastline	coastal

a. For robustness, also calculated using Heston (2006).
b. Provides longest consistent time series for tourism.
c. For robustness, also calculated per surface area.

Source: Authors.

TABLE 7.5
Countries Included in the Sample

Africa	Asia & Pacific	Europe & North America	Latin America & Caribbean	Middle East
Benin	Australia	Albania	Antigua and Barbuda	Algeria
Botswana	Bangladesh	Austria	Argentina	Bahrain
Burkina Faso	Bhutan	Belgium	Belize	Egypt, Arab. Rep.
Burundi	China	Bulgaria	Bolivia	Jordan

(continued next page)

TABLE 7.5 *continued*

Africa	Asia & Pacific	Europe & North America	Latin America & Caribbean	Middle East
Cameroon	Fiji	Canada	Brazil	Kuwait
Central African Republic	Hong Kong SAR	Cyprus	Chile	Libya
	India	Denmark	Colombia	Mauritania
Chad	Indonesia	Finland	Costa Rica	Morocco
Comoros	Iran, Islamic Rep.	France	Dominica	Oman
Congo, Dem. Rep.	Japan	Germany	Dominican Republic	Saudi Arabia
Congo, Rep.	Kiribati	Greece	Ecuador	Sudan
Cote d'Ivoire	Malaysia	Hungary	El Salvador	Syrian Arab Republic
Gabon	Myanmar	Iceland	Grenada	
Gambia, The	Nepal	Ireland	Guatemala	Tunisia
Ghana	New Zealand	Israel	Guyana	
Guinea	Pakistan	Italy	Haiti	
Kenya	Papua New Guinea	Malta	Honduras	
Lesotho		Netherlands	Jamaica	
Liberia	Philippines	Norway	Mexico	
Madagascar	Singapore	Portugal	Nicaragua	
Malawi	Solomon Islands	Romania	Panama	
Mali	Republic of Korea	Spain	Paraguay	
Mauritius	Sri Lanka	Sweden	Peru	
Namibia	Thailand	Switzerland	St. Kitts and Nevis	
Niger	Vanuatu	Turkey	St. Lucia	
Nigeria		United Kingdom	St. Vincent and the Erenadines	
Rwanda		United States		
Senegal			Suriname	
Seychelles			Trinidad and Tobago	
Sierra Leone			Uruguay	
South Africa			Venezuela R.B.	
Swaziland				
Togo				
Zambia				
		Number of countries:		*Total:*
33	24	27	30	13	127

Source: Authors.

Appendix II: Additional Robustness Checks

TABLE 7.6
Robustness to Using Various WHL

Variables	(1) Growth	(2) Growth	(3) Growth
Tourism	0.013**	0.013*	0.015**
	[0.006]	[0.007]	[0.006]
Income	–0.082	–0.083	–0.081
	[0.069]	[0.070]	[0.070]
Education	0.158**	0.158**	0.156**
	[0.066]	[0.067]	[0.066]
Distance	0.013***	0.013***	0.013***
	[0.004]	[0.004]	[0.004]
Constant	–0.027	–0.026	–0.037
	[0.433]	[0.435]	[0.435]
Cut-off year for instrument	2002	1997	1992
Kleibergen-Paap rk Wald F statistic	19.724	10.759	10.161
Stock-Yogo weak ID test critical values (10 percent maximal IV size)	16.38	16.38	16.38
Stock-Yogo weak ID test critical values (15 percent maximal IV size)	8.96	8.96	8.96
Observations	96	96	96
R-squared	0.212	0.212	0.204

Robust standard errors in brackets
*** $p<0.01$, ** $p<0.05$, * $p<0.1$
Source: Authors.

TABLE 7.7
Robustness to Using Only Cultural Sites

Variables	(1) Growth	(2) Growth
Tourism	0.013**	0.015***
	[0.006]	[0.005]
Income	–0.082	–0.082
	[0.069]	[0.070]
Education	0.158**	0.156**
	[0.066]	[0.067]

(continued next page)

TABLE 7.7 *continued*

Variables	(1) Growth	(2) Growth
Distance	0.013***	0.013***
	[0.004]	[0.004]
Constant	–0.027	–0.036
	[0.433]	[0.437]
Instrument coverage	Overall	Cultural only
Kleibergen-Paap rk Wald F statistic	19.72	18.33
Stock-Yogo weak ID test critical values (10 percent maximal IV size)	16.38	16.38
Stock-Yogo weak ID test critical values (15 percent maximal IV size)	8.96	8.96
Observations	96	96
R-squared	0.212	0.205

Robust standard errors in brackets.
*** p<0.01, ** p<0.1, * p<0.1.
Source: Authors.

TABLE 7.8
Robustness to Removing Various Centuries from the WHL

Variables	(1) Growth	(2) Growth	(3) Growth	(4) Growth	(5) Growth	(6) Growth	(7) Growth	(8) Growth
Tourism	0.015***	0.015***	0.016***	0.017***	0.017***	0.022***	0.022***	0.022***
	[0.005]	[0.005]	[0.005]	[0.005]	[0.005]	[0.005]	[0.005]	[0.006]
Income	–0.082	–0.081	–0.081	–0.082-0	–0.079	–0.079	–0.078	–0.076
	[0.070]	[0.070]	[0.070]	[0.070]	[0.070]	[0.071]	[0.071]	[0.071]
Education	0.156**	0.156**	0.154*	0.152**	0.15	0.150**	0.145**	0.145**
	[0.067]	[0.067]	[0.067]	[0.067]	[0.067]	[0.067]	[0.067]	[0.067]
Distance	0.013***	0.013***	0.013***	0.013***	0.013***	0.013***	0.013***	0.013***
	[0.004]	[0.004]	[0.004]	[0.004]	[0.004]	[0.004]	[0.004]	[0.004]
Constant	–0.037	–0.038	–0.047	–0.054	–0.058	–0.064	–0.073	–0.090
	[0.437]	[0.437]	[0.438]	[0.439]	[0.439]	[0.442]	[0.442]	[0.445]
Century cut-off point for cultural sites	All	XX	XVIII	XV	XIII	X	V	V BC
Kleibergen-Paap rk Wald F statistic	19.72	18.23	18.20	65.439	66.91	17.28	17.77	18.92
Stock-Yogo weak ID test critical values (10 percent maximal IV size)	16.38	16.38	16.38	16.38	16.38	16.38	16.38	16.38
Stock-Yogo weak ID test critical values (15 percent maximal IV size)	8.96	8.96	8.96	8.96	8.96	8.96	8.96	8.96

(continued next page)

TABLE 7.8 *continued*

Variables	(1) Growth	(2) Growth	(3) Growth	(4) Growth	(5) Growth	(6) Growth	(7) Growth	(8) Growth
Stock-Yogo weak ID test critical values (20 percent maximal IV size)	6.66	6.66	6.66	6.66	6.66	6.66	6.66	6.66
Observations	96	96	96	96	96	96	96	96
R-squared	0.205	0.204	0.196	0.1960	0.187	0.171	0.171	0.152

Robust standard errors in brackets.
*** $p<0.01$,** $p<0.05$, * $p<0.1$
Source: Authors.

TABLE 7.9
Robustness to Using Additional Instruments for Tourism

Variables	(1) Growth	(2) Growth	(3) Growth	(4) Growth
Tourism	0.013**	0.015**	0.015**	0.015**
	[0.006]	[0.006]	[0.006]	[0.006]
Income	−0.082	−0.081	−0.081	−0.081
	[0.069]	[0.070]	[0.069]	[0.069]
Education	0.158**	0.155**	0.155**	0.155**
	[0.066]	[0.066]	[0.066]	[0.066]
Distance	0.013***	0.013***	0.013***	0.013***
	[0.004]	[0.004]	[0.004]	[0.004]
Constant	−0.027	−0.038	−0.044	−0.040
	[0.433]	[0.434]	[0.432]	[0.429]
Instrument coverage	UNESCO	UNESCO, coastline	UNESCO, coastline, coastline interacted with distance	UNESCO, coastline, coastline interacted with distance, and coastline squared
Kleibergen-Paap rk Wald F statistic	—	11.45	9.04	8.58
Stock-Yogo weak ID test critical values (5 percent maximal IV size)	—	—	13.91	16.85
Stock-Yogo weak ID test critical values (10 percent maximal IV size)	—	19.93	9.08	10.27

(continued next page)

TABLE 7.9 *continued*

Variables	(1) Growth	(2) Growth	(3) Growth	(4) Growth
Stock-Yogo weak ID test critical values (20 percent maximal IV size)	—	8.75	6.46	6.71
Hansen-J test (p value)		0.31	0.58	0.78
Observations	96	96	96	96
R-squared	0.212	0.203	0.199	0.202

Robust standard errors in brackets.
*** $p<0.01$, **$p<0.05$, * $p<0.1$.

Source: Authors.

TABLE 7.10

Robustness to Using Different Measures of GDP

Description Variables	(1) GDP, PPP (constant 2005 international $) World Bank growth	(2) Real GDP chain per worker unit: I$ per worker in 2000 constant prices, PWT 6.2 growth rgdpwok pwt	(3) Real GDP per capita (constant prices: Laspeyres) unit: I$ in 2000 constant prices, PWT 6.2 growth rgdpl pwt	(4) Real GDP per capita (constant prices: chain series) unit: I$ in 2000 constant prices, PWT 6.2 growth rgdpch pwt	(5) Real GDP chain per equivalent adult unit: I$ per eq. adult in 2000 constant prices growth rgdpeqa pwt
Tourism	0.013**	0.024***	0.022***	0.021***	0.022***
	[0.006]	[0.007]	[0.007]	[0.007]	[0.007]
Income	-0.082				
1 ncome_rgdpwok_pwt	[0.069]	-0.162**			
		[0.070]			
Income_rgdpl_pwt			-0.075		
			[0.081]		
1 ncome_rgdpch_pwt				-0.079	
				[0.081]	
1 ncome_rgdpeqa_pwt					-0.093
					[0.082]
Education	0.158**	0.093	0.148*	0.149*	0.139*
	[0.066]	[0.071]	[0.079]	[0.079]	[0.079]
Distance	0.013***	0.015***	0.012***	0.012***	0.012***
	[0.004]	[0.004]	[0.004]	[0.004]	[0.004]
Constant	-0.027	0.767	-0.107	-0.086	0.035
	[0.433]	[0.511]	[0.562]	[0.561]	[0.586]

(continued next page)

TABLE 7.10 *continued*

Description Variables	(1) GDP, PPP (constant 2005 international $) World Bank growth	(2) Real GDP chain per worker unit: I$ per worker in 2000 constant prices, PWT 6.2 growth rgdpwok pwt	(3) Real GDP per capita (constant prices: Laspeyres) unit: I$ in 2000 constant prices, PWT 6.2 growth rgdpl pwt	(4) Real GDP per capita (constant prices: chain series) unit: I$ in 2000 constant prices, PWT 6.2 growth rgdpch pwt	(5) Real GDP chain per equivalent adult unit: I$ per eq. adult in 2000 constant prices growth rgdpeqa pwt
Kleibergen-Paap rk Wald F statistic	19.72	16.28	16.36	16.36	16.45
Stock-Yogo weak ID test critical values (10 percent maximal IV size)	16.38	16.38	16.38	16.38	16.38
Stock-Yogo weak ID test critical values (15 percent maximal IV size)	8.96	8.96	8.96	8.96	8.96
Stock-Yogo weak ID test critical values (20 percent maximal IV size)	6.66	6.66	6.66	6.66	6.66
Observations	96	97	98	98	98
R-squared	0.212	0.127	0.161	0.162	0.150

Robust standard errors in brackets.
*** $p<0.01$, ** $p<0.05$, * $p<0.1$.

Source: Authors.

Notes

The authors wish to thank Daron Acemoglu, Thomas Chaney, Decio Coviello, Pieran-gelo De Pace, Fuad Hasanov, Camelia Minoiu, Xavier Sala-i-Martin, and James Stock for stimulating discussions and helpful comments. We also thank Mileva Radisavljević and Latoya McDonald for editorial assistance. All remaining errors are ours.

1. The coefficient of correlation associated with figure 7.1 is equal to 0.27.
2. We further discuss the relevance of exploiting the "between" rather than the "within" variation.
3. We use different normalizations, including population in 1980 and surface area. We also use an additional instrument based on the kilometers of coastal area.
4. More and more tourism brochures use the label WHL to advertise for a destination. We further disentangle the "advertising effect" from the "testimony effect" by using the "flow" of sites added rather than the "stock" of sites in a given year when using first-differences.
5. Sites are dated according to their century of creation. Where specific dates are unavailable, sites are dated according to the corresponding civilization's period of peak influence.
6. Note also that some sites are historic markets or harbors that still have an economic relevance.
7. We use different methodologies to define voting coincidence amongst all UN General Assembly votes, as shown in table 8.2. Thacker (1999) codes votes in agreement as 1, votes in disagreement as 0, and abstentions or absences as 0.5. Barro and Lee (2005) use the fraction of times a country votes in accordance with the country of interest (either both voting yes, both voting no, both abstaining, or both absent). Kegley and Hook (1991) compute a similar fraction but disregard abstentions and absences. See Dreher and Sturm 2006 for data and a more detailed discussion of these different methodologies.
8. We also looked at countries that have been under UN embargo or the target of sanctions. We find that overall these countries have a number of sites greater than the median.
9. A controversy has emerged surrounding the creation of such areas and the resulting rural population displacement and associated land tenure insecurity.
10. Tourism arrivals are also available from World Tourism Organization. However, the economic impact of tourism arrival can differ radically depending on the source and destination countries of tourism (that is, regional versus international tourism). The focus of this chapter being to quantify the impact of international tourism specialization on economic growth, we use tourism receipts to be able to measure the reliance of a country on tourism in its exports of goods and services. For robustness, we also define *Tourism* as the average of tourism receipts as a share of GDP and obtain similar results.
11. Taking the average of tourism receipts over the whole period instead of the first ten years yields similar results.
12. For example, Sala-i-Martin et al. (2004) determined a ranking of variables according to their significance in growth regressions using a Bayesian averaging methodology. The independent variables we chose are based on the top five variables of this list.

13. We subtract tourism receipt from the numerator of *Trade*.
14. We further test the robustness of our results by using versions of the WHL from different years.
15. The results are available from the authors upon request. The Hansen-J test associated with those regressions indicates that the over identifying restrictions are not valid when all those instruments are used. In addition, F-tests also indicate that the instruments are weak.
16. Results discussed in this section but not presented are available from the authors upon request.
17 The total number of observations dropped is less than 5 percent of the total sample.
18. We tested for non-linearities along countries' population size. We found no such evidence.
19. Both tails of the distribution of countries' populations pull the result in a different direction.
20. One has to be cautious not to exclude small population countries from the regression sample without considering the population distribution.
21. We use as the instrument for change in *Tourism* the change in the number of sites added to the WHL, thus only capturing the "advertising effect" as opposed to the "testimony effect."

References

Acemoglu, D., and V. Guerrieri. 2008. "Capital Deepening and Nonbalanced Economic Growth." *Journal of Political Economy* 116 (3): 467–98.
Acemoglu, D., V. Guerrieri, S. Johnson, and J. Robinson. 2001. "The Colonial Origins of Comparative Development: An Empirical Investigation." *American Economic Review* 91 (5): 1369–401.
Aitken, B., G. Hanson, and A. E. Harrison. 1997. "Spillovers, Foreign Investment, and Export Behavior." *Journal of International Economics* 43 (1): 103–32.
Alcala, F., and A. Ciccone. 2004. "Trade and Productivity." *Quarterly Journal of Economics* 119 (2): 612–45.
Barro, R. J., and J.-W. Lee. 2000. "International Data on Educational Attainment: Updates and Implications." CID Working Paper No. 42. Cambridge, MA: Harvard University.
Barro, R. J., and J.-W. Lee. 2005. "IMF Programs: Who Is Chosen and What Are the Effects?" *Journal of Monetary Economics* 52: 1245–69.
Baumol, W. 1967. "Macroeconomics of Unbalanced Growth: The Anatomy of Urban Crisis." *American Economic Review* 57: 415–26.
Besley, D. A., E. Kuh, and R. E. Welsch. 1980. *Regression Diagnostics: Identifying Influential Data and Sources of Collinearity.* New York: John Wiley.
Blomstrom, M., and A. Kokko. 1997. "How Foreign Investment Affects Host Countries." Policy Research Working Paper No. 1745: Washington, DC World Bank.
Borensztein, E., J. De Gregorio, and J.-W. Lee. 1998. "How Does Foreign Direct Investment Affect Economic Growth?" *Journal of International Economics* 45 (1): 115–35.

Chao, C.-C., B. R. Hazari, J.-P. Laffargue, P. M. Sgro, and E. S. H. Yu. 2006. "Tourism, Dutch Disease, and Welfare in an Open Dynamic Economy." *Japanese Economic Review* 57 (4): 501–15.

Copeland, B. R. 1991. "Tourism, Welfare, and De-Industrialization in a Small Open Economy." *Economica* 58: 515–29.

Davidson, R., and J. G. MacKinnon. 1993. *Estimation and Inference in Econometrics.* New York: Oxford University Press.

Dollar, D., and A. Kraay. 2003. "Institutions, Trade, and Growth." *Journal of Monetary Economics* 50: 133–162.

Dreher, A., and J.-E. Sturm. 2006. "Do IMF and World Bank Influence Voting in the UN General Assembly?" KOF Swiss Economic Institute, Working Paper No. 137. Zurich: ETH.

Frankel, J. A., and D. Romer. 1999. "Does Trade Cause Growth?" *American Economic Review* 89 (3): 379–99.

Guiso, L., P. Sapienza, and L. Zingales. 2008. "Long Term Persistence." NBER Working Paper No. 14278. Cambridge, MA: NBER

Hall, R. E., and C. I. Jones. 1999. "Why Do Some Countries Produce So Much More Output Per Worker Than Others?" *Quarterly Journal of Economics* 113 (4): 1119–135.

Heston, A., R. Summers, and B. Aten. 2006. *Penn World Table Version 6.2.* Center for International Comparisons of Production, Income and Prices. Philadelphic: University of Pennsylvania.

ITB World Travel Trends Report. 2009. *International Tourism Challenged by Deteriorating World Economy.* March. Berlin: ITB.

Johnson, S., W. Larson, C. Papageorgiou, and A. Subramanian. 2009. "Is Newer Better? The Penn World Table Revisions and the Cross-Country Growth Literature." Unpublished paper.

Kegley, C. W., Jr., and Steven W. Hook. 1991. "U.S. Foreign Aid and UN Voting: Did Reagan's Linkage Strategy Buy Defense or Defiance?" *International Studies Quarterly* 35 (3): 295–312.

Klenow, P. J., and C.-T. Hsieh. 2007. "Relative Prices and Relative Prosperity." *American Economic Review* 97 (3): 562–85.

Lucas, R. E., Jr. 1993."Making a Miracle." *Econometrica* 61 (2, March): 251–72.

Oulton, N. 2001. "Must the Growth Rate Decline? Baumol's Unbalanced Growth Revisited." *Oxford Economic Papers* 53: 605–27.

Political Risk Services. 2009. *International Country Risk Guides East Syracuse, NY: Political Risk Services.*

Sachs, J. 2003. "Institutions Don't Rule: Direct Effects of Geography on Per Capita Income." NBER Working Paper No. 9490 (February). Cambridge, MA: NBER

Sala-i-Martin, X., G. Doppelhofer, and R. I. Miller. 2004. "Determinants of Long-Term Growth: A Bayesian Averaging of Classical Estimates (BACE) Approach." *American Economic Review* 94 (4): 813–35.

Sequeira, T. N., and P. Macas Nunes. 2008. "Does Tourism Influence Economic Growth? A Dynamic Panel Data Approach." *Applied Economics* 40: 2431–41.

Singer, H. 1950. "The Distribution of Gains Between Borrowing and Investing Countries." *American Economic Review* 40: 473–485.

Stock, J. H., and M. Yogo. 2002. "Testing for Weak Instruments in Linear IV Regression." NBER Technical Working Paper No. 284 (November). Cambridge, MA: NBER

Tabellini, G. 2007. "Culture and Institutions." CEPR Discussion Papers 6589. Washington, DC: CEPR

Thacker, S. C. 1999. "The High Politics of IMF Lending." *World Politics* 52 (3): 181–205.

UNESCO. 2008. "Operational Guidelines for the Implementation of the World Heritage Convention." Paris: UNESCO World Heritage Center.

World Bank. 2004. *World Development Indicators*. Washington, DC: World Bank.

World Bank. 2008. *World Development Indicators*. Washington, DC: World Bank.

8

Financial Mechanisms for Historic City Core Regeneration and Brownfield Redevelopment

Francesca Romana Medda

Associate Professor of Applied Economics, University College of London (UK), with Simone Caschili, and Marta Modelewska

This chapter examines innovative financial funding mechanisms that can spur private-sector investment in urban heritage regeneration projects. In recent years, the scope of urban heritage interventions has broadened to address both natural and cultural heritage; therefore, the definition of "brownfield" must be extended to include not only natural brownfields, such as contaminated sites, but also areas with cultural heritage assets, as for example, underutilized historic districts. Given the public good characteristics of brownfield investment, the private sector may undervalue the commercial returns and overvalue the related costs of projects, thereby leading to market failures and the undersupply of urban heritage redevelopment projects. The public sector must act as a catalyst to foster private investment in heritage brownfield regeneration by creating financial solutions, such as debt leveraging, local revolving funds, and tax abatements/credits to create continuous stimulus and incentives that can help diminish the incidence of market failure in these types of investments. This is especially critical in developing countries. While private-sector funding for urban brownfield projects (especially natural heritage sites) is increasing, these actors need to assume a greater role in investing in urban cultural brownfield projects. Against this background, this chapter analyzes four models of financing urban heritage brownfields: (1) public-private partnerships, (2) land value finance mechanisms, (3) urban development funds, and (4) impact investment funds. Various case studies to corroborate the statements are presented.

Introduction

The scope of urban cultural heritage conservation has broadened considerably since the adoption of the Venice Charter of 1964, with the United Nations Educational, Scientific and Cultural Organization (UNESCO) and International Council on Monuments and Sites (ICOMOS) at the forefront of this change. There has been a shift away from the conservation of objects and sites as an end in itself, to also considering the environmental dimensions and social factors of heritage conservation as well as the intangible values of heritage assets. However, there are still varied approaches to the rehabilitation and conservation of cultural heritage in historic urban cores, often using in their operational applications the concept of cultural heritage as spatially well-identified sites or as a series of discrete groups of remains. Within these different types of interpretations, cultural heritage areas are still sometimes mainly seen as belonging to the past, disconnected from the present and from each other within the urban landscape (Moylan et al. 2009).

Worldwide, at both national and regional levels, there are also notable differences in the scope and thus the legislative framework dedicated to urban heritage conservation; for instance, in China, heritage is defined as "immovable physical remains [...] that have significance" (ICOMOS 2000), whereas in Vietnam cultural heritage comprises both tangible and intangible elements (ASEAN 2000). These differences in definitions and approaches contribute to the difficulty of attracting financial support, particularly from the private sector, for cultural heritage conservation (Starr 2010). And so, it can be a challenging and complicated task to devise creative financial solutions for the revitalization and rehabilitation of historic urban areas by leveraging a combination of available resources from the private and public sector.

If one interprets urban heritage as an evolving interrelationship between history, ecosystems, and culture, this interaction must be seen as a multilayered integration of natural and cultural heritage. However, projects concerned with urban natural assets—which include soils, geology, and geomorphology—tend not to suffer the financial obstacles and restrictions that urban cultural heritage projects do. In fact, over the past 20 years, an extensive set of best practices has been developed for the rehabilitation of urban natural brownfields, including a thorough range of financial supports and mechanisms for site management (RESCUE 2004; U.S. EPA 1999).[1] From this perspective, the present chapter aims to extend the interpretation and approaches applied to urban natural brownfields to the regeneration and conservation of historic districts.

An urban brownfield can be defined as any land in a city that has been used in the past and is not now available for immediate use without some type of intervention (Alker et al. 2000); urban brownfields are areas that may be partially occupied or vacant. This chapter extends the definition of brownfield often used in the United

States; that is, contaminated land usually as the result of former industrial activity (Syms 1999). Instead, the approach of this chapter is to examine urban brownfields where there is continuity between the past and the present and between natural and manmade environments (De Sousa 2000; NRTEE 2003; RESCUE 2004; UK DETR 1999). From this perspective, urban areas that are blighted and idle but that have cultural heritage, such as the historic city cores of Asmara and Massawa in Eritrea, can also be identified as urban brownfields (see figure 8.1 and box 8.1).

If the value capital of a city is its urban heritage, this implies that in both cases of brownfields (natural and cultural) there is a depreciation of this urban capital, either due to site contamination (in the natural brownfield) or to its derelict and blighted status (in the case of cultural brownfield). The area of Makina in Medina Fes (Morocco), for example, combines these two aspects; it is in need of conservation and rehabilitation of its historic housing stock, but in the area of Ain Nokbi, a remediation plan has been developed to reduce the land's contamination and pollution resulting from copperware activity.

FIGURE 8.1
Types of Urban Brownfields

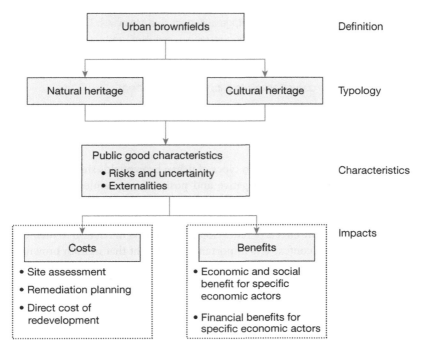

Source: Authors.

> **BOX 8.1**
>
> ## Rehabilitation of Historic Urban Brownfields Is Part of Nation Building and Economic Development in Eritrea
>
> **Eritrea Cultural Assets Rehabilitation Project** (Project number 058724)
> Total Project Cost: US$5.4 million
> Total Loan Amount: US$5 million
> Approved: July 2001 – Closed: July 2007
>
> As Eritrea began the process of rebuilding its economy after the conflict with Ethiopia, the World Bank supported a pilot project to test the potential of more fully integrating cultural heritage conservation into economic development. One focus of this project was the rehabilitation and conservation of the unique architectural heritage in the historic city cores of Asmara and Massawa. Both were suffering from severe deterioration as a result of natural and human forces. The work included developing new zoning regulations for the city cores and conservation plans for key historic buildings. The project also supported the production of a number of important publications and studies on Eritrean cultural heritage, particularly related to the built heritage of Asmara and Massawa. These publications have become popular among residents, scholars, and tourists, thereby increasing local awareness, international interest, and tourism. The project also supported archiving ancient manuscripts and recording oral history as part of the investment in cultural assets to support nation building.
>
> *Source:* Eritrea Cultural Assets Rehabilitation Project Implementation and Completion Report.

As shown in figure 8.1, the two types of urban brownfields share public good characteristics relative to the negative and positive externalities and the risks and uncertainty of redevelopment projects. The next section of this chapter will examine in greater detail the public good features of urban brownfields, and in so doing will consider the effects of redevelopment projects in relation to their costs and benefits. In this context it is important to highlight that in both brownfield definitions, the costs and benefits of the interventions are very hard to predict because they relate to three activities unique to brownfield redevelopment: site assessment, site remediation plan, and actual redevelopment effort.

From a financial vantage point, remediation and redevelopment activities should be viewed as brownfield development potentials; as Groenendijk argues, "it is important to be flexible about the end use of the site [...]. Making (minor) changes to the site plan may result in much more cost-efficient reclamation"

(Groenendijk 2006). Therefore, the costs and benefits of brownfield interventions are always linked to the actual end use of the site.

Bartsch warns that brownfield remediation is a financial "twilight zone" and thus developing adequate and affordable financing mechanisms is the most significant barrier against reusing brownfield heritage in urban areas (Bartsch 2002). With Bartsch's caveat in mind, this chapter will review different financial mechanisms dedicated to redeveloping cultural and natural heritage brownfields, which include the intervention of the private sector. It will first provide some background with a discussion of the risks and externalities associated with investment in urban brownfield development. Next, it will address the role of public administration as the catalyst for the development of urban brownfield sites. In so doing, it will consider the private sector as the primary source for urban brownfield funding, and will discuss four specific financial mechanisms: public-private partnerships (PPPs), land value finance mechanisms, urban development funds, and impact investment funds. Each section will offer a case study of a project that has used the considered financial mechanism. The chapter will end with conclusions including policy recommendations.

Public Good Assets and Private Intervention

The difficulty of obtaining financial resources for redeveloping natural and cultural heritage brownfields is often related to their public good features. This analysis focuses on urban brownfield areas that have development potential due to their heritage status but that are also imbued with significant risks and externalities of development; therefore, by following the three-tiered model of the National Round Table of the Environment and the Economy (NRTEE) framework; these areas are labeled as B-sites (see figure 8.2). The uncertainty and externalities are two specific market failures that dominate the development of B-sites.

In addition to the normal risks that one may confront in an urban development—including site risk, construction risk, and operating risk—two other risks are added in the case of brownfield investments: uncertainty about the actual redevelopment costs and uncertainty about future land value. These two types of risk instigate various other risks associated with the financial lenders, particularly loan and credit risk, which correspond to the inability of borrowers to make loan payments; for example, in case the value of the property which may be given as security is eroded. These types of risk are particularly troublesome in developing countries where there is seldom a well-developed credit system and there may also be limited experience in the business of borrowing for brownfield projects (Meyer 2000). Moreover, Bartsch notes that, because the transaction costs related to brownfield project underwriting have tripled in the last decade, lenders

FIGURE 8.2
Brownfield Classification

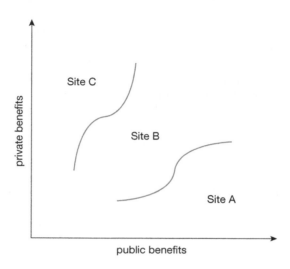

Source: Authors.

have begun to impose informal "rules of thumb" as specific conditions for urban brownfield redevelopment; for instance, developers must have a minimum of 25 percent equity in the project to guarantee sufficient capital risk (Bartsch 2002). Other financial risks, such as collateral risk, are in general associated with the characteristics and size of the project; in this case small loans may have proportionally higher fixed costs of foreclosure and resale than large loans, and thus the associated exposure to these risks has a greater impact on projects in developing countries where size of project and size of investment are often limited to under US$2 million (Yount and Meyer 1997). In these circumstances, private developers may undervalue their own commercial returns and overvalue the related costs of the brownfield project, and this will determine the market failure effect; that is, brownfield redevelopment may be undersupplied.

Urban brownfields and therefore historic urban areas also experience the impact of negative and positive externalities. In general, site development can have negative externalities because the project may cause considerable disturbance for the surrounding area and its inhabitants. Most significantly, urban brownfield redevelopment relates to substantial positive externalities for the city and society at large (De Sousa 2000). Renewal of the historic area, thereby reducing the pressure for new development, can help to contain urban sprawl, and as a consequence of the intervention there may be a reduction of commuting, transport pollution, and congestion. But particularly important in this kind of heritage project is the improvement in the quality of life, livability, attractiveness, and reduction of urban poverty, and subsequently the possibility to stimulate a sense of urban belonging. As Lee observes, the main toll for living in blighted urban areas is paid by the most destitute of urban households in terms of greater exposure to crime, poorer residential quality, higher prices of consumer goods, and inferior provision of education and health services (Lee 1996). Moreover, as in the case of the area of al-Azhar, situated in the old city in Cairo, the inhabitants of urban brownfields are often new migrants with limited financial means, which hinders the maintenance and conservation of the old fabric of the city (Sedky 2009). The private sector, however, also generally fails in this case to capture and internalize the collective benefits related to environmental and cultural heritage.

Experience shows that the development of both cultural and natural urban brownfields must generate a cash flow stream for the private sector and be linked with the sale and commercial operation of the redevelopment property. Private actors will examine their revenue and investments in relation to their corporate social responsibility, mainly as a marketing strategy, but they are only likely to do so with investments that have a high financial rate of return.

Given the public good characteristics of brownfield investments, the economic justification for public-sector investment is well established, since the private sector would provide suboptimal brownfield redevelopment and under provision of investments due to the presence of risks and externalities, and sometimes due to coordination problems among private agents (Isham and Kaufmann 1999). However, the redevelopment of cultural and natural heritage is a form of hybrid public good investment, so it may be unreasonable to expect the public sector to be the sole investor in and provider of urban brownfield redevelopment (Dasgupta and Serageldin 2000).

There is disagreement about the best ways to finance urban brownfield projects, including regarding the allocation of the public investments. Of particular concern is that public investments can crowd out private investments; public and private investments can coexist, but the balance between the two will vary depending on the project scheme and context. For instance, the authors of an analysis of Indian public investments observe that if the investment of the public sector is through market borrowing rather than deficit financing, this leads to a rationing of bank credit for the private developers and thus imposes crowding out of the private investments (Pradhan et al. 1998). (See figure 8.3.)

Another distinctive effect in urban brownfield investments is associated with public-sector institutions. An extensive study of 116 developing countries, covering the period 1980–2006, analyzed how different forms of public investment may render different effects, particularly in investments for urban heritage brownfields that have tangible and intangible

FIGURE 8.3
"Vicious Circle" of the Process that Limits Investments

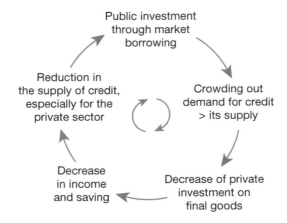

Source: Authors.

features (Gomez-Ibanez 2007). The authors argue that the crowding-out effect is increased by weak institutions saddled with problems of coordination between local and central government, uncertainty about legal liability, insufficient practical knowledge, high fiscal evasion, and corruption. It is evident that such administrative and legal deficiencies will discourage the intervention of the private sector.

To spur private-sector investment in urban brownfields, it is therefore necessary to create continuous stimuli and incentives to diminish the market failures present in these types of investments, and this is especially needed in developing countries. Private-sector funding for urban brownfields (especially natural heritage sites) is increasing, and numerous foundations and private companies have a long tradition of patronage of urban cultural heritage (Kurdila and Rindfleisch 2007, see box 8.2.) These actors need to assume a relevant role in the strategic investment in urban brownfields. For instance, nonprofit corporations with tax-exempt status have often accomplished brownfield development with the use of revolving funds provided by private capital. Another possible solution is to spread insurance risks across a number of small investments through the use of portfolio investments. An example is provided by the private equity fund known as the GINKGO fund, which is dedicated to acquiring a portfolio of natural brownfield projects in France and Belgium. The French fund has been created by the Caisse des Depots, the European Investment Bank, the Compagnie B. de Rothschild, and other private investors. The fund was established in 2010, with an eight-year

---

BOX 8.2

International Partnerships Promote Regeneration Efforts in Mostar, Bosnia and Herzegovina

Pilot Cultural Heritage Project (Project number 059763)
Total Project Cost: US$15.8 million
Total Loan Amount: US$4 million
Approved: June 1999 – Closed: December 2004

This post conflict project aimed to improve a reconciliation process among the peoples in Bosnia and Herzegovina through recognition and rehabilitation of their common cultural heritage in the city of Mostar. The partnership that was formed, and the contributions of many governments and organizations, greatly increased the effectiveness and outcomes of the work. Before project planning began, extensive studies had been prepared for the reconstruction of the Mostar bridge and the adjacent buildings by UNESCO. The Aga Khan Trust for Culture (AKTC), the World Monuments Fund (WMF), and UNESCO had helped develop a plan for the revitalization of the historic city core. The preliminary work provided a solid basis for proceeding with the project design and implementation. The implementation included these activities: (1) UNESCO formed and facilitated an International Committee of Experts, which provided valuable guidance; (2) AKTC and WMF assisted with the reconstruction and conservation of the historic neighborhood; and (3) the governments of Italy, the Netherlands, Croatia, Turkey, France, and the Council of Europe Development Bank contributed with financing and in-kind services. Even more importantly, soon after project completion, thanks to the framework established during project implementation, private owners of heritage buildings on the two sides of the bridge started rehabilitating their properties. These owners converted them into small businesses, with a significant impact on job creation, especially for the poor, and in particular for women. The bridge has thus become an attractor of private investments and an asset to brand the city nationally and internationally.

Source: Bosnia and Herzegovina Pilot Cultural Heritage Project Implementation and Completion Report.

---

investment horizon and initial capital of €100 billion. Its objective is to lease and acquire brownfield sites—in France alone there are more than 250,000 potentially polluted industrial sites—in order to implement cleanup, remediation, and construction of energy-efficient buildings.

Understanding the context, objectives, and constraints of the different private actors is, as Serageldin observes, like a Rubik's cube that "requires patience, dedication and imagination" to figure out (Serageldin 1999). Although it is difficult, it is certainly feasible to pursue and mobilize private-sector investment and form partnerships with the public sector for the development of urban brownfield sites. The next sections of this chapter highlight the role of the public sector as prime mover and catalyst in leveraging resources and programs, and then examine four types of financial partnership between the public and private sectors for urban brownfield investments.

The Catalyst Player: The Role of Government

Addressing urban brownfields presents particular challenges to national and regional policy-makers due to these sites' significant heritage legacies (cultural or natural) and potential for further development. These areas are often left abandoned due to contamination, decay from lack of maintenance, limited access to transport, and depressed local economies. As numerous examples indicate (for instance, in Latin America; Marker et al. 2007), the high cost of facilitating the reintegration of rehabilitated sites—including natural areas and historic districts—into the property market and the lack of expertise in this field often slow the process of transforming brownfields into new uses (Jackson and Garb 2002). In general, public-sector financial assistance is needed to make a site-reuse project economically viable, because remediation and preparation costs render many projects economically uncompetitive, at least initially (Kurdila and Rindfleisch 2007; Meyer and Lyons 2000; Wernstedt et al. 2006). This can be overcome, however, by providing a range of coordinated inputs (e.g., policies, instruments, planning, funding, and training) to increase site attractiveness to the point where the market will take hold of the sites and exploit their potential, especially given their central locations. (See box 8.3.)

The management of an increasing stock of derelict land and structures in inner-city locations is a pressing concern for urban planners and property-related private stakeholders. When one considers the ongoing consumption of open space for housing, retail, and industry, it is clear that the goal of maintaining a sustainable built environment cannot be met without reintegrating brownfields into the property market and encouraging development back into central urban locations (RESCUE 2004). When new developments are built on city peripheries, the historic and post-industrial quarters in city centers almost always remain abandoned or partially occupied; for instance, this process is especially evident in the Central and Eastern Europe and the Baltic countries, as in the case of Tallin, the capital of Estonia (Cocconcelli and Medda 2010).

BOX 8.3

Public Investments Act as a Catalyst for Private-Sector Involvement in Urban Regeneration in Lahore

Pakistan Punjab Urban Development Project (Project number 010305)
Total Project Cost: US$145.2 million
Total Loan Amount: US$90 million
Approved: April 1988 – Closed: March 1998

In the 1980s, many buildings and much of the infrastructure of the Walled City of Lahore (WCL) were at risk, threatened by overcrowding, inappropriate zoning, pollution, and physical decay. Consequently, the government of Pakistan, with the World Bank's assistance, prepared a project that sought to (1) improve the WCL's basic infrastructure, and (2) demonstrate the value of coordinated area upgrading. Because of the WCL's important historical and cultural endowments, the project also supported heritage conservation that included sanitation, restoration of schools and community centers, and conservation of city gates and historic buildings. An evaluation conducted at the end of the project indicated that property values had increased, fostering business activities, private-sector investments in housing, retail, and service more in general, and improving service delivery in the area.

Source: Pakistan Punjab Urban Development Project Implementation and Completion Report.

Numerous examples around the world show that innovative approaches are needed to financially structure and manage urban brownfield projects (Wernstedt et al. 2006). Where possible, the government can play a catalyst role by using public funds judiciously to leverage the investment of private capital into deprived neighborhoods (ODPM 2002). For many brownfield heritage areas, ring-fencing the revenue they generate, rather than seeing it disappear into the central revenue fund, would provide redevelopment projects with more financial security; however, it could also reduce the ability to apply revenue from well-known sites to cross-subsidize less-known but equally important ones. A successful case of post-industrial heritage redevelopment is that of Eskişehir, Turkey, a market-oriented brownfield regeneration process with government assistance that has allowed industrial buildings to be preserved as part of Turkey's 20th-century architectural heritage (Cahantimur et al. 2010).

In recent decades, public authorities have developed a wide range of financial tools—including grants, loans, revolving loan funds, tax incentives, and other financial mechanisms—to stimulate the reuse and redevelopment of brownfield urban areas and make them more attractive to private investors. In countries such as India and Egypt, the regeneration of brownfields mostly relies on government grants, which are to date the most successful instruments in facilitating regeneration projects and attracting private investors.

Local governments, more than regional and central governments, are in the best position to foster heritage brownfield regeneration as well as to lead and facilitate brownfield efforts in the community. Local authorities may create financial solutions to the brownfield financing problem by leveraging a combination of available national and local funds and private money. Local government programs usually offer one or more of several types of incentives. Some of these include regulatory relief, liability relief, grants and loans, insurance, waivers of development fees, property tax abatements and remediation tax credits, public investments in infrastructure and amenities, and changes in regulatory procedures among others. Table 8.1 briefly presents financial tools broadly used by local authorities for brownfield projects. These financial mechanisms are used particularly for natural heritage projects but can certainly be applied to cultural heritage brownfields or historic city areas.

National government programs, in general, require that beneficiaries meet special eligibility criteria, many of which are intended to combine public funding with private sources, thereby creating barriers against applying for funds. However, central authorities' initiatives provide a solid foundation upon which local governments are able to build their own brownfield financing strategies.

The foregoing analysis indicates that the public sector must be the initiator of urban brownfield projects for the regeneration of blighted and underused urban areas and historic city areas. In summary, the public financing initiatives must usually employ one or more of the following strategies:

- *Reduce the risks on the lender site,* to make capital more available for brownfield redevelopment. Incentives, such as loan guarantees or companion loans, can ensure a minimum return by limiting the borrower's exposure to unforeseen problems that can affect the value of collateral or the borrower's ability to pay.
- *Reduce the borrower's financing costs,* to make capital more affordable. Local authorities can subsidize interest costs through tax-exempt financing and low-interest loans, and can reduce loan underwriting and documentation costs through loan packaging assistance and technical support.
- *Improve the borrower's financial situation.* The project's cash flow can be improved through tax credits, tax abatements, or repayment grace periods, easing the way for the project to show the expected profitability.

TABLE 8.1

Local Financial Tools Used for Brownfield Financing

Tax increment financing (TIF)	TIF is the most common form of local support and a key part of a strategy to address financing gaps. The TIF mechanism uses anticipated growth in property taxes from a development project to finance public-sector investments in that project. It is usually used in economically distressed or abandoned areas. TIF bonds are issued for the specific purposes of the redevelopment, such as acquiring and preparing the site; cleanup; upgrading utilities, streets, or parking facilities; as well as carrying out other necessary site preparations and improvements.
Special service areas or taxing districts	Cities can delineate a "special service area," for instance the historic city core, and use it as a way to raise cash to finance additional services, improvements, or facilities to benefit the targeted area. The property owners in a special service area agree that a special property levy or special fee will be imposed, with the proceeds used to pay for the defined services or activities. The jurisdiction uses this additional revenue to finance the improvements, by either earmarking it directly for the area or using it to issue bonds to fund the projects.
Tax abatements	These are reductions of, or forgiveness for, tax liabilities. There are usually two forms of tax abatement: (1) a reduction in rates for a specified period (5–10 years), or (2) a freeze on property values, usually at a pre-improvement stage. It is a workable, flexible incentive that helps influence private investment decisions, but it has to be carefully designed to target intended beneficiaries without offering unnecessary subsidies, which can be a difficult feat. Tax abatements are commonly used to stimulate investments in building improvements or new construction in areas where property taxes or other conditions discourage private investment.
Local revolving loan funds	Revolving funds are usually established to meet specific objectives of the city. They can be used, for example, for cleanup, removal of debris and leftover equipment, and so on. After the loan is repaid to the fund, money is available for new projects.
General obligation bonds	General obligation bonds can be issued for any proper public purpose that pertains to the local government and its affairs. These bonds can be used to support brownfield cleanup and reuse projects as well as for acquiring land, preparing sites, and making infrastructure improvements.
Debt leveraging	Debt leveraging is a strategy that increases the return on equity when the investment is financed partially with borrowed money. In the case of brownfields, a public entity can serve that purpose by fronting the capital to make private investment less risky. This strategy has not been used much, but it has been effective in attracting private capital to brownfield sites.
Fees or fines for brownfield activities	The collected inspection fees or fines can be devoted to urban projects instead of having these resources disappear into the general local fund.

Source: Authors based on Bartsch 2002; NALGEP 2004.

- *Provide direct financial assistance* in the form of grants and forgivable loans, to make projects more attractive for private investors. This strategy is increasingly popular among local authorities, especially for site assessment and environmental cleanup (Bartsch 2002).

After having highlighted the public sector as the catalyst for urban brownfield redevelopment, this chapter will next examine four specific financial mechanisms that can be applied to urban heritage brownfield redevelopment and historic districts regeneration.

Public-Private Partnerships

The World Bank and the Public-Private Infrastructure Advisory Facility (PPIAF) define brownfield projects under PPPs as being concerned with abandoned and polluted areas and also with poorly maintained infrastructure service systems. This restricted definition of brownfield does not include historic districts, as has been proposed in this chapter. The World Bank Private Participation in Infrastructure (PPI) Project Database identifies three types of PPP contracts (or concessions) regarding brownfield projects in developing countries: rehabilitate, operate, and transfer (ROT); build, rehabilitate, operate, and transfer (BROT); and rehabilitate, lease, and transfer (RLT). Some brownfield projects that have utilized the ROT concession are the Lianyungang Wastewater concession in China (US$16.9 million), the Linyi City Salcon Water concession in China (US$4.4 million), and the Caticlan Airport concession in the Philippines (US$52 million). Examples of brownfield rehabilitation under the BROT concession include such projects as Aguas de San Andres in Colombia (US$9.3 million) and EMFAPA Tumbes in Peru (US$72 million). Figure 8.4 shows the distribution of brownfield concessions for the time periods 1990–99 and 2000–2009. BROT and ROT types dominate in both periods in relation to RLT concessions.

A growing number of brownfield projects are being initiated in the Latin America and China-India regions. PPP mechanisms are generally viewed by governments in industrial and developing countries as a feasible financing alternative when governments lack sufficient financial resources on their own, and also as a way to involve and transfer to the private sector the management and ownership of assets previously understood merely as public assets. Among many successful examples is the project led by Porto Vivo (Sociedade de Reabilitacao Urbana), a public entity established in 2004 for the rehabilitation of the historic city core of Baixa Porto (Portugal). The agency played a critical role in the redevelopment because its responsibilities cover the collection of urban taxes; the definition of incentives and compensation; and the sale, demolition, renting, and

FIGURE 8.4
Brownfield Concession Trends

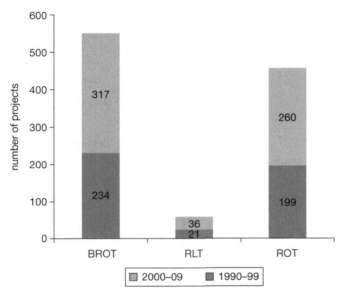

Source: Authors based on World Bank data.

rehabilitation of the historic building stock. These activities were carried out in cooperation and in formal partnerships with the private sector.

Another interesting redevelopment project was carried out in the former Poznanski's cotton factory in Lodz (Poland). In this case, the PPP mechanism was structured under an informal framework whereby the private actor was the main investor (cost of the whole investment estimated at €120 million) and the local authorities (city hall, marshal's office, and provincial heritage conservator) were involved in the design works and execution of the building renovation. The project included creation of a multifunctional center, which opened in 2006 under the name Manufaktura, housing entertainment, commercial, and cultural activities (including the National Museum of Modern Art, cofinanced by the EU). The Manufaktura project has provided significant impetus to the economic regeneration of the city core by focusing on an extensive derelict area (27 hectares) and has also had an important impact on the economy of the city as a whole. For instance, 2,500 people were employed for the redevelopment, and 3,500 are now working in the center.

Formal PPP arrangements usually have a robust structure composed of different parts that each play a key role in the implementation of a project. Figure 8.5 presents a sample schema of the agents, parts, and relationships involved

FIGURE 8.5

Special Purpose Vehicle Schema for a Public-Private Partnership

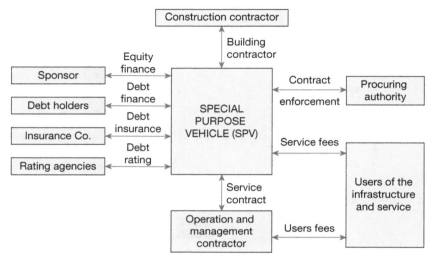

Source: Authors based on EIB 2010.

in a PPP, in accordance with the special purpose vehicle approach, described next (EIB 2010).

The special purpose vehicle (SPV) is typically a consortium of financial institutions and private companies responsible for all PPP activity (including the coordination of the financing and the service delivery). In the case of urban brownfields, the SPV creates a series of contracts with the procuring authority (such as the government), users of the service, building and operation contractors, and the investors and financiers. Each of these contracts poses a potential source of conflict and risk to the project that must be managed. The SPV's degree of independence and the financial and political condition of the government are important factors that affect the level of risk.

As described previously, several risk factors specific to brownfield projects may increase the yields demanded by the private sector for investing in urban redevelopment; these aspects are particularly onerous in developing countries. In some other cases, a number of urban brownfield heritage projects have encountered problems of cash flow at the implementation stage (Annez 2006; Leighland 2008). The cash flow problem relates mainly to an overestimation of profitability as well as poor project preparation, which neither accurately accounts for the real condition of the sites nor for the pollution problems. The decline of concessions for natural heritage brownfields is especially evident in Latin American countries. Moreover, the short investment horizon was also one of the problems with brownfield concessions in Latin America during the 1990s (Sirtaine et al. 2004). Investors should begin to expect profits only after 10 years from the start of operating the project. Thus, for local investors cash flow appears to be the main reason driving the renegotiation—or even the cancellation of—brownfield contracts.

It is also critical that there be close cooperation among the different partners involved in PPP arrangements for urban brownfield projects. It is particularly important to involve and consult with the local residents of the project area. In the case of the regeneration of solid waste disposal sites in Istanbul, Turkey, a main obstacle to the financial success of the project was the lack of consultation with the local resident population, who had strong negative feelings attached to these sites. The role of public partners can be vital in these cases to ensure that brownfield projects generate positive feedback, especially from those who will mainly benefit from the urban investment—namely, those households living at or near the site.

Case Study: Sumidouro Project in São Paulo, Brazil

The Sumidouro project, located in the district of Pinheiros, São Paulo, Brazil, is an example of a successful brownfield project with a cultural heritage focus. The project, entitled Praça Victor Civita, has been financed through a public-private partnership as the main instrument. The project concept, developed according to the schema presented in figure 8.6, aimed to do environmental remediation work in the old central waste incinerator Sumidouro in order to build a recreational area for cultural and educational activities. The project covers 13,648 meters of land that had been contaminated by heavy metals found in the soil and ground water. In addition, dioxins and furanes were found in the main building. Private investors financed the remediation activities and the creation of a new public park, called Victor Civita Square, as well as an educational and cultural center (Motta 2006).

Figure 8.5 indicates the stakeholders that participated in the project. The PPP was established between the municipality of São Paulo and the private investors. Other public stakeholders who played a relevant role in the project were the municipal environmental department, in charge of the elaboration and monitoring of the remediation and revitalization plans, and the state environmental agency (CETESB), in charge of licensing, establishing remedial goals and supporting investigation, logistics, and technology developments. GTZ, the German development agency, acted as facilitator and technical consultant for the soil and groundwater cleanup.

FIGURE 8.6

Stakeholder Map of the Brownfield Development Project "Sumidouro"

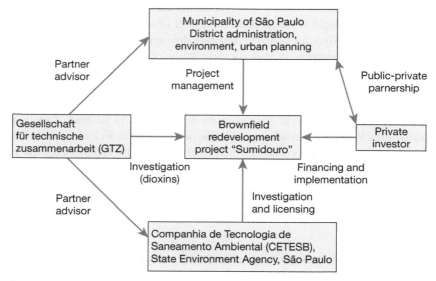

Source: Authors based on Marker et al. 2007.

The Sumidouro project was completed in March 2009 after four years of negotiation between public and private bodies and two years of environmental remediation activity[2] for a total cost of about R$6 million. The Praça Victor Civita is currently used for several activities including lectures, school visits, workshops on environmental education, concerts, indoor and outdoor sports, and elderly daycare programs in the center.

Land Value Finance

The basic approach of land value finance (LVF), also called land value capture finance, is to recover the capital cost of the urban investment by capturing some or all of the increments in land value increases resulting from the investment. There is much literature on this approach, and numerous applications around the world (Andelson 2000; Bowes and Ihlanfeldt 2001; Medda 2008; Smith and Gihring 2006). LVF is a flexible mechanism that can be used to finance a broad range of urban development and regeneration project types, including in historic districts; for instance, transportation infrastructure, affordable housing, cultural restoration, and community amenities enhancement.

The increases in land value may be captured directly or indirectly through their conversion into public revenues as fees, taxes, exactions, or other fiscal means. In general, in its fiscal form the land value capture mechanism satisfies equity principles, because it recoups the investment in the urban brownfield and returns the profits resulting from the redevelopment of economically idle urban areas back to the public (that is, the source of the intervention). Since one can estimate the levy in accordance with the land market situation and target specific landowners, such as in commercial and business land use, LVF plays a potentially progressive role. In its different forms, LVF can facilitate the development of abandoned or underutilized urban properties along with promoting wider public goals, such as discouraging urban sprawl; it can also work effectively alongside other financial instruments such as urban development funds, PPPs, and joint ventures.

However, an annual levy on land value may instigate land price spirals as well as distortions in land supply by, for example, inducing landowners who are rich in land but poor in capital to sell their land. This is a significant problem in developing countries with high inflation rates and low economic growth rates. An example of this is seen in the Desepaz housing development project in Colombia, where one of the project goals was to rehabilitate housing estates for the city's poor. In this case the LVF approach has resulted in various economically detrimental effects due to the phenomenon of speculation, which effectively restricted the realization of the social objectives (Otoya and Loaiza 2000).

Among the various LVF techniques that can raise capital for urban brownfield investments, the most successful are:

- *Special assessment.* This is a tax assessed against parcels identified as receiving a direct and unique benefit as a result of a public project.
- *Tax increment financing.* This mechanism allows the public sector to "capture" growth in property tax (or sometimes sales tax) resulting from new development and increasing property values. Tax increment finance mechanisms operate in two ways: through fiscal incentives such as tax relief or through tax disincentives to encourage urban development.
- *Joint development.* This is a mechanism of cooperation and risk-sharing between the public and private sectors, usually applied to transport investment to promote efficiency and benefit equity among participants, thus creating a win-win situation.
- *Developer/impact fee.* A fee assessed on new development within a jurisdiction provides a means of defraying the cost to the jurisdiction of expanding and extending public services to the development.

As many successful examples have proven, LVF techniques can be a powerful mechanism to finance redevelopment of urban heritage brownfields. One can draw lessons from a number of effective brownfield projects (especially for natural heritage sites) in the United States, where tax increment mechanisms in particular have gained much public-sector attention (Calgary City Council 2005; Dye and Merriman 2006; Smolka 2000). For instance, among the various financial programs supporting urban brownfield projects in New York State, the redevelopment tax credit is an interesting example of LVF with a broad urban focus. The redevelopment tax credit has three components that accrue credit between 10 percent and 22 percent: site preparation credits, tangible property credits, and onsite groundwater credits. The participants in the scheme can either be owners or operators of the urban brownfield areas. Significantly, the credits are increased from their basic level in relation to the number of employees the developer hires; this tactic aims to reduce poverty and unemployment. However, it should be underlined at this point that no standardized model of LVF may be replicated across cities, because usually the most successful applications are cases in which the financial tools are tailored to the specific objectives and needs of a project.

Case Study: Akaretler Row Houses in Istanbul, Turkey

A mixed-use development project in the center of Istanbul, Turkey, is a successful example of the application of LVF to leverage public money and renovate a city's heritage buildings. The group of residences, known as the Akaretler Row Houses, was originally built as housing for palace workers in the 19th century; with its neoclassical frontage design the ensemble is one of the city's best examples of 1870s civil architecture. The possibility of restoring the houses' historical value and bringing new life to this area was hindered for many years by strict regulations for the preservation of historical buildings owned by a national public-sector owner, the Turkish Foundation, in conjunction with tedious procedures for obtaining construction permits for development, and the absence of effective incentives. However, by the time the General Directorate of the Preservation of Cultural and Historic Heritage and the General Directorate of the Turkish Foundation approved the development plans, the economic potential for development had become obvious. In addition, real estate and tourism tax breaks given to this project helped to create market demand and potential value.

The public sector agreed with a project developer, the Bilgili Group, on several ways in which the value was to be captured: local taxation, private-led real estate renovation, and local service agreements. As a result of negotiated conditions, the locally generated tax collected by the municipality successfully funded the infrastructure improvements on the site, while the private investor, the Bilgili Group, led the direct restoration of the culturally valuable Akaretler Row Houses. The company also helped to market the area through its involvement in other renovation projects nearby (at the State Naval Museum) and also assumed the management of surrounding public spaces as part of an agreed basic service provision, including cleaning and gardening within a small local park.

Thanks to this investment, a nationally significant cultural site in Istanbul has become available for visitors and, more importantly, for its residents. The project has also contributed to the creation of new jobs in the area and supports local businesses due to rising numbers of tourists. It is noteworthy that the LVF mechanism has successfully maintained both the internal and external rates of return. The net return on investments in 2009 for the Bilgili Group was projected at €8.1 million, compared to the total cost estimation of €51 million.

All construction and restoration projects in Turkey are subject to prior written approval of several institutions—the General Directorate of the Preservation of Cultural and Historic Heritage, the General Directorate of the Turkish Foundation, the District Municipality, plus in this case the metropolitan municipality, since the project entailed infrastructure development—therefore, it was essential to retain good relations with key players. This approach helped all stakeholders to capitalize on opportunities and overcome challenges while the project was being carried out. It shows that a strategic approach, with the involvement of the actors, is necessary to implement all components of a project to the highest possible standards.

Urban Development Funds

In the last decade, there has been a significant rise in the number of urban investment funds. These funds have provided the vehicles for a range of investors to gain exposure to real estate markets by committing incremental and small amounts of money. The funds focus on all forms of urban investments; they operate in diverse geographic areas and have different maturity dates that offer considerable choice to investors. Infrastructure funds and real estate funds have been used increasingly for urban investments in recent years, but there have been some limitations to using them for brownfield projects. These funds generally do not focus on urban regeneration issues such as brownfield redevelopment, and they lack the potential for being integrated with other city development strategies. Particularly in the case of real estate funds, these funds often seek high financial returns on a short-term investment horizon.

Urban development funds (UDFs) integrate in their structure many positive features of the previously described funds. The inclusion of brownfield investments into a UDF portfolio reflects several positive features of such projects:

- The income return is a strong component of total returns.
- Income expectations are less volatile in the short term due to the length of leases.

- Brownfield redevelopment projects can generate value through active management (for example, by adding leisure activities such as the development of the hotel network system of Paradores in Spain).
- Urban brownfield projects are seen as a means of achieving greater diversification in portfolios due to their low volatility and long-term returns.

Urban brownfield investments in developing countries can, however, face certain obstacles. One problem may be the income return, which is inflation hedged; this problem can be solved through regulation and negotiation of the pricing mechanisms to adjust the income for inflation. Furthermore, investors may be put off by the long-term commitment required for brownfield projects. Therefore, it is vital that these investments should benefit local economies, thus resulting in sustainable returns, and at the same time help private investors meet their financial goals.

There are many examples of urban development funds dedicated to urban brownfields, especially in the Unites States. There, a development fund known as the Environmental Protection Agency (EPA) Brownfield Revolving Loan Fund (BRLF) finances the remediation activities of redevelopment projects through low-interest or even no-interest loans for brownfield cleanup. By 2006 funds were given to approximately 190 projects. There are also heritage funds established in European countries: in Ireland the Hearth Revolving Fund is mainly a privately financed fund designated for the restoration of listed heritage buildings for resale, usually as dwellings; in the Netherlands a revolving fund, a joint initiative entitled Brownfields Beter Benut (Brownfields Better Used), provides low-interest loans for the promoters of brownfield projects.

Regarding financing the redevelopment of historic districts, it is worth discussing the European Commission policy initiative Joint European Support for Sustainable Investment in City Areas (JESSICA), developed by the European Investment Bank and supported by the Council of Europe Development Bank (CEB). The recent financial crisis and increasingly scarce public budgetary resources have stimulated exploration of the best ways to employ European Union Structural Funds (SFs)—aimed at reducing regional disparities in income, wealth, and opportunity—in order to meet the growing development needs of EU member states. As a result, the JESSICA initiative was launched to provide new opportunities to authorities responsible for the implementation of SFs (JESSICA was promoted through the EU 2007–13 programming cycle). The primary objective of JESSICA is to define a system of financial urban development funds by using revolving financial instruments to support sustainable urban development (that is, renewal and regeneration projects). Such financial vehicles build portfolios of revenue-generating projects by providing them with loans, equity, or guarantees that are then repaid by project revenues or cost savings over a given period.

One of the features of this specific urban development fund is the capacity to use the SF contribution, thereby ensuring long-term sustainability for the urban development. By leveraging additional resources from the private sector, the fund is able to create stronger incentives for better performance of the final recipients, increasing the efficiency and effectiveness of public resources. However, JESSICA represents a specific policy tool whose wider financial impact would need to be tailored if it were to be implemented in countries outside the European Union.

Taking the above into consideration, significant potential exists for the creation of urban development funds dedicated to urban heritage brownfields that would provide both appropriate funding for the project and risk coverage for investors. Several financial mechanisms may be considered:

- *Guarantee fund,* which could act as a guarantee to financiers in case a developer should prove unable to meet his obligations (for example, the European Agricultural Guidance and Guarantee Fund).
- *Insurance program,* which could provide security by protecting against cost overruns and unforeseen risks.
- *Revolving fund* from which a developer could obtain low-interest loans; redemption and interest flow back into the fund and could cover residual risks and institutional controls after remediation is completed (for example, the National Restoration Fund in the Netherlands).

Urban development funds based on a revolving financial mechanism could make funds available at a low interest rate to attract investors, and these funds, through self-supporting mechanisms, may be reinvested or made available to cover residual risks. The revolving funds could supplement already existing traditional urban development instruments such as grants and loans, particularly in developing countries. The establishment of a revolving fund within the structure of an urban development fund for historic urban heritage projects could significantly improve both the quantity and duration of urban brownfield redevelopment.

Case Study: Silesia and Other Regions in Poland

Poland is investing in JESSICA in four of its regions: Wielkopolska, West Pomerania, Pomerania, and Silesia. It decided to create revolving vehicles and dedicate part of the SFs to finance urban renewal and regeneration projects in the cities of these regions, particularly historic districts. Because of its history, for many years Poland did not participate in the debate over regeneration needs and policies in Europe.

The Silesia region is a highly industrialized area with numerous postproduction and postindustrial sites, many of which have high historical value;

for example, in Katowice, the regional capital. The general directive on managing those sites, resulting from Polish environmental policy, stipulates that they should be used as soon as possible for other functions, such as for recreation grounds and for urban or industrial development. However, there is not enough money to proceed. JESSICA's revolving mechanism will address this and narrow the financial gap in the region. The fund will provide loans or guarantees to projects aimed at revitalizing degraded town centers and city districts, as well enhancing the physical features of former military and industrial areas in small and big cities (including comprehensive preparation of land for economic activity). Approximately €60 million of SFs is dedicated from the Silesia Managing Authority to be used through the JESSICA program, with the possibility of leveraging additional private resources.

Impact Investment

In emerging and developing countries with weak economies, it is often difficult to secure large investments for brownfield projects that will give rise to social spin-offs and attract further investment, thereby helping to generate wealth and reduce poverty. In this regard, philanthropic foundations have been the cornerstones of numerous urban revitalization projects in economically distressed areas when the goals aim to meet social and environmental targets. However, as Judith Rodin, the president of the Rockefeller Foundation, observes, "charitable donations do not provide enough capital to solve pressing social and environmental challenges at scale" (Bridge Ventures and Parthenon Group 2010).

In recent years a new form of investment, known as impact investment funds, has emerged in the market. The impact investment funds are designed as socially responsible investments that are not driven exclusively by profit and are generally targeted toward addressing environmental and social issues. The impact investments are defined as "actively placing capital in businesses and funds that generate social and/or environmental good and a range of returns, from principal to above market, to the investor" (Bridge Ventures and Parthenon Group 2010).

Impact investment funds can be differentiated from socially responsible investments (SRIs) although they originate from the same roots. The main drawback of SRI funds (that is, ethical funds) is that they do not specifically emphasize urban investment. In particular, although financial advisers report that investors show interest in SRIs, that has not led to robust and sustained flows of investor resources into these funds. This may be due to the often disappointing performance of SRI funds; in fact, by having a restricted investment range, SRI funds cannot always hold the best-performing assets in their portfolios. For this reason, it has been necessary for the financial market to create an investment option that addresses the cultural, social, and environmental aspects of urban brownfield regeneration and also delivers consistently satisfactory financial performance to investors.

In the case of impact funds, investors are keen to achieve social and environmental goals through their investments (for example, by investing in urban areas with high unemployment and contaminated properties, such as with "base of pyramid" populations—BoPs) (Hammond et al. 2007),[3] but they are also interested in generating profits. In this context investors can decide if they prefer to prioritize social returns (impact-first investors) and accept lower financial returns, or prioritize profits (financial-first investors), which also includes social and environmental returns. Between these two kinds of investors there is the so-called layered structure, in which both types of investors (impact and financial-first investors) work together and combine different financial and socially or environmentally oriented goals.

Urban brownfield projects, geared toward sites of either natural or cultural heritage, can certainly fit into the investment strategies of such funds because such projects can generate social and environmental benefits and, at the same time, generate significant returns to investors. An example of this is the cultural heritage project aimed at revitalizing the old district of Hafsia in Tunis, assisted by a World Bank loan, which is a double award–winning project.[4] The consortium of the credit impact fund supporting the project is composed of private-sector investors and the Municipality of Tunis, the Association pour la Sanvegarde de la Medina, and the Agence de Rehabilitation et Renovation Urbaine. The success of this fund, which has produced an economic rate of return of about 11 percent, also included the conservation of the old town and revitalization of the economic structure of the area, safeguarding the social mix of inhabitants, and helping to accomplish a resettlement scheme (Kaul et al. 1999). An interesting example of the use of impact funds for redevelopment of a natural brownfield site is provided by India's Byrraju Foundation and Water Health International.[5] The aim of this fund is to implement water filtration businesses and provide access to purified water at about half the price these populations are accustomed to paying for purified water (O'Donohoe et al. 2010).

The impact investment funds may therefore "out-perform" other types of social funds, because they are integrated across many industries and provide flexibility in investing in assets with performance potential. In conclusion, impact investment funds used for brownfield projects must satisfy two basic conditions: (1) they must seek private-sector involvement, and (2) they cannot be dedicated exclusively to short-run, profit-driven investments, but rather they must have a balanced investment portfolio that engages in socially and environmentally responsible and/or ethical investments in cities, particularly in brownfield areas.

Case Study: Pine Ridge Reservation in South Dakota, United States

The Pine Ridge Reservation in Shannon County, South Dakota, provides an example of the successful application of impact funds to improve social and heritage conditions in an abandoned and depressed area. The Lakota Fund initially began to serve the Pine Ridge Reservation in 1993 after Shannon County was listed as the poorest county in the United States. The Pine Ridge Reservation comprises an area of 6,985 square kilometers and had a population of 15,521 in 2000.

In 1995, not only did Shannon County residents have an average income about four times lower than the national average, with a 36 percent unemployment rate in the county, but they also suffered the worst life expectancy in the nation (56.5 years for males). Most of the population (80 percent) lived in rural areas far from services and had to travel between 60 and 290 miles to meet with their bank advisers (Mushinski and Pickering 2007).

The Lakota Fund is a community development financial tool established to provide "culturally appropriate strategies, including business loans, technical assistance, and targeted community and business development."[6] The fund has had a loan portfolio since 2008 and has disbursed more than 660 micro- and small-business loans totaling more than US$4.7 million. A number of educational and cultural programs have been launched to increase the skills of the Oglala Lakota people. The fund has, moreover, developed the first Native American–owned tax-credit finance for affordable housing projects and the first Native American Chamber of Commerce.

Today Shannon County is no longer the poorest county in the United States; it now ranks 43rd. The population's capacity to generate wealth is certainly associated with the Lakota Fund's good performance, which has, on average, a 2.5 percent rate of interest annually. The Lakota Fund is regarded as a valuable example of the integration of both natural and cultural heritage and, as stated in the Lakota Fund's 2011 mission statement: "its success is to build up the world of creative entrepreneurship for Lakotas following their dreams, goals and opportunities while maintaining strong connections to their land and rich cultural heritage of productivity and trading" (Malkin 2003).

Conclusion

The dynamics of urban areas reflect the broader economic and social forces of a country, because cities are often referred to as a nation's engine of economic growth and opportunity. In recent decades cities worldwide have faced intense pressures caused by the acceleration of urban growth and by decline processes. Moreover, the recent economic crisis of the latter 2000s, due to the accumulation of massive debt, much of it in the property sector, calls for innovative funding mechanisms to support sustainable urban development, in particular redevelopment of urban brownfields. In this chapter, the authors have extended the definition of urban brownfield by including not only natural brownfields, such as contaminated sites, but also cultural heritage sites, as, for example, derelict historic districts.

Urban brownfield redevelopment projects have proven public good characteristics; for that reason, the public sector is typically the driving force and facilitator in balancing the relationship between public interests and private objectives. This calls for the need to strengthen administrative institutions to foster private investment. Public authorities also need to take into account the interaction between natural and cultural heritage and be able to attend to the needs of the present inhabitants and activities in targeted areas.

Two important factors must be considered carefully before proceeding with such projects. First, project planners must explore the contextual element; that is, what city redevelopment, and specifically what type of brownfield investment is proposed? Second, crucially, all stakeholders must understand the economic relationship between the investment(s) and the real estate market. From this perspective, promoting arrangements for formal partnerships—with transparency and greater participation of all stakeholders in the decision-making—should be preferred above the informal partnerships often in use. In particular, policies that encourage decentralization for financing and implementing brownfield redevelopment may allow for a better response to city needs by offering more flexible tools and alternative forms of fiscal and fund incentives to develop the poorest city areas.

The main potential benefit of the private intervention methodologies reviewed in this chapter is their flexibility in adapting the structure of incentives and spreading risk to specific features of a brownfield project, and to the economic and institutional environment. Brownfield redevelopment and financing are less common in developing countries than in the United States and in Europe, where EU Structural Funds are available. The Milken Institute, for instance, has prepared a plan to alleviate the problem of scarce financial resources for a significant number of heritage sites in Israel. The various funding models developed include provision of microfinance for communities, which may leverage loans and donations to finance conservation works for local heritage sites; venture capital funding that links archaeological conservation with tourism, small business, and retail industries; and the sale of low-risk archaeological development bonds to provide long-term project financing.

Accordingly, the integrated urban land management policies related to heritage brownfield regeneration should focus on market-led incentives, including indirect incentives and gap-funding, and enable public intervention with direct funding and public-driven development where necessary (Thornton et al. 2007). Policies should be explicitly designed to:

- Broaden the scope of heritage brownfield redevelopment projects by including sites of both natural and cultural heritage;
- Eliminate legal obstacles to heritage brownfield redevelopment;
- Provide direct and indirect financial incentives to encourage heritage brownfield development and discourage greenfield development; and
- Create incentives that lead to brownfield redevelopment.

To design new financial mechanisms aimed at regeneration and/or development of urban brownfields with private-sector intervention, it is paramount to thoroughly assess the long-term risks and benefits of such investments. In particular, one must evaluate the performance potential of city assets by examining the sustainability of the urban interventions across generations, income, and groups, and in so doing analyze methods for capturing the value of undervalued and vulnerable brownfield assets, which are the city's latent capital.

Notes

1. "Brownfield" is the generic name used to designate remains of old urban manufacturing.
2. http://www.pracavictorcivita.org.br.
3. BoP refers to people who earn less than US$3,000 per year.
4. The Tunisia Third Urban Development Project, 1982–1993.
5. Known as "Water Health," which operates in India, Ghana, and the Philippines.
6. http://www.lakotafunds.org.

References

Alker, S., V. Joy, P. Roberts, and N. Smith. 2000. "The Definition of Brownfield." *Journal of Environmental Planning and Management* 43 (1): 49–69.

Andelson, R. V. 2000. *Land-Value Taxation Around the World*. Malden, MA: Blackwell.

Annez, P. C. 2006. *Urban Infrastructure Finance from Private Operators: What Have We Learned from Recent Experience?* Policy Research Working Paper 4045. Washington, DC: World Bank.

ASEAN Foreign Ministers. 2000. *ASEAN Declaration of Cultural Heritage*. Bangkok: ASEAN.

Bartsch, C. 2002. "Financing Brownfield Clean-up and Redevelopment." *Government Finance Review*, February.

Bartsch, C., and B. Wells. 2005. *State Brownfield Financing Tools and Strategies*. Washington, DC: Northeast-Midwest Institute.

Bowes, D. R., and K. R. Ihlanfeldt. 2001. "*Journal of Urban Economics* 50: 1–25.

Bridge Ventures and Parthenon Group. 2010. *Investing for Impact: Case Studies Across Asset Classes.* Rockefeller Foundation. http://www.rockefellerfoundation.org/uploads /files/d666caa9-9093-4f75-8502-9017a89a5dc7.pdf

Cahantimur, A. I., R. B. Oztürk, and A. C. Oztürk. 2010. "Securing Land for Urban Transformation Through Sustainable Brownfield Regeneration: The Case of Eskişehir, Turkey." *Environmental and Urbanization* 22 (1): 241–58.

Calgary City Council. 2005. *The U.S. Experience with Tax Increment Financing (TIF): A Survey of Selected U.S. Cities.* March. Calgary: Calgary City Council.

Cocconcelli, L., and F. R. Medda. 2010. *Transport Infrastructure Finance Through Land Value Capture: Application to Estonia.* Luxembourg: European Investment Bank.

Dasgupta, P., and I. Serageldin, eds. 2000. *Social Capital: A Multifaceted Perspective.* Washington, DC: World Bank.

De Sousa, C. 2000. "Brownfield Redevelopment Versus Greenfield Development: A Private Sector Perspective on the Costs and Risks Associated with Brownfield Redevelopment in the Greater Toronto Area." *Journal of Environmental Planning and Management* 43 (6): 831–53.

Dye, R. F., and D. Merriman. 2006. "Tax Increment Financing: A Tool for Local Economic Development." *Land Lines* 18 (1).

European Investment Bank (EIB). 2010. *Public and Private Financing of Infrastructure: Evolution and Economics of Private Infrastructure Finance.* Report 15 (1). Luxembourg: European Investment Bank.

Gomez-Ibanez, J. A. 2007. *Private Infrastructure in Developing Countries.* Paper presented to the Commission on Growth and Development at the Workshop on Global Trends and Challenges, September 28–29. New Haven: Yale Center for the Study of Globalization.

Groenendijk, N. 2006. *Financing Techniques for Brownfield Regeneration.* Department of Legal and Economic Governance Studies. Enschede, Netherlands: University of Twente.

Hammond, A., W. J. Kramer, J. Tran, R. Katz, and C. Walker. 2007. *The Next 4 Billion: Market Size and Business Strategy at the Base of the Pyramid.* World Resources Institute. http://www.wri.org/publication/the-next-4-billion

Huxley, J. 2009. *Value Capture Finance: Making Urban Development Pay Its Way.* London: Urban Land Institute.

International Council on Monuments and Sites (ICOMOS) China. 2000. *Principles for the Conservation of Heritage Sites in China.* Chengde: ICOMOS.

Isham, J., and D. Kaufmann. 1999. "The Forgotten Rational for Policy Reform." *Quarterly Journal of Economics* 114 (1): 149–84.

Jackson, J., and Y. Garb. 2002. *Financing Brownfield Redevelopment in Central Europe.* New York: Institute for Transportation and Development Policy.

Kaul E. I., I. Grumberg I., and M. Stern, eds. 1999. *The United Nation Development Programme.* Oxford: Oxford University.

Kurdila, J., and E. Rindfleisch. 2007. "Funding Opportunities for Brownfield Redevelopment." *Environmental Affairs* 34: 479–502.

Lee, C. 1996. *Environmental Justice, Urban Revitalization and Brownfields.* Washington, DC: U.S. Environmental Protection Agency (EPA).

Leigland, J. 2008. *The Rise and Fall of Brownfield Concessions: But Some Signs of Recovery After a Decade of Decline.* Trends and Policy Options series. Washington, DC: World Bank and Public-Private Infrastructure Advisory Facility (PPIAF).

Malkin, J. 2003. *Financial Literacy in Indian Country*. Longmont, Co: First Nations Development Institute.

Marker, A., A. Nieters, and D. Ullrich. 2007. "Contaminated Site Management and Brownfield Redevelopment in Latin America." In *Proceedings 2nd International Conference on Managing Urban Land*, April 25–27. Stuttgart.

Medda, F. R. 2008. *Land Value Mechanism in Transport PPPs: Investment in Urban Mass Transit Systems*. Washington, DC: World Bank.

Meyer, P. B. 2000. "Lessons from Private Sector Brownfield Redevelopment." *JAPA* 66 (1): 46–57.

Meyer, P. B., and K. Mount. 2005. *Brownfields Insurance for Public Sector–Led Development Projects: Experience and Methods*. Louisville: Northern Kentucky University, University of Louisville.

Meyer, P. B., and T. S. Lyons. 2000. "Lessons from Private Sector Brownfield Redevelopers: Planning Public Support for Urban Regeneration." *Journal of the American Planning Association* 66 (1): 46–57.

Motta, M. T. 2006. *Estudo de Caso: Revitalização de Brownfield na Area do Antigo Incinerador Pinheiros*. http://www.cetesb.sp.gov.br/rede/documentos/encontro_lat_americano/sumidouro.pdf

Moylan, E., S. Brown, and C. Kelly. 2009. "Toward a Cultural Landscape Atlas." *International Journal of Heritage Studies* 15 (5): 447–66.

Mushinski, D. W., and K. A. Pickering. 2007. "Heterogeneity in Informal Sector Mitigation of Micro-enterprise Credit Rationing." *Journal of International Development* 19 (5): 567–81.

Nae, M., and D. Turnock. 2011. "The New Bucharest: Two Decades of Restructuring." *Cities* 28 (2): 206–19.

National Association of Local Government Environmental Professionals (NALGEP). 2004. *Unlocking Brownfields: Keys to Community Revitalization*. Washington, DC: NALGEP.

National Round Table of the Environment and the Economy (NRTEE). 2003. *Cleaning Up the Past, Building the Future*. Ottawa: NRTEE.

O'Donohoe, N., C. Leijonhufvud, Y. Saltuk, A. Bugg-Levine, and M. Brandenburg. 2010. *Impact Investments: An Emerging Asset Class*. JP Morgan Global Research 29 November. http://docbk.com/2011/09/impact-investments/

Office of the Deputy Prime Minister (ODPM). 2002. *The Government's Response to the Transport, Local Government and the Regions Select Committee Report: The Need for a New European Regeneration Framework*. London: ODPM.

Otoya, L. B., and J. G. Loaiza. 2000. *Application of New Land Value Capture in Colombia*. Research Report LP00Z2. Cambridge, MA: Lincoln Institute.

Pradhan, M., L. Rawlings, and G. Ridder. 1998. "The Bolivian Social Investment Fund." *World Bank Economic Review* 12 (3).

RESCUE. 2004. *Regeneration of European Sites in Cities and Urban Environment*. http://www.rescue-europe.com.

Sedky, A. 2009. *Living with Heritage in Cairo*. Cairo: American University in Cairo Press.

Serageldin, I. 1999. "Cultural Heritage as Public Good." In *Global Public Goods*, ed. E. I. Kaul, I. Grumberg, and M. Stern. Oxford: United Nation Development Programme, Oxford University Press.

Sirtaine, S., M. E. Pinglo, J. L. Guasch, and V. Foster. 2004. *How Profitable Are Infrastructure Concessions in Latin America? Empirical Evidence and Regulatory Implications, PPIAF Trends and Policy Options.* Washington, DC: World Bank.

Smith, J. J., and T. A. Gihring. 2006. "Financing Transit Systems Through Value Capture." *American Journal of Economics and Sociology* 65 (3): 751–86.

Smolka, M. O., and D. Amborski. 2000. *Value Capture for Urban Development: An Inter-American Comparison.* Working paper. Cambridge, MA: Lincoln Institute.

Starr, F. 2010. "The Business of Heritage and the Private Sector." In *Heritage and Globalisation,* ed. S. Labadi and C. Long. New York: Routledge.

Syms, D. 1999. "Redevelopment Brownfield Land." *Journal of Property Investment and Finance* 17 (5): 481–500.

Thornton, G., M. Franz, D. Edwards, G. Pahlen, and P. Nathanail. 2007. "The Challenge of Sustainability: Incentives for Brownfield Regeneration in Europe." *Environmental Science and Policy* 10: 116–34.

UK Department of the Environment, Transport and the Regions (DETR). 1999. *Quality of Life Counts.* London: DETR.

U.S. Environmental Protection Agency (EPA). 1999. *A Sustainable Brownfiled Model Framework.* Report EPA500-R-99-001. Washington, DC: EPA.

Wernstedt, K., P. B. Meyer, and A. Alberini. 2006. "Attracting Private Investment to Contaminated Properties: The Value of Public Interventions." *Journal of Policy Analysis and Management* 25 (2): 347–69.

Yount, K. R., and P. B. Meyer. 1997. *The Loan Application Process for Brownfield Financing.* Report. Washington, DC: EPA.

9

Mapping Heritage Economics for Spatial Analysis in Historic City Cores

Christian Ost

Professor in Economics, ICHEC Brussels Management School (Belgium)

The identification of economic values in historic city cores, and their measurement with the use of indicators, aims to provide the basic material for a mapping process. Availability of reliable data makes the identification of statistical units to measure economic values a key element in the mapping process. The identification of thematic maps is related to the definition of economic values, and this chapter identifies tentative thematic maps belonging to several categories of values: non-use values, use values related to the real estate market, use values related to cultural tourism, and use values related to impacts on local economy. Showcasing the geographic information provided by economic values on maps requires the identification of patterns, connections, and relationships between indicators of all categories of values. This process is two-fold: first, the analysis of indicators related to categories of values; second, the analysis of aggregated values to summarize and map the information. Mapping of selected key indicators describes the relationship between public intervention and economic values. Finally, an economic landscape map is made of compounded values measured for an entire area. Successive layers of values have been laid on top of each other, the first layer being a base map. The final product visualizes the economic landscape of the city. A detailed case study on Mali is presented to apply the concepts described in the chapter.

Introduction

"Venice is now becoming a very uncomfortable city, largely because there are so many tourists in the summer. [...] In another 20 or 30 years, it will actually be the thinking man's Disneyland, a millionaires' playground. But there won't be any people there; it will just be a museum city."[1] (John Julius Norwich, history writer) "When a town is put on the World Heritage List, it means nothing should change. But we want development, more space, new appliances—things that are much more modern. We are angry about all that."[2] (Abba Maiga, homeowner, speaking about the World Heritage city of Djenné in Mali)

Both statements illustrate the intricacy and complexity of the challenges that World Heritage Sites face today. Some historic city cores suffer from excesses of mass tourism, despite the considerable potential for bringing economic returns, or fail to provide sound and balanced economic growth; yet others strive to be included on the United Nations Educational, Scientific and Cultural Organization (UNESCO) list of World Heritage Sites. Most local governments lack institutional capacity and/or funds to cope with preservation management activities necessary for upkeep of their heritage assets while simultaneously faced with the array of priority investments needed for social and economic development.

Most experts concur that the protection and promotion of cultural heritage assets can be important to spur local economic development. Worldwide, institutions acknowledge today the need for a new urban strategy that includes cultural heritage serving as a platform or even acting as an engine of economic growth and sustainable urban development (World Bank 2009).

The aim of this chapter is to contribute to the assessment of economic values in historic city core regeneration.[3] The focus is on the city, and on mapping its heritage values. "The cultural heritage nature of conservation in historic cities [...] adds a dimension that standard urban economics is ill-equipped to address. Many of the benefits of cultural heritage do not enter markets, or do so only imperfectly" (Serageldin 1999, 24). As a practical tool for spatial analysis, the mapping process of heritage economics aims to provide a common base for the array of specialists and stakeholders participating in the urban conservation process, including local and city administrators, tourism planners and managers, conservation specialists, experts, academics, residents, and local business.

The mapping tools described in this chapter are intended as instruments and not products for their own sake. The use of mapping tools is rather an attempt to improve the understanding of the complexities of historic conservation in city cores, and develop better ways to implement policy measures. Examples with fictional and real maps are used to help illustrate the effectiveness of the mapping process for spatial analysis, applied to diverse situations found in cities of developing countries.

Historic Cities Face New Challenges

Historic cities are endowed with heritage capital of both cultural and economic values, which if properly harnessed have a potential for promoting economic growth. These cities often face the particular financial challenge of preserving their vast array of heritage assets. Most cities seek to promote their patrimony of monuments and sites to be considered by UNESCO for the World Heritage List, in the belief that this may bring international recognition and, with it, prospects for future economic gains. However, social and economic benefits that may be derived from heritage are often hard to achieve. Conflicting issues may arise between protection rules applied to the heritage and alternative economic opportunities emerging one or two decades after the nomination, in particular in times of economic crisis and increased competition between cities. (See box 9.1.)

Business cycle and long-wave theory aim to explain how a time-adjusted initiative may succeed in turning into a growth opportunity. It describes alternating periods of higher growth and cyclical downturns. It shows that a competitive context can alternatively be considered as an opportunity or a threat. Historic city cores have developed over the years alongside such long-term economic perspectives. However, not all historic city cores have been successful in harnessing sustained economic growth, let alone social and economic development of the place. Cultural goals and economic welfare must go hand in hand, notwithstanding how propitious the global context.

Historic monuments, sites, and city cores have been protected first by national conservation policies and then by international regulations for the last 40 years. Among the different charters, declarations, and memoranda, there is consensus regarding the complexity of historic city core planning and management. Of particular value are the Charter for the Conservation of Historic Towns and Urban Areas (Washington Charter, 1987) and the Declaration on the Conservation of Historic Urban Landscapes (Vienna Memorandum, 2005). The Washington Charter stipulates that "in order to be most effective, the conservation of historic towns and other historic urban areas should be an integral part of coherent policies of economic and social development and of urban and regional planning at every level."

Initially, conservation expertise tended to cover single buildings, monuments, or sites. Today more emphasis is put on the economic and social impact of conservation projects on the city core as a whole. A concept such as the historic

---

BOX 9.1

The Opportunities and Challenges of Urban Heritage Are Documented Worldwide

Historic Cities and Sacred Sites: Cultural Roots for Urban Futures

The World Bank started the debate on the importance of conservation and regeneration of historic city cores and cultural heritage decades ago. A flagship World Bank publication, called *Historic Cities and Sacred Sites: Cultural Roots for Urban Futures*, was published in 2001 and included more than 50 essays by a wide range of researchers and practitioners working in developed and developing countries. This publication aimed at exploring such topics as the governance, planning, and management of urban heritage and the challenges for heritage conservation during periods of economic transition. This book aimed especially to contribute to the understanding of culture's function in nurturing economic development by addressing one element of identity—the sense of place. It explored the sense of place and the historic continuity of socio-cultural roots that can inspire a positive civic culture, city image, and energy for urban development and transformations. This concept of roots emphasizes the importance of conserving meaningful physical dimensions of locations—historic buildings, streetscapes, and open spaces that have special significance to people and that help create a sense of belonging.

Source: Serageldin, I., E. Shluger, and J. Martin-Brown, eds. 2001. *Historic Cities and Sacred Sites: Cultural Roots for Urban Futures.* Washington, DC: World Bank.

---

urban landscape was appropriately enhanced at a time when decision makers in historic city cores were confronted with sustainable development priorities. It is now widely accepted that "economic aspects of urban development should be bound to the goals of long-term heritage preservation," as indicated in the Vienna Memorandum. This emphasis on including heritage concerns within economic planning can help historic city cores face their specific challenges.

Part of the challenge is to attract investment and generate wealth. When industrial development emerged in the western countries, geographical factors were often key to success: communication crossroads, means of transportation, access to rivers and seas, proximity of raw material and coal mines, labor resources, local skills, and so on. Economic growth today relies less on these physical attributes, but more on high-tech state-of-the-art communication networks. Nevertheless, cultural factors such as amenities, beautiful architectural settings, and better quality of life can be successful in attracting companies and investment. As compared with the industrial era, this era fortunately allows many countries in the world to participate in the major competition game, boosting economic opportunities, cultural resources, and sustainable development all at once.

Sustainable growth is an important issue today on the political agenda. Regeneration of historic city cores and conservation of cultural heritage assets match perfectly the objective of sustainability: built heritage is immutable, and nominated sites are distributed across the world.[4] In fact, heritage represents an exception among economic resources: rich and poor countries possess them, and the monuments cannot be displaced. But sustainability is not an easy goal to achieve, because a rapid urbanization process poses a key challenge in the integration of cultural heritage conservation within the development of contemporary city planning systems.

Stewardship of heritage assets requires up-to-date information on their economic value, and on the economic impacts and outcomes of their conservation. Providing accurate data can help the decision-making process, but will not bridge the gap between conservation ideals and reality. Heritage is a definite asset for developing cities in the long run. But the optimal path toward balanced development requires accurate tools, as well as an open-minded attitude from various stakeholders.

Economic Values and Indicators

Heritage economics, based on database and information systems, can contribute to achieving two objectives. The first is to monitor the stock of cultural heritage assets in the historic city core, assessing its economic values and analyzing the nature, the local distribution, and the evolution of such values over time. Heritage indicators and maps are key elements in this analysis. They can display excess or lack of values, unbalanced distribution of values across the city, or values not in phase with sustainable development. The second objective is to feed into the field of planning and the decision-making process, and in particular investment appraisal techniques applied to conservation. Economic data provide useful information to assess the magnitude of impacts expected from projects.

Today, measuring economic values has become a standard process in economics either for assessing the benefits of investing in cultural capital, or for evaluating and selecting conservation and management projects. Use and non-use values express the tangible and non-tangible aspects of the built heritage. In economic terms, use and non-use values are distinguished by the marketable or non-marketable aspects of the heritage. The peculiar characteristic of heritage, as a physical asset (e.g., a building, a monument) with a value that clearly goes beyond the asset itself, requires such a meaningful distinction. The measurement of use and non-use values aims to develop simultaneously quantitative and qualitative approaches to heritage conservation.

Use values are identifiable, often measurable with great accuracy, and widely represented in historic city cores: there are use values related to the real estate market, existing within but independently from the heritage (e.g., housing, shops, offices, or public services); and there are use values related to tourism, either directly (e.g., visits to the site, museum, or monument) or indirectly (e.g., lodging, food, shops, and services on site and off site).

Economists are able to measure induced use values (category of macroeconomic values) as a result of the macroeconomic multiplier, which creates a range of benefits in the vicinity of the heritage, taken as a whole. The relevance of these values depends mainly on methodological factors, and the values are measured for larger areas only.

Non-use values are a prerequisite to use values. Because they are not marketable, non-use values are not directly measurable in monetary terms. Non-use values can be identified in relation to individual monuments, objects, architectural ensembles, or public spaces, or in relation to a historic district as a whole. In the last decade, economists have developed techniques to assess the economic value of non-market exchanges. These non-market valuation techniques are used to build indicators, and can be classified into two categories:

• Revealed preference methods draw and analyze data from the existing market or past behavior for heritage-related goods and services.
• Stated preference methods rely on the creation of hypothetical markets in which survey respondents are asked to make hypothetical choices.

Heritage performance as a contributor to economic values can be measured by indicators, which are today consistently used as an integrated approach for measuring and monitoring cities. They are considered a perfect tool to test city performances. Indicators are used to communicate information and to make predictions on future performance. They can simplify the interpretation of complex systems and help decision makers. The use of indicators does not substitute for the use of databases. However, it is a very effective and pragmatic approach when direct documentation would be too costly and time intensive.

Heritage indicators also express how economic values may be consistent with sustainable development goals. This aspect is now commonly addressed in the wake of the publication of "Our Common Future," known as the Brundtland Report.[5] As noted in the report, sustainable development is based upon a paradigm that brings together three different perspectives: economic, social, and environmental.

This paradigm advances the notion that heritage conservation and economic growth can be compatible, when there is consideration that the world is their common stage (conservation is a form of cultural globalization), and that the long term is their common timeline (to the extent that actions move in an environmentally sustainable way). Hence, heritage conservation constitutes an obvious choice for sustainable development for historic city cores.[6] Generally speaking, the best indicators are those that suit the purpose of the analysis. Table 9.1 provides an indicative set of indicators for different types of values.[7]

The choice of selected heritage indicator in each category of the stream of values is based on available data, expert opinion surveys, or subjective assessment. The metrics of the judgment can be based on a scoring process (for example, on a scale from 1 to 5, with 1 = indication of lowest value, and 5 = indication of highest value), or an ordinal scale (such as "low, medium, high," or "bad, poor, fair, good"). Selected indicators can be listed in a dashboard to provide a monitoring tool to specialists and city managers.

Mapping Economic Values

The physical conditions of the urban fabric and its surroundings are mapped to provide useful management information to decision makers and project promoters. The mapped information seldom includes social or economic attributes of the heritage. The identification of economic values in historic city cores, and their measurement with the use of indicators, aims to provide the basic material for a mapping process. Unfortunately, mapping hinges greatly on the quality of input data. As suggested with the Djenné test case (see later section in this chapter), the

TABLE 9.1

Heritage Indicators for Non-Use and Use Values

Types of values	Example of indicators
Non-use values	Willingness to pay, awareness of heritage significance, and visitor preferences
Use values related to the real estate market	Property values, rental values, vacancy rate, housing affordability, number of sales, and sustainable housing
Use values related to tourism (direct)	Admission fees, number of visitors, monument carrying capacity, number of guides, and consumer satisfaction
Use values related to tourism (indirect)	Souvenir sales, average time spent, tourist expenditures, number of hotel nights stayed, and car parking
Use values related to impacts on the local economy	Fiscal revenues, jobs in cultural sector, heritage-related events, local growth, and quality-of-life index

Source: Author.

availability of data makes the identification of statistical units to measure economic values a key element in the mapping process.

Available mapping software programs (e.g., ArcGIS, Mapinfo, and Maptitude) are commonly used and are reliable tools for the purpose of drawing economic maps. The most common method of data creation is digitization, which provides a visual display of values or indicators. A Geographic Information System (GIS) captures, edits, and analyzes data, which are linked to specific locations. This technology of spatial data handling has developed with the growing use of information systems and personal computers.

In general, a digitalized map provides the base for a mapping system in which parcels, blocks, or neighborhoods are attributed successive layers of data for individual components of economic values. Specialists and researchers may face the problem of a lack of suitable data to fit the technical requirements of mapping, and so have to rely on larger statistical units. The precision of a geographic base map depends on data availability, which differs considerably among countries in the world. Digital base maps and extensive databases for economic values are often hard to find, since they depend largely on the quality and availability of national and regional or city statistics. Highly sophisticated mapping techniques for heritage should be considered as an optimal solution, a goal to achieve in the long run, when a city is committed to putting time and resources into this initiative. However, cities with lesser resources and technologies can still find relevant utility for mapping done through more basic base maps that use simpler technology.

The identification of thematic maps is related to the definition of economic values. Economists may disagree on the process of breaking down the values attached to the heritage. Accordingly, the selection of thematic maps is not a standardized process, but is always related to what the spatial analysis is intended to address (e.g., tourism assessment, project evaluation). It is also related to data availability and practical experiences. Tentative thematic maps belonging to four categories of values are described below.

Non-Use Values

Non-use values are not traded in markets and are difficult to measure. Hence, non-use values indicators do not perfectly adapt to mapping techniques. However, non-market valuation methods are reliable enough to map non-use values indicators, in particular when survey results are available in great quantity. In addition to surveys, participatory methods might provide information to make intangible heritage "visible" and encourage participation from local stakeholders.

Non-use values include option values (i.e., the option of visiting the heritage some day in the future), existence values (i.e., the value attributed to the existence of the heritage), or bequest values (i.e., the value of passing inherited heritage to future generations). Mapping economic non-use values can be summarized by asking "the right question on the right heritage items to the right people." Values are measured through multiple techniques, either revealed preference methods (e.g., impact analysis, hedonic price, travel cost) or stated preference methods (e.g., contingent valuation, choice modeling).

One of the most popular methods for measuring stated preferences is the contingent valuation method, which aims to estimate residents' willingness to pay for the conservation of the heritage (J. Paul Getty Trust 2000, 74–76). Mapping the preferences requires that the survey specify some spatial attributes in the questionnaire.

The mapping of the results could be two-fold:

1. Preferences (hence, non-use values) are geo-referenced on maps; respondents' preferences are shown according to their place of residence. Map 9.1A shows a fictional example based on five samples of residents covering different neighborhoods in a city. People are asked to express their willingness to pay for the conservation of a monument in the city. The color-coded map shows differences between willingness to pay. It helps to identify awareness of, and concern for, the same heritage item among the inhabitants.
2. Preferences are displayed on maps in terms of the heritage being surveyed. Map 9.1B shows a fictional example where willingness to pay is asked for three monuments. A color-coded map visualizes the discrepancy of willingness to pay between several heritage items (darker tones = higher values). A similar survey could be conducted among a sample of tourists or visitors, and results could be mapped similarly.

Alternative measures for non-use values are made by the use of surrogate markets, revealing people's preferences, and can be described as follows:

- *Hedonic pricing method* aims to estimate non-use values as a quality-adjusted price or an implicit price. If people consider a heritage building as having twice the quality of regular houses, then the hedonic price must be twice the actual real estate price. The hedonic price is based on attributes that can be located specifically. Mapping non-use values with the hedonic price method involves selecting the buildings (or the parcels) with attributes (e.g., prestigious location, proximity to a monument, specific significance or authenticity) and showing non-use values by identifying the parcels where hedonic prices differ from the actual estate value.
- *Travel cost method* uses the cost incurred by individuals for traveling to the city as implicit price. This method is rather applied to non-resident visitors on a regional scale. Color-coded maps indicate the accessibility to the city,

MAP 9.1
(A) Fictionalized Map Showing Residents' Willingness to Pay for Conservation of a City Monument, by Neighborhood (B) Fictionalized Map Showing Residents' Willingness to Pay for Conservation of Three Different City Monuments

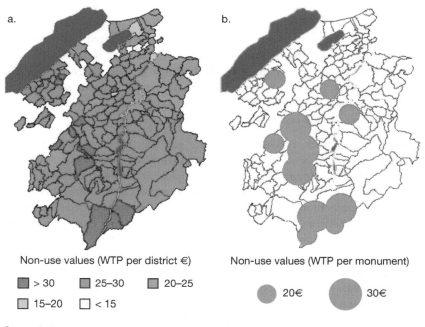

a.

b.

Non-use values (WTP per district €)

▧ > 30 ▧ 25–30 ▧ 20–25

▧ 15–20 ☐ < 15

Non-use values (WTP per monument)

● 20€ ● 30€

Source: Author.

considering travel time starting from the city center. We assume that high travel time (= high travel cost) is an indication of high non-use values. The same kind of map, but on a very large scale, can describe non-use values for foreign visitors flying and further travelling to a remote country for visiting the heritage. We expect that the farther away they come from, the higher they consider the non-use values.

Use Values Related to Real Estate

Economic values in historic city cores are embedded in the urban fabric. Heritage buildings and monuments have an economic significance not just related to the past but also to future opportunities of the city. In fact, economic values often allow heritage to keep its cultural significance as the city develops.

By adapting and re-using outstanding monuments for contemporary needs, cities seek to capture economic values to better preserve and utilize their cultural assets. Covent Garden, in central London, is an example of continuous rethinking and reuse of an urban fabric for changing needs. Originally an abbey—the Convent of St. Peter—the site was also a major source of fruit and vegetable production in London. The land was redeveloped by the early 17th century and became an architectural ensemble, with an open air market in its center. The site needed a redevelopment by the end of the 1960s when the market moved to a new location. With many of the buildings protected through heritage designation, the site was redesigned as a shopping center and tourist attraction.

Many historic buildings have a residential function. The expression of a use value from buildings and monuments is given by real estate values, measured by property values or rental values (e.g., actual rental values for tenant-occupied housing, imputed rental value for owner-occupied housing). Many historic buildings and monuments also provide services to the city government (a historic town hall, for example) or serve as museums or performing arts venues.[8] Real estate values are thus market indicators of individual and collective demand for the use of historic buildings and monuments. Mapping of rental or property values requires the recording of heritage buildings and monuments to provide the baseline data onto which values will be visualized. Rental and property values are expressed in monetary terms or in indices. When individual or cadastral databases are not available, real estate values are estimated in average terms for blocks or building groups across the city.

The mapping of real estate values requires comparing physical and architectural attributes of heritage buildings to rental or property values. The mapping of the following selected indicators describes the relationship between occupancy of heritage buildings and use values:

- Occupancy versus vacancy of heritage buildings;
- Use of buildings;
- Rental and property values;
- Property values (heritage versus non-heritage buildings);
- Housing affordability;
- Nonresident occupation (seasonal occupation, vacation rental housing);
- New residents versus initial population; and
- Conditions of conservation.

The mapping aims to evaluate economic values as they are related to building occupancy, but also emphasizes such urban processes as gentrification or poverty alleviation. Mapping side-by-side housing affordability, incoming new residents, and property prices highlights the relationship between the status of the heritage in the historic city core and its social or economic impact on the population. Spatial analysis provides a preemptive tool for dealing with urban development issues in historic conservation. (See box 9.2.)

The following (fictionalized) maps represent the historic center of Uzès in France. This example shows a city with a highly dense area of heritage buildings. Rental values (map 9.2A) are indicated in green (darker tones = higher values), evidencing that more moderately priced housing is found in the southeast of the city.

Map 9.2B indicates the occupancy of buildings in the city (buildings occupied or not). Although most of the city has a high occupancy rate, there is a concentration of unoccupied buildings in the southeast area of the city. Map 9.2C indicates how property prices for housing can be spatially distributed, when compared to an average value for the city as a whole. Parcels in blue indicate housing prices lower than the average, and parcels in red indicate housing prices higher than the average. Again, more moderate housing prices are in the southeast area. Map 9.2D indicates the state of conservation of heritage buildings.

BOX 9.2

GIS Supports Detailed Analysis and Targeted Approach to Problem Solving in the Fes-Medina

Morocco, Fes-Medina Rehabilitation Project (Project number 005524)
Total Project Cost: US$27.6 million
Total Loan Amount: US$14 million
Approved: October 1998 – Closed: November 2005

The primary objectives of this World Bank–supported project were to assist in the conservation and rehabilitation of the Fes-Medina (especially its historic housing stock) and to use the rehabilitation process to alleviate poverty. In cooperation with the local Agency for the Rehabilitation of Fes-Medina (ADER-Fès), the project work built a solid base of information for this effort. Extensive data on the composition, status, and income of the Fes-Medina's population and the actual physical condition of the built environment were integrated into a Geographic Information System (GIS). This GIS-based information was a significant factor in project design, because it dispelled earlier assumptions and allowed a targeted approach to problem solving.

Source: Fes-Medina Rehabilitation Project Appraisal Document and Implementation and Completion Report.

MAP 9.2A
Rental Values in Uzès, France
Darker tones = higher values

MAP 9.2B
Occupancy of Buildings
Darker tones = higher values

MAP 9.2C
Property Prices for Houses
Red = higher than average; Blue = lower than average

MAP 9.2D
State of Conservation of Heritage Buildings
Green = good condition; Yellow = fair condition; Red = bad condition

Source: Author.

Categories include "good condition" (green), "fair condition" (yellow), and "bad condition" (red). This kind of assessment aims to find a correlation between housing prices and the state of conservation of buildings. As it appears on the map, lower-than-average conditions are concentrated in the east of the city.

The different layers of data clearly indicate a correlation between the economic factors explaining the economic value of the cultural heritage of the historic city core. Indeed, most of the indicators show a similar pattern of overvalued heritage in western areas of the city and undervalued heritage in eastern areas. Additional indicators related to other components of use values confirm this situation.

Use Values Related to Cultural Tourism

Historic city cores often rely on visitors as a source of revenues and income to the city. Some cities can easily handle more cultural tourism; some experience negative impacts from mass tourism. By nature, most tourism is from outside of the city, including from abroad. However, city residents also visit heritage sites or take part in heritage-related recreational activities. Although small and big cities face distinct tourism challenges, the issues involved in tourism management are similar to those of major cultural or natural sites, and they parallel the handling of tourism development on a national scale. Many developing countries rely on revenues from cultural tourism to obtain foreign exchange to finance imports and growth.

Access and visits to buildings and monuments characterize the economic contribution of the heritage to the city economy. Even if buildings or monuments have no open access (and so, no admission fees), tourists enjoy their beauty from the outside and end up spending in their proximity. When there is admission fee, this is an economic expression of one direct use value of heritage; that is, the visitation service provided by the buildings' and monuments' heritage. It represents a flow estimate measured over a time period (a day, a month, a year).[9]

The mapping process starts with a presentation of all monuments and heritage buildings in the historic city core that could possibly be attractive to visitors. In historic city cores, it is difficult to isolate heritage items from other attractions (e.g., museums, parks, natural sites, gardens). (See box 9.3.) Direct use values for visits are measured by the amount of revenues as a result of visits, including the admission fees. Accordingly, actual economic values are only attributed for places open to the public and where there is a charge for the visit.

An alternative representation visualizes the economic reality in terms of the number of visitors, because mapping economic values only with admission fees can sometimes lead to a misleading interpretation. For example, churches attract many visitors and are among the most visited places; although they do not generate direct economic benefit to the city, they attract visitors. Counting visitors at places where there are no admission fees remains a meaningful contribution to

BOX 9.3

GIS Documentation Provides the Basis for Cultural Tourism Routes in Lahore

Pakistan, Punjab Municipal Services Improvement Project (Project number 083929)
Total Project Cost: US$58.9 million
Total Loan Amount: US$50 million
Approved: June 2006 – Ongoing

The cultural heritage component of this World Bank–assisted project is focused on preparing a more comprehensive urban regeneration project for the Walled City of Lahore with the aim of making it a world-class tourist destination. The project is providing assistance for (1) undertaking studies to recommend positive changes in heritage management and legislative frameworks; and (2) creating a heritage trail, to demonstrate the connections between heritage conservation, cultural tourism, and income generation. The trail, extending from the Delhi Gate to the Lahore Fort, will link a variety of monumental buildings, private residences, traditional bazaars, and open spaces as a sequence of experiences in the historic built environment. As part of the preparation for both activities above, a GIS system has been established, with assistance from the Aga Khan Trust for Culture (AKTC), Pakistan, and an inventory of all buildings in the Walled City of Lahore has been completed, with documentation of land use and building ownership, age, and historic value.

Specifically, the project achieved the following:

Topographical survey: Between 2008 and 2009, the AKTC carried out a topographical survey of the entire Walled City of Lahore, measuring 2.56 square kilometers. This survey covered all streets, including the 1,835 street segments less than 1.5 meters wide, measuring a total of 14.255 kilometers. The survey was conducted entirely at night using EDM Total Station technology.

GIS database: The topographical survey became the base spatial data for the preparation of a GIS database in which all 21,800 individual land parcels and the buildings standing on them are included. Basic photographic data was generated for individual properties. Moreover, the database covers some 172 attributes for each building, including date of construction, structural condition, height, land and building use, type, ownership type, tenure, occupation density, and more. This GIS database is operational and can be used as a municipal geospatial, fiscal, ownership, and heritage database subject to the incorporation of the relevant additional data.

Source: Project update note by Bank staff. 2012.

the city and site management. First, it allows comparison of visitor flows across the city; second, it provides data in case a city wants to evaluate the opportunity of imposing limits due to the carrying capacity of a site, or for the purpose of considering entry charges.

Additional indicators for visits can be used for mapping. Carrying capacity of a site (i.e., maximum possible number of visitors per day) and visitor rate (i.e., number of visitors as a percentage of carrying capacity) are useful tools to describe the "visit market" of the historic city core. Derived from a straightforward demand-supply relationship, the indicator of visitor rate highlights excess of demand (hence, a risk for the heritage) or excess of supply (hence, a potential for economic values).

As noted earlier, use values related to visitors and tourism are of two types: direct use values (i.e., visits to the site, museum, or monument) and indirect use values (i.e., expenditures made by visitors or tourists on lodging, food, and souvenirs).

Indirect use values are the most complex to identify, to measure, and to map. Indirect use values are measured by heritage-related expenditures made by residents or visitors. Some of these expenditures are easily traceable and can be inscribed on maps, because they are specifically and completely related to the heritage (a museum of the monument, a souvenir shop, and such). Other expenditures are more difficult to assess, or must be estimated as average values for entire blocks, streets, city areas, or meaningful economic areas. When specific places can be identified or located with precision, the mapping of indirect use values consists of an exhaustive recording and documenting of all such places across the city. This requires extensive gathering of information from hotels, restaurants, shops, visitor information centers, transportation services, guide agencies, and such, which is a task probably applicable to only a small city or a district. Big cities have staff, equipment, and resources to undertake such recording, but the economic impact measured is not exclusively related to the heritage. The need for measurement by sampling is inevitable.

Modern technology (e.g., GIS, GPS, Geocoding) will soon offer ways of better managing tourism in historic city cores. These tools will improve site management and prevent congestion where cities struggle with excess tourism. Similar mapping techniques will help city authorities increase the economic impact from tourism. Assessing indirect use values requires relying on both sampling and mapping. Tourist expenditures for lodging, food, transportation, and goods or services are market transactions defined by a supply and a demand side. Appraisal of these transactions can be two-fold:

- A demand-side analysis is undertaken through a sample survey among visitors, to analyze the consumer's behavior and to estimate expenditures per person, per day. Expenditures can also be segmented between per-day trip and per-overnight trip. One can either measure individual averages for trip spending and length of stay from the sample, or measure the overnight spending on a case-by-case basis and then average across all samples.

- A supply-side analysis is undertaken through a sampling survey among the suppliers/producers. Retail shops, hotels, restaurants, parking lots, transportation businesses, and guided tour offices should be part of the sample. When the historic city core is small in size, it is possible to undertake a comprehensive recording and mapping of all the places where tourism expenditures are anticipated. Such a supply-side map will display the economic potential of the city, or the capacity of supplying accommodations, goods, and services to visitors. It also displays how the heritage and the economic features connect spatially.

The mapping of tourism-related use values relies on a variety of indicators. Although admission fees are the proper data for measuring economic values, it is helpful to collect additional indicators for explaining and emphasizing the true meaning of values generated by tourism; among them:

- Access to the heritage: all-year-round, seasonal, once or twice a year;
- Admission fees (including free access);
- Carrying capacity and visitor rate as a percentage of carrying capacity;
- Number of visitors;
- Assisted and guided visits, availability of audio-tours, museum of the monument, monument store;
- Visitor behavior (satisfaction, time spent);
- Availability of parking, public transportation, guided tours;
- Average expenditures per visitor per day (time spent in the city, number of stays);
- Sales related to visitors; and
- Heritage-related events organized in the city (festival, exhibition, artistic performance).

Mapping aims to provide a comprehensive vision of these indicators, adding together the different layers. It depicts a city map that summarizes all factors and impacts on tourism generated by heritage. It explains how use values are generated by tourism, and presents the areas where they occur. Maps of tourism-related use values have to be analyzed together with maps of non-use values, to emphasize the places where use values could be higher.

The following example (of a fictional town) illustrates the potential of mapping direct and indirect use values as they are related to cultural tourism, and serves to visualize connections between maps. Maps 9.3A and 9.3B show the monuments (direct use values) and the hotels, restaurants, shops, and services (indirect use values).[10]

MAPS 9.3A-B
**Fictional Town Showing (A) Direct Use Values and
(B) Indirect Use Values**

A

B

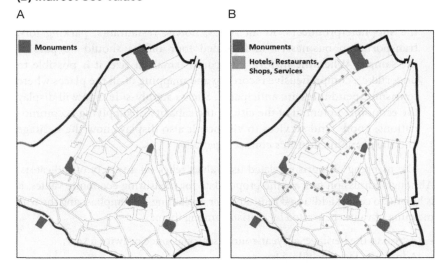

Source: Author.

Map 9.3C shows the buffer zones that are tentatively drawn around the monuments (in blue), and around the commercial activities, where we expect to measure indirect use values (in red). Map 9.3D shows the selected direct plus indirect
use values areas related to tourism. Estimates of the values inside of the areas are
represented by a color-coded map (higher, medium, and lower values). Indicators are used to estimate these values (ratio between visitor sales and total sales,
number of shops, turnovers, visitors). This map visualizes the higher and lower
economic areas in the historic city core.

Use Values Related to Impacts on Local Economy

Victor Hugo once said: "L'usage d'un monument appartient à son propriétaire,
mais sabeauté appartient à tout le monde" (The use of a monument belongs to
its owner, but the beauty of a monument belongs to all). This exemplifies the
heritage as a collective good. Many monuments or historic sites are public or collective goods through their physical presence, in the sense that, being part of a
local, national, or world cultural heritage, they "belong" to everyone.

This economic definition is consistent with the cultural value and the various
levels of protection of the heritage: on a local level (low cultural value), cultural

MAPS 9.3C–D

Fictional Town Showing (C) Buffer Zones around Monuments and (D) Higher and Lower Economic Areas in the Historic City

C   D

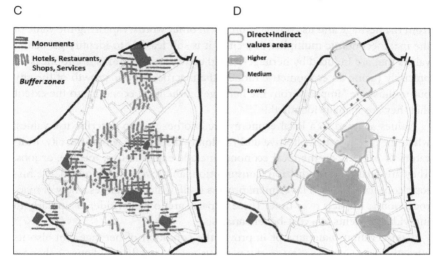

Source: Author.

heritage is a public good to the local inhabitants and its conservation is managed at that level (cultural associations, groups of volunteers); on a national level (high cultural value), cultural heritage becomes a nation's public good and its conservation is dealt with at the national level (national heritage list); on a world level (outstanding cultural value), cultural heritage is a universal public good and its conservation is a world issue (World Heritage List).

A typical feature of public goods is the existence of externalities, benefits, or costs that are not accounted for by some kind of market transaction. Economists customarily look to government for solutions to market failure for heritage goods, or even to remedy the total absence of a market.[11]

Given the public good dimension of historic city cores and the large amount of externalities, an economic analysis that provides a broad vision on issues such as growth, development, employment, urban planning, or transportation is important. Therefore, a macroeconomic analysis may sometimes be an appropriate tool for an integrated vision of the multiple components of a historic city core, offering a holistic approach to optimizing the economic value of the city's heritage. Such an approach may be more or less suitable, depending on the size of the city core: a sufficiently large entity is required to reflect a macroeconomic reality. A large size embeds the critical mass of economic agents and diversified activities.

A small historic village or a historic core will not easily suit the macroeconomic perspective because most of the economic activities we want to measure as economic values appear outside of the city.

Despite the methodological difficulty of capturing macroeconomic impacts from the heritage and its conservation (or in other words, capturing the value of the macroeconomic multiplier in a city), it is still feasible to identify particular values that are induced by heritage-related activities. The aim is not to measure precisely (using an econometric model) the macroeconomic growth of the city but to illustrate "impacts from the heritage on the local economy, to the extent that they are spatially identifiable."[12]

Values accrued to a local economy are another way to describe use values, when they are mostly collective and randomly distributed across the city. Indicators of impacts on the local economy include expenditures, income, or jobs. They are related to production, consumption, and investment. Indeed, the historic conservation is an investment process itself, which generates a flow of macroeconomic impacts over time. These impacts are to be considered similarly to individual benefits in a cost-benefit analysis.

Conservation maintains or improves the condition of heritage, but also its attractiveness. Conservation creates new businesses, stabilizes old ones, enhances the quality of life in the city, and provides benefits to many stakeholders—tourists and residents included. Economic values sprawl around the heritage, and cover an undetermined area. A convenient analogy is the economic hinterland, or a zone coming under the economic and commercial influence of an urban center. There is no absolute rule in tracing a hinterland: economic impacts do not necessarily propagate in concentric circles with decreasing intensity; they could disseminate further and in other directions than anticipated. Mapping units refer to where the initial impulse takes place, and where the impacts and values are distributed.

Table (9.2) gives some examples of factors inducing an impact, the corresponding macroeconomic indicators, and spatial identification (mapping units).

Map 9.4 displays three mapping features combined: (1) a base map of an indicator of impacts on the local economy (e.g., change in number of jobs, or change in income growth) in a grey-color progression; (2) the boundary of the heritage protected area (as a brown line); (3) the spatial identification of new investment during the previous period (red dots). Adding together the three mapping tools visualizes the expected correlation between private business investment, its impact on the local economy, and the heritage. Map 9.5 displays four areas selected in the inner historic city of Diest in Belgium. Impacts on the local economy are assessed for all areas, on the basis of local surveys.

TABLE 9.2

Examples of Ways to Map the Impact of Heritage Activities on Local Economies

Heritage-related activity	Indicators of impacts on the local economy	Mapping units
Festival, heritage open day	Expenditures made during the event (use values)	Place where the festival is organized, and streets where expenditures take place
Income from tourist-related activities re-spent in the economy (multiplier effect)	Number of jobs, income generated in related sectors	Locations where jobs and income generation take place**
Property values for non-heritage buildings	Property values (use values)	Parcels or blocks of properties (heritage vs. non-heritage properties)
Private investment and new business start due to historic status, or heritage conservation projects*	Jobs created, income generated	Locations of projects, of new business, and its impact

*Either a positive impact (higher income, new job) or the absence of a negative impact (no job lost, no foreclosures).
**In Djenné, Mali, for example, this can be fairly clearly identified because neighborhoods historically have been organized by the various professional groups (e.g., fishermen, masons, merchants, guides), and still are to a certain extent today.
Source: Author.

Impacts on the local economy are the result of individual decisions or of collective decisions taken by the public authorities. In the economic literature, macroeconomic impacts are commonly related to public initiatives.[13] Most of the macroeconomic impulses being directed at heritage or its conservation by public authorities (at the city, regional, or national level) induce a large array of benefits and values. Mapping these values is similar to the previous analysis.

In today's world, the debate between supporters of profit-oriented (private) and government-supported (public) cultural activities still persists. Public intervention remains common in the domain of culture, as the collective dimension of heritage implies collective responsibility, which is endorsed by community representatives. Economists agree that the market system is more efficient in resource allocation, but only to the extent that conditions of fair competition prevail. In the field of cultural heritage and conservation activities, conditions of perfect competition rarely exist.

Accordingly, public or public-private partnership arrangements are allowed to correct dysfunctions resulting from free market mechanisms. Efficiency in resource allocation and equity or equal access to major resources are important considerations. To provide equality of access to cultural goods for everyone, public authorities need to take an active part in heritage management. City administrators can act in various capacities: as owner and caretaker of heritage buildings, as manager of heritage-related cultural activities, as levier of local taxes, as provider of public subsidies or fiscal incentives, and as initiator and entity in charge of the implementation of urban and legal regulations.

An intervention by city, regional, or national authorities in heritage management or conservation is measured by the ensuing local expenditures (local public consumption and investment) or alternately by tax exemption.

The mapping of economic values related to public intervention requires comparing the public attributes of the heritage to these values. Mapping of the following selected indicators describes the relationship between public intervention and economic values:

- Publicly owned buildings;
- Public use of buildings, and public services;
- Public financing, subsidies, and tax reductions (by tax parcels or by individual properties);
- Public-regulated development and conservation projects;
- Local expenditures and jobs (spatial identification of projects); and
- Public benefits from heritage-related initiatives: poverty alleviation, sanitation, crime reduction, and improved public safety and wellbeing.[14]

Economic Landscapes

The mapping process emphasizes the spatial distribution of economic values related to heritage. Components of use values and non-use values do not always show similar patterns or a consistent spatial distribution. They should be shown separately or in combination, to provide a comprehensive view of the economic values of the city heritage. This facilitates the identification of economic values that are distributed across the area. Spatial information then provides an economic landscape context to the historic city, with a high potential for policy applications.

Explaining and summarizing the geographic information provided by economic values on maps requires the identification of patterns, connections, and relationships between indicators of all categories of values. The process is twofold, as described in figure 9.1: first, the analysis of indicators related to categories of values; second, the analysis of aggregated values to summarize and map the information.

MAP 9.4
Display Combining Three Mapping Features
Grey-color progression = impacts on the local economy (change in number of jobs, or change in income growth)
Brown line = boundary of the heritage protected area
Red dots = new investment

Source: Author.

MAP 9.5
Four Areas Selected for Study in the Historic City Core of Diest, Belgium

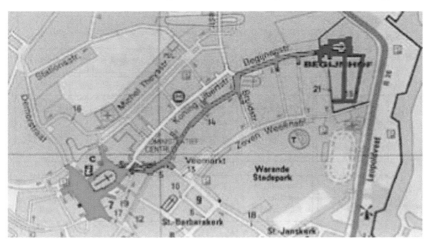

Source: Author.

This process is consistent with the fact that urban planners and architects consider the city as a comprehensive entity. They emphasize a holistic approach to dealing with heritage, taken as built structures organized in space, and revealed by its own scale and perspective in the surrounding area. Spatial analysis aims to identify the organization in space of heritage economic values, from the material provided by the mapping process. Spatial identification is conditioned by many factors: physical features (natural, artificial, or both), road and communication connections, urban density, and so on. The analysis takes into consideration both the location of the economic values (buildings, monuments) and the impact of these values on the surrounding area (streets, public spaces, non-heritage buildings), thus arriving at the shape and boundary for each category of economic values.

Individual indicators are often merged into a composite index. Spatial analysis can be more effective by displaying and visualizing a comprehensive economic landscape. The purpose is to draw areas of total economic values on a base map, by selecting different layers of values (successive thematic maps) and by adding up the layers into a single map. The map visualizes the aggregate economic value of heritage, or an economic landscape of heritage. The economic landscape appears on a single color-coded map (with darker tones for higher values), and identifies the places with the lowest and with the highest values.

FIGURE 9.1

How to Organize, Explain, and Synthesize Geographic Information about Values

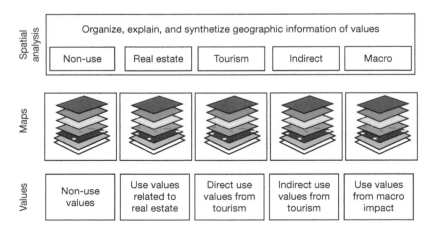

Spatial analysis	Organize, explain, and synthetize geographic information of values				
	Non-use	Real estate	Tourism	Indirect	Macro

| Maps | | | | | |

| Values | Non-use values | Use values related to real estate | Direct use values from tourism | Indirect use values from tourism | Use values from macro impact |

Source: Author.

It also displays a continuity of values into successive leveled areas. Historic city cores exemplify this approach, which is consistent with the assessment of an aggregate economic value.

The process of adding up layers of values is not an obvious one. First, there is a risk of double counting by adding similar indicators, or data that envision the same reality through separate assessment. Then, any composite or aggregate index requires a sound weighting process: Are non-use values more significant than use values? Are direct use values more important than indirect use values? Finally, individual maps display indicators, with no standardized metric or unit of account.[15]

An economic landscape map is made of compounded values measured for an entire area. Successive layers of values have been laid on top of each other, the first layer being a base map. The final product visualizes the economic landscape of the city (map 9.6).

Economic landscapes change over time. Although values are connected to a static urban fabric, the economic decisions and behavior of stakeholders determine how values get transformed, and how these changes shift across the city in dynamic ways. The economic landscape is also an identification mark for a historic city core, its pattern revealing how the heritage and the city economy are connected. Various patterns of economic landscapes are

MAP 9.6

Multi-layered Map of the Economic Values of Diest, Belgium, Laid over the Base Map

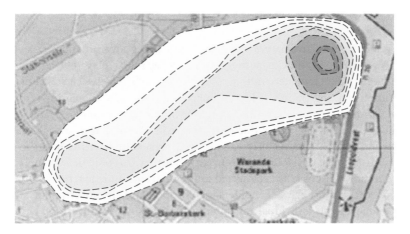

Source: Author.

FIGURES 9.2
Various Patterns of Economic Landscapes

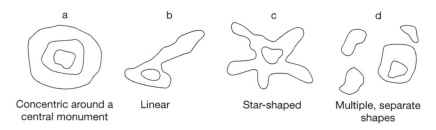

a	b	c	d

Concentric around a   Linear   Star-shaped   Multiple, separate
central monument   shapes

Source: Author.

expressed through different shapes, showing how economic values are organized in space: a landscape can be concentric around a central highly attractive monument (figure 9.2a); a landscape can be drawn following linear (figure
9.2b) or star-shaped areas (figure 9.2c); and shapes can also be multiple and
separated from each other (figure 9.2d).

Regional mapping of monuments and sites may be processed in the same way.
The aim is to develop GIS network approaches and frameworks, such as establishing the linkages between several urban sites to create tourism circuits or to
diffuse mass tourism from highly concentrated spots. In addition, such GIS network approaches could reveal accessibility indicators such as travel time.

Enhancing Urban Spatial Function

The public or collective nature of the heritage justifies government intervention
on behalf of its citizens. City authorities have a key role to play in bringing heritage stakeholders together, finding solutions to conflicts between stakeholders,
and implementing policy including managing trade-offs. Increasing non-use
values with an improved external image for the city, increasing use values with
economic incentives, and reducing macroeconomic leakages are all actions
that contribute simultaneously to improved preservation of the heritage and
to the sustainable development of the city. But they can only be accomplished
if a societal consensus is established among citizens and stakeholders of the
city's heritage. Heritage stakeholders include local and city governments, tourism management, individual inhabitants, local businesses, investors, heritage
administrators, conservation project managers, and site managers. In historic

city cores listed as World Heritage, stakeholders include local, national, and international communities, as well as future generations.

The identification and mapping of cultural heritage indicators may be used for assessing conservation projects and assisting authorities or heritage caretakers in project implementation. These are tools to identify and measure the economic returns of conservation decisions, to show the geographic impacts of conservation projects, and to adopt a comprehensive approach to site management in the urban context. Data on economic values attached to various stakeholders are brought together into impact analysis, social cost-benefit methods, or alternative project evaluation tools. Although the mapping of economic values is not itself a decision-making tool, it certainly provides a useful reference to assist in the decision-making process.

Figure 9.3 combines a summary of identification of stakeholders; the impact from the project variables; and their significance in terms of economic values,

FIGURE 9.3

Mapping Elements for the Evaluation and Assessment Process

Stakeholders	Items	Values	Indicators	Maps (page 277)
Residents	Occupation	Use values from real estate	Rental values	Map 9.7C
Visitors	Benefit from the visit	Use values from tourism	Admision fees, visits	Map 9.7E
Population at large	Existence, bequest values	Non-use values	Willingness-to-pay	Map 9.7B
Bussiness, shops, services	Residents and visitors expenditures	Indirect use values, macro use values	Jobs, income	Map 9.7F

Source: Author.

indicators, and maps selected for the analysis. It provides elements for the evaluation and assessment process. The figure indicates each stakeholder's own perspective on the project, as visualized by its geographic display.

Mapping provides elements toward the interpretation of heritage-related economics. It provides additional data, and may assist in identifying features critical to historic conservation. It determines the relative contribution of categories of economic values to the city's growth and welfare. One interesting feature of map analysis is the possibility it offers to detect imbalances of economic benefits within a given historic city core. Thematic maps, as economic landscape maps for aggregate economic values and can identify imbalances of categories of economic values across the historic city core. Those imbalances between use and non-use values, between direct and indirect use values, and between economic values and conservation costs are representative of inequity between heritage stakeholders. Imbalances in spatial distribution of economic values reveal how the existing maintenance and use conditions of the heritage stock, or heritage conservation, bring benefits to some stakeholders and costs to others.

The purpose is to provide city authorities with development schemes of heritage economics, offering key references to decision makers to prevent or to correct value imbalances within the historic city core. Accordingly, the mapping of heritage economics becomes a tool for urban and land-use planning. By enhancing urban spatial functions, it contributes to preserving the economic value that makes the heritage a sustainable cultural asset.

Key possible findings of mapping schemes are the following:

- *Absence of or few non-use values.* The awareness of cultural values for the heritage is dim, or not revealed within the preferences of people. This does not mean that the heritage does not carry architectural value, or does not comply with criteria such as integrity or authenticity. This situation denotes that the citizenry does not really care about the continued existence of the city's heritage, or would not be willing to pay to preserve the option of visiting it at some time, while the city may not be regarded as possessing significant cultural heritage. Given the lack of non-marketable benefits, the economic value of the heritage is potentially low.

  Map analysis may reveal an extended lack of non-use values, or a focus of non-use values around a single outstanding building or monument or a compound of them. This is typical for cities that have preserved their heritage as isolated objects, but failed to develop an integrated approach to their historic core. So far, heritage economics has mostly focused on individual buildings or monuments.

- *Scarce or few use values found.* Spatial analysis may confirm that cultural and economic values go hand in hand in the historic city core. Residents acknowledge the cultural value of the heritage, and people's preferences indicate their willingness to preserve this heritage. However, most of the economic values are non-marketable, which implies that the city faces a challenge in bringing into the market the heritage's economic potential values (transforming preferences into exchanges and transactions).

Map analysis may indicate trends where use values could arise. It could enable the city to develop initiatives at places where non-use values are high. It could bring recommendations on fostering use values related to the real estate market, or use values related to tourism. Globally the city should integrate heritage preservation activities (non-use values) with economic development framework (use values) and urban planning.

- *Use values are predominantly attached to a single type of activity.* Use values are predominantly the product of the real estate market or the tourism economic activities. A lack of diversification of use values prevents the city from achieving balanced growth. Spatial analysis reveals such imbalances across the city with places that are largely focused on an extensive development of the real estate market or the tourism market. When a city "puts all its eggs in one basket," it faces the risk of unbalanced and unsustainable growth. Spatial analysis could recommend where to diversify use values in the city, as an integrated approach with historic conservation.

  Tourism-related use values provide a significant example of unsustainable development when tourism grows beyond the capacity of the city. Again, spatial analysis will pinpoint the places or the neighborhoods where an extensive growth of tourism becomes a threat for safeguarding of the heritage assets.

- *There are few indirect use values related to tourism specifically.* Cultural and architectural values are acknowledged and economically revealed by the preferences of consumers and by preferences expressed by visitors from around the world. This finding denotes that transportation services and mobility options exist so that a large number of visitors come to the city. But while the city experiences high use values, it may fail to supply the economic conditions to provide lodging, food, and other commercial and public services to incoming visitors. Spatial analysis indicates the places where most use values occur, and leads to recommendations on the development of new accommodations to match the visitor demand. This raises tourism management issues.

  As we know, an overextended development of indirect use values can impede sustainable development. The city needs to maintain a diversified and balanced economy. Spatial indicators related to housing affordability, or to the number of grocery stores for residents versus the number of souvenirs shops, demonstrate how imbalances in indirect use values can impede sustainable growth.[16]

An additional issue is that the city may fail to capture the benefits of indirect and induced outcomes from tourism.[17] Spatial analysis will help local authorities to organize the growth of indirect use values, to keep as much economic value as possible contained in the city, and to ensure that fiscal revenues are collected locally.

- *There are few use values related to impacts on the local economy in general.* Poor private or public initiatives in conservation, or in the enhancement of the heritage, ensues little macroeconomic impact in terms of income or jobs. However, the main reason for feeble economic impact is because benefits are captured mostly by non-residents.

Local authorities strive to keep as much economic values as possible within the city. A historic city core loses its use values when residents drive out of the city for shopping, when tourists cannot find lodging or dining places in the city, when activities in the city are managed by non-resident individuals or companies, when goods and services are imported, when conservation jobs go to non-local workers, and when the tax on heritage properties or the admission fees do not benefit the city budget.

Leakages do not reduce heritage economic value, they just displace them and shift them to other beneficiaries. In this case, the solution is to redirect values to the benefit of the city, after first measuring the size of the leakages. A better knowledge of such losses—for example, how much fiscal revenue is generated by an archaeological monument or city heritage to the benefit of the national budget—can help city administrators in political negotiations with other levels of government. Other means are increasing the propensity of inhabitants to consume inside the city, reallocating tax income (e.g., transfer payments, public expenditures, investment), maintaining jobs in the city, and enticing businesses to stay in the city.[18]

Case Study: The World Heritage City of Djenné in Mali

A test case for Djenné, Mali, a listed World Heritage Site since 1988, aimed to collect data to test the mapping technique, with the purpose of showing the distribution of the economic value of Djenné's heritage. The ancient town of Djenné is located 600 kilometers northeast of Bamako, the capital of Mali, West Africa, and has a population of about 20,000 inhabitants (2008 estimate). It receives roughly 15,000 tourists per year, of which 3,000 stay overnight in the town (2008 estimate).

Djenné's earthen architectural style reflects centuries of acquired knowledge, building know-how, traditions, and lifeways of its populations. The organic character of its earthen architecture is in harmony with its surrounding natural landscape and river. For its unique character, the old town of Djenné was inscribed on the World Heritage List in 1988. Its tangible cultural heritage consists of the Great Mosque (the largest earthen building in the world), an architectural ensemble of earthen houses, and four archaeological sites outside the city's perimeter. The urban heritage of Djenné's historic center includes 1,858 houses (with 12,000 inhabitants), of which some 50 two-story houses are built in the traditional "djennenké" style. Djenné was a center of Islamic learning and pilgrimage, one of the most important in West Africa, and its Mosque, originally built during the 13th century and said to be the biggest earthen construction in the world, dominates the market square.

The government of Mali attracted an important collaboration involving the Aga Khan Trust for Culture, Dutch Restoration Project and the European Union to preserve the unique architecture of the town. The urban perimeter is quite limited by the river surrounding it, yet it is estimated by UNESCO that in 2025 the population in the historic city core will have increased by 45 percent (from 13,000 to 19,000). In recent years, the city has faced the following economic and urban challenges, which affect its heritage: a gradual impoverishment of the population due to increased droughts, which makes the maintenance of the traditional earthen facades more difficult to afford, resulting in building abandonment and collapses; exodus of the young to bigger cities; struggle to keep the mason profession alive, with sufficient work and a transition of knowledge to younger generations; modernization of the traditional houses, with the introduction of water and modern amenities; new constructions in modern styles and with new materials; infrastructure, sewage, and water evacuation issues; unstable tourism (after a steady increase, it has stopped due to terrorist activity in the Northern Malian desert). (See box 9.4.)

The Djenné test case aimed to collect data to test the mapping techniques.[19] Non-market benefits were not addressed specifically in the survey, but are known to be significant to the city of Djenné. These were grossly estimated. Survey questions were structured to roughly capture the use values of Djenné's heritage for the year 2008. With reference to use values, neighborhoods (parcels data were not available for housing), historic buildings, and heritage-related business (hotels, restaurants, transportation by punt, art and crafts, masons, guides) were identified on a digitalized base map (map 9.7A).

Individual thematic maps illustrate each category of economic values:

- *Non-use values* (map 9.7B): Spatial analysis areas were drawn on the original map to identify places with the highest values. Contingent valuation method was not applied to Djenné. Nevertheless, the whole historic city core has substantial non-use values. The Mosque appears in darker tones because of its status as Djenné's architectural landmark, and as a monument with outstanding cultural value.

BOX 9.4

Mapping Identifies One of the Main Challenges in Djenné

Mali Urban Development and Decentralization Project (Project number 001750)
Total Project Cost: US$141 million
Total Loan Amount: US$80 million
Approved: December 1996 – Closed: June 2005

At the request of the government of Mali, the World Bank assisted in the design of a project to improve institutional capacity and infrastructure for the provision of basic services in several of the country's cities (Bamako, Sikasso, Ségou, Timbuktu, and Djenné). To help conserve Mali's historic cities and monuments, the project also supported the establishment of strategic long-term physical, spatial, and environmental management plans. As part of this work, an inventory and map of infrastructure in Djenné showed that one of the city's main challenges at the time was to address storm water drainage. Consequently, the project helped improve a system with 6.5 kilometers of extension of drainage trenches on 20 streets. The project also supported the conservation and promotion of an archaeological site in Djenné and provided office equipment for the city's cultural mission.

Source: Mali Urban Development and Decentralization Project Implementation and Completion Report.

- *Use values related to the real estate market (mainly the housing market)* (map 9.7C): Spatial distribution of rental values are shown per neighborhood (darker tones are highest values). The increase in population feeds a demand for housing in the historic city core. The average annual rental value (averaged per neighborhood, as data are not available for individual units or parcels) was (Mali francs) CFAF200,000 (US$400) in 2008. This indicates strong economic values from the heritage occupancy. The highest value is 250 percent higher than the lowest value.
- *Direct use values related to tourism* (map 9.7D): Djenné possesses many attractive places for visitors, such as public and private buildings, mostly not accessible inside and not charging an admission fee. They cover almost the entire area of the Old Town of Djenné. In trying to link the sites together, the map displays tours or visitor walking paths across the city

MAPS 9.7

Maps of Djenné, Mali, Showing Different Non-Use and Use Values

MAP 9.7A

Base Map for Djenné, Mali

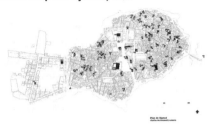

MAP 9.7B

Non-Use Values
Darkest tones = highest values

MAP 9.7C

Use Values Related to Real Estate
Darkest tones = highest values

MAP 9.7D

Direct Use Values Related to Tourism
Light yellow = tours and visitor walking paths

MAP 9.7E

Indirect Use Values Related to Tourism
Red = main places with estimated indirect use values (food and lodging)

MAP 9.7F

Use Values Related to Impacts on the Local Economy
Estimate of the spatial distribution of macroeconomic impact (jobs, income) from investments

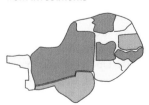

MAP 9.7G

Economic Landscape
Darkest tones = highest values

Source: Author.

(light yellow on the map). This indicates the highly concentrated nature of the city heritage.

- *Indirect use values related to tourism* (map 9.7E): The main places with estimated indirect use values are identified in red on the map. Inside the city, there are eight places for lodging and food, plus the Monday market. Indirect use values include also the sales of 27 tourist guidebooks. Outside of the city, there are the ferry transportation services and lodging at Djenné Djenno hotel. Tentative mapping of indirect use values (for the known business locations) shows that most of the lodging business is concentrated north of Yroboukaina, not far from the Mosque and the marketplace.
- *Use values related to impacts on the local economy* (map 9.7F): The test-case study did not address specifically macroeconomic impact from conservation projects. The volume of investment in the 12 neighborhoods amounted to CFAF140 million (US$280,000) in 2008, mostly from private funds. The map shows an estimate of the spatial distribution of macroeconomic impact (jobs, income) from investments.
- *Economic landscape* (map 9.7G): An economic landscape map combines shapes of data displayed in the individual maps.[20] The economic landscape map for Djenné indicates how overall economic values are distributed across the city, and reveals areas of concentration of values (darker tones indicate higher values). Two darker spots show intensive values, respectively the marketplace with the Mosque (bottom) and the "Campement" area with multiple accommodations. Apart from the location of heritage points of interest, the absence of visit charges at many locations and the limited lodging facilities may in part explain the less intensive values found elsewhere.

An important lesson learned from this test case is that, despite the fact that GIS techniques require very large databases to perform at their best, it is still meaningful to use this method on a digitalized base map, and to identify the relevant vector elements given the available data.

The mapping exercise in Djenné reveals the economic impact of a particular project; namely, the Mosque restoration assisted by the Aga Khan Trust for Culture. The project employed local masons, apprentice masons, carpenters, wood suppliers, potters, and water carriers. Construction teams are lodged in long-term rental units or small hotels; eat at particular restaurants; hire cooks, guards, carriers, and helpers; and purchase local building materials. Upon completion of the project, the attractiveness of the Mosque has been enhanced, to be enjoyed externally by foreigners (non-Muslims are not allowed inside the Mosque, and this is likely to stay unchanged). A community center might be built in the city and neighborhood of the Mosque to present and explain earthen architecture and the Mosque restoration project, thus increasing tourist traffic. Improved earthen coating developed for this project, and overall economic opportunities, may become more permanent by extending the benefits of the technique employed by the project to the city's houses.

Additional analysis may reveal the gradient of households at the various neighborhoods (measured by income, rental values) since neighborhoods are still predominantly structured around professional affiliations. The economic cost of the annual house recoating expenses will be incurred by owners.[21] Houses vary in styles, sizes, and according to neighborhoods, and therefore vary in maintenance costs.

Finally, the mapping exercise helps to define the framework for possible future adaptation of specific conservation zones within the UNESCO and national protection zone, by mapping these zones and their respective targeted conservation regulations, costs, and investments.

Conclusion

There was a time when discussing heritage conservation and management in terms of economic values was inappropriate: economic tools were inadequate for addressing the peculiar features of heritage; heritage conservation and economic growth were treated in isolation; and projects involved conservation specialists, not stakeholders. Today experts recognize that "[t]he variety of values ascribed to any particular heritage object—economic value, aesthetic value, cultural value, political value, educational value—is matched by the variety of stakeholders participating in the heritage conservation process. Balancing these values is one of the most difficult challenges in making conservation decisions that satisfy the needs of many stakeholders" (Mason 1998, 2).

Although the fields of cultural economics and heritage economics have advanced considerably in the last decades, there is still a lack of empirical economic tools flexible enough to suit the variety and complexity of economic realities, particularly when applied to heritage assets in historic city cores. This chapter puts forward uses of new tools for decision makers in the field of heritage conservation, to provide a typology of how heritage economics are applied to value heritage assets in historic city cores. It also proposes to review methods in use to coalesce the many stakeholders involved in the conservation process: decision makers, experts, residents, visitors, and conservation specialists. Mapping data and visualizing the tangible and intangible aspects of investments in conservation of patrimony may help to bring about a comprehensive understanding of the values of heritage. As a preamble to spatial analysis, the mapping process enhances the scope of economic analysis and provides the additional insight of cultural economics.

Policy implications of spatial analysis are the next level of inquiry. It is true that valuation techniques have greatly improved in the last decades. It is true that cultural economics provide us today with better tools to evaluate and assess values in historic cities. Ultimately, economics of conservation will remain as imperfect as economics or conservation still are today. Specialists, students, and citizen will rely on maps, figures, and indicators to understand the ever-changing spatial and economic relations in urban settings and ways to assess the value of heritage. Nevertheless, we must not overlook the essential importance of alternative approaches with regard to the economic role of heritage assets in the future.

Mapping techniques of urban heritage assets and monuments provide an effective way to create an information base for monitoring public policies, programs, and projects aimed at local social and economic development.

Notes

1. http://heritage-key.com/blogs/sean-williams/lord-norwich-tourism-venice-reaching-meltdown.
2. http://www.nytimes.com/2011/01/09/world/africa/09mali.html.
3. This chapter is a follow-up to *Guide for Heritage Economics: Values, Indicators, Maps, and Policies*, research conducted by the author at the Getty Conservation Institute, Los Angeles, in 2008–09. The guide was intended to provide fundamental economic principles and guidelines for historic cities' stakeholders to help in the decision-making process.
4. In the last 30 years, 242 cities were inscribed onto the UNESCO list of World Heritage Sites. These entries differ considerably. They include highly populated cities, national capitals, and small villages, economically poor and rich. Their spatial distribution is: in Africa (3.7 percent), in the Arab States (9.1 percent), in Asia and the Pacific (11.6 percent), in Europe and North America (59.5 percent), and in Latin America and the Caribbean (16.1 percent). Estimates of these cities' GDPs vary broadly between US$38 million and US$143 billion.
5. Commission on Environment and Development, United Nations 1983.
6. Sustainability indicators were measured for the city of Siena, Italy. Among other results, indicators show how clean transportation in the city, water consumption per inhabitant, and the degree to which people suffer from lack of urban safety have changed over 10 years (Semboloni 2005).
7. Among many other rankings based on city indicator analysis, the Mercer Quality of Living Survey compares 215 large cities with 39 criteria. New York is the standard reference (score of 100), and other cities are rated in comparison. Criteria include safety, education, hygiene, recreation, political or economic stability, and public transportation. Several World Heritage cities are among the best-rated cities (2009 Survey): Vienna (ranked 1), Bern (9), Brussels (14), Berlin (16), Luxemburg (19),

Paris (33), and Lyon (37) (http://www.mercer.com/articles/quality-of-living-survey-report-2010).

8. The Vieux Lyon quarter in France (Old Lyon, World Heritage Site since 1998) covers 74 acres (30 hectares), including 500 buildings, 3,000 housing units, and 7,000 residents. This represents a high use value for the city and its residents. Most buildings are used for housing, but Old Lyon includes other economic functions: hotels, restaurants, retail shops, offices, and cultural venues. As a whole, the historic city core provides many services to its inhabitants: job opportunities; commercial options; cultural activities and administrative, health, and education services. With a particularly high rate of occupancy, heritage buildings play a very important role in promoting the city's growth and welfare.

9. Rome remains one of the top destinations for tourism in Italy. The number of visitors (mostly related to heritage sites) was 29.7 million in 2008, of which 43 percent were from Italy and 57 percent from abroad. These visitors provide substantial revenues in terms of admission fees to access monuments and heritage sites. More than half of the visits are estimated to be free of charge, which leaves a huge potential consumer surplus (= amount of consumers who benefit for free). The Cathedral of Notre-Dame, in Paris, a World Heritage city since 1991, is the most visited monument in France. It is noteworthy that the two most visited monuments in Paris are Notre-Dame and the Basilique du Sacré-Coeur (respectively, 13.6 and 10.5 million visitors in 2007) (Office de Tourisme de Paris). The Eiffel Tower comes third, and charges for the visit, which is not the case for both churches.

10. An alternative way to display values is drawing bubbles centered on the spot that is measured. The bubble radius is proportional to the number of visitors and represents the attractiveness of the place. Similar tools can be applied to commercial activities, indicative of a commercial buffer zone.

11. Inhabitants of the Mont-Saint-Michel in France (a few dozens in the last census) experience simultaneously positive and negative externalities: residents enjoy the setting as a wonderful living place and are annoyed by tourists. Both externalities need public regulations. On one hand, the setting is protected to maintain positive externalities, and these regulations are sometimes considered as a burden for inhabitants. On the other hand, the mass of tourism has to be regulated to avoid exposing the monument to undue risks, and these regulations are sometimes considered as a burden for visitors.

12. When an annual event is organized to enhance the city heritage, privately owned buildings are exceptionally open to the public. Most of the visitors are city residents and meet for that occasion in restaurants and cafes in the city. Impacts on the local economy of this heritage-related initiative could be measured through food and drink expenditures, those in excess of the regular daily sales.

13. Macroeconomics is often connected to John Maynard Keynes, who set the general principles of this discipline in the 1930s. Keynes also advocated for strong public interventions in the economy. This principle seems consistent with a public goods approach to conservation.

14. It is unclear how accurate the spatial identification and mapping of these outcomes from development and conservation projects can be. Although they represent increasing economic values for the city inhabitants, they are not totally linked to heritage policy, and are not always identifiable spatially.

15. Developing methods to build reliable aggregate maps goes beyond the scope of this chapter. The process of adding up thematic maps drawn on a set of overlaying sheets, revealing colored-coded areas, was initiated by landscape architect Ian McHarg, who pioneered geographic information analysis before computers were available. The process is described in McHarg's book *Design with Nature* (1992).

16. Regulating stores in historic district illustrates the question in point. "The strictest laws regulating tourist shops are placed on two of Venice's most famous sites, the Rialto Bridge and San Marco Square. Store licenses from other areas are non-transferable to these two regions. This limit does not apply exclusively to tourist shops in these areas, but bars and restaurants as well. If a shop closes in this area, then another is able to move in, but the absolute number of stores in the area is fixed (870 stores in the district of San Marco)." (Venipedia, the Free Encyclopedia of Venice, Italy; http://Venipedia .org; see retail sales.)

17. In Venice, the masses of tourists brought in by giant cruise ships are known to spend very little time or money in the city, injecting almost no compensation.

18. Macroeconomic leakages are known to be significant when the relevant entity is small. But large countries can face similar issues of keeping heritage economic values from going abroad. Tourism revenue leakages in developing countries are seen when the lodging or transportation activities are managed by international corporations, with very little local economic impact.

19. The test-case study was conducted by Kathleen Louw (Getty Conservation Institute, Los Angeles) in March–April 2009, and coordinated by Yamoussa Fané (Cultural Mission of Djenné).

20. The formula used to draw map 9.7G was applied to the same "parcel" base map as the one used in maps 9.7C and 9.7E. The formula calculated a weighted average of the five layers, maps 9.7B to 9.7F. An equal weight of 20 percent was given to the following scores: 1 to 2 (map 9.7B), 1 to 4 (map 9.7C), 1 to 2 (map 9.7D), 1 to 2 (map 9.7E), and 1 to 4 (map 9.7F), as the color-coded maps reveal. The range of scores was divided into five levels, as indicated on the color-coded map of 9.7G. The result was redesigned to fit a symbolic map similar to the transparent overlay sheets of McHarg's day.

21. This maintenance, called "crépissage," must be done each year before the rainy season to ensure house stability, and is the full responsibility of each owner.

References

Abler, R., J. Adams, and P. Gould. 1971. *Spatial Organization–The Geographer's View of the World*. Englewood Cliffs, NJ: Prentice-Hall.

Avrami, E. C. 2004. "Cultural Heritage Conservation and Sustainable Building: Converging Agendas". *Industrial Ecology*. Dec. 2004: 11–14.

Coccossis, H., and A. Mexa, eds. 2004. *The Challenge of Tourism Carrying Capacity Assessment, Theory and Practice*. Farnham, UK: Ashgate.

Capello, R., and P. Nijkamp, eds. 2004. *Urban Dynamics and Growth: Advances in Urban Economics*. Amsterdam: Elsevier.

Donaire, J. A., and N. Gali. 2008. "Modeling Tourist Itineraries in Heritage Cities, Routes Around the Old District of Girona." *Revista de Turismo y Patrimonio Cultural* 6.

Duranton, G. 2008. "Spatial Economics." In *The New Palgrave Dictionary of Economics*, 2nd ed., ed. S. N. Durlauf and L. E. Blume. London: Palgrave

Fotheringham, A. S., and P. A. Rogerson. 1993. "GIS and Spatial Analytical Problems." *International Journal of Geographical Information Systems* 7.

Fusco Girard, L., B. Forte, M. Cerreta, P. De Toro, and F. Forte, eds. 2003. *The Human Sustainable City*. Farnham, UK: Ashgate.

Greffe, X. 1999. *La Gestion du Patrimoine Culturel*. Paris: Anthropos.

Jamieson, W. 2008. "The Use of Indicators in Monitoring: The Economic Impact of Cultural Tourism Initiatives." *ICOMOS Canada Bulletin* 4 (3).

J. Paul Getty Trust. 2000. *Assessing the Values of Cultural Heritage*. Research report. Los Angeles: The Getty Conservation Institute.

Lichfield, N. 1988. *Economics in Urban Conservation*. Cambridge: Cambridge University Press.

Mason, R. 1998. "Economics and Heritage Conservation: Concepts, Values, and Agendas for Research." In *Economics and Heritage Conservation, a Meeting Organized by the Getty Conservation Institute*. Los Angeles Getty Conservation Institute.

Mason, R. 2005. *Economics and Historic Preservation: A Guide and Review of the Literature*. Washington, DC: Metropolitan Policy Program, The Brookings Institution.

McHarg, I. L. 1992. *Design with Nature*. New York: John Wiley & Sons Inc.

Monmonier, M. 1996. *How to Lie with Maps*. Chicago: University of Chicago Press.

Nijkamp, P., and P. Riganti. 2004. "Valuing Cultural Heritage Benefits to Urban and Regional Development." In *ESRA Conference Papers*, 44th European Congress of the European Regional Science Association: Regions and Fiscal Federalism, University of Porto, Portugal.

Ost, C. 2009. *Guide for Heritage Economics: Values, Indicators, Maps, and Policies*. Scholar research. Los Angeles: The Getty Conservation Institute.

Rypkema, D. 2003. *The Economics of Historic Preservation: A Community Leader's Guide*. Washington, DC: National Trust for Historic Preservation.

Rojas, E. 1999. *Old Cities, New Assets: Preserving Latin America's Urban Heritage*. Washington DC, Baltimore: Inter-American Development Bank, John Hopkins University Press.

Semboloni, F. 2005. *Case Study on Siena*. Working Paper, European Foundation for the Improvement of Living and Working Conditions, Dublin.

Serageldin, I. 1999. *Very Special Places: The Architecture and Economics of Intervening in Historic Cities*. Washington, DC: World Bank.

Serageldin, I., E. Shluger, and J. Martin-Brown, eds. 2001. *Historic Cities and Sacred Sites, Cultural Roots for Urban Futures*. Washington, DC: World Bank.

Throsby, D. 2001. *Economics and Culture*. Cambridge: Cambridge University Press.

Van Oers, R. 2007. "Towards New International Guidelines for the Conservation of Historic Urban Landscape." *City & Time* 3 (3): 34–51.

World Bank. 2009. *Systems of Cities, Harnessing Urbanization for Growth and Poverty Alleviation. The World Bank Urban and Local Government Strategy*. Washington, DC: World Bank.

Index

Boxes, figures, maps, notes, and tables are indicated by b, f, m, n, and t following the page number.

ECO-AUDIT
Environmental Benefits Statement

The World Bank is committed to preserving endangered forests and natural resources. The Office of the Publisher has chosen to print *The Economics Of Uniqueness* on recycled paper with 50 percent postconsumer fiber in accordance with the recommended standards for paper usage set by the Green Press Initiative, a nonprofit program supporting publishers in using fiber that is not sourced from endangered forests. For more information, visit www.greenpressinitiative.org.

Saved:
- 15 trees
- 7 million Btu of total energy
- 1,293 lb. of net greenhouse gases
- 7,012 gal. of waste water
- 469 lb. of solid waste

CPSIA information can be obtained at www.ICGtesting.com
Printed in the USA
LVOW02s1633151013

357039LV00018B/42/P

UNIVERSITIES AT MEDWAY LIBRARY

9 780821 396506